NATIONAL ASSOCIATION
FOR PHYSICAL EDUCATION
IN HIGHER EDUCATION

PROCEEDINGS

NATIONAL ASSOCIATION
FOR PHYSICAL EDUCATION
IN HIGHER EDUCATION

CURRENT CHALLENGE:
Revitalization
or Obsolescence?

Annual Conference
College Park, Maryland
January 5-8, 1984

Volume V

National Association for Physical Education in Higher Education
Annual Conference Proceedings

Volume V	January 5-8, 1984	College Park, Maryland
Volume IV	January 6-9, 1983	Indianapolis, Indiana
Volume III (out of print)	January 8-10, 1982	San Diego, California
Volume II	June 5-8, 1980	Brainerd, Minnesota
Volume I	June 1-3, 1979	Milwaukee, Wisconsin

Editor
Nancy L. Struna, PhD
Department of Physical Education
University of Maryland
College Park, MD 20742

Copyeditor: Peg Goyette; **Typesetters:** Yvonne Sergent, Angela Snyder, Aurora Garcia; **Text Layout:** Janet Davenport.

Library of Congress Catalog Number: 81-646183

ISSN: 0276-461X

ISBN: 0-931250-88-9

Copyright © 1984 by the National Association for Physical Education in Higher Education

Printed in the United States of America

Human Kinetics Publishers, Inc.
Box 5076, Champaign, IL 61820

CONTENTS

Current Challenge:
Revitalization or Obsolescence?

Section 1

Physical Education
And Higher Education:
Missions and Potential

Perspectives On The Mission
Of Higher Education

Martha E. Church
Hood College

All of us recognize the importance of preparing our students, regardless of age, to take on the mantle of career and life. We know, too, that most institutions of higher education have made great, or at least moderate, strides in addressing ways of modifying our educational goals and practices to prepare both women and men better for their varied futures and their realization as fully participating, caring citizens.

We have just emerged from an era of incredible growth in student, faculty, and staff numbers, and in programs, services, and facilities. We have also witnessed a dramatic shift in areas of curricular interest, especially for women. Soft money permitted us to respond to curricular needs and to rapidly expanding research requirements. This was also the era in which the federal government and most of our states entered the student financial aid picture, thereby opening access in ways heretofore unknown anywhere in the world. We also recognized and began to respond to the needs of lifelong learners, while we watched opportunities for learners grow dramatically outside academia. Of growing concern to us were social issues, including educational opportunities for the handicapped, affirmative action, and issues of access and equity. Our institutions responded well to these issues and concerns, and they did so within the confines of our commitment to prepare our students for productive lives as responsible citizens.

As we move into the mid-1980s, our colleges and universities face monumental societal issues while the very foundations of these institutions are being buffeted by economic tides of gigantic proportions. We have witnessed a fundamental shift from basic commodity-producing industries to the newer service-oriented and high technology sectors. This shift has produced a radically changed work scene for which we must both prepare our students and retrain older workers. As those of us from steel making areas know all too well, some workers will never return to jobs in the steel and auto industries. Most, if not all, of our students will enter or reenter the world of work and are likely to change positions four to six times, which may involve considerable retraining. As Commodore Grace Murray Hopper, USN, the "godmother of computers," remarked at Hood's 1983 Commencement, educators will need retraining, too, especially as they recognize the importance of working better with mature learners.

3

Yet, as we move into the mid-1980s, there are persisting problems for women workers—professionals and nonprofessionals alike, regardless of marital status, age, or race. These concerns are well known to women and relate to being paid less than men, needing more help at home, needing some assistance in child care, lacking opportunities for training for better jobs, and having virtually no leisure time at all (working women spend at least 26 hours a week on housework, according to a recent study of the National Commission on Working Women). Institutions committed to erasing biases still have much to accomplish in this era of diminished fiscal resources.

Your profession has a remarkable opportunity for leadership as you and I seek to influence not only the nature of work within our institutions and elsewhere but also what people expect to derive from work. Sports have powerful lessons to share, and many of you guide these efforts. The literature summons us to encourage our students to be risk-takers. We hear from men such as Alan Pifer, president emeritus of the Carnegie Corporation, about the necessity of encouraging courage. Because you understand what is involved in risk-taking and know the ingredients of courage, you are perhaps among the best equipped to help institutional leaders and colleagues rethink how we can all better accomplish our institutional missions as we move into the future.

Let me suggest areas in which physical educators could and should assume leadership: We need to redefine growth for ourselves and our students—bigger is not necessarily better. We need to think in terms of growth in spirit, growth in our humane treatment of others, and growth in our partnership with others—beginning within our families, moving into our educational institutions, and finally entering our places of work and/or volunteer service. There are frustrations to be alleviated and better feelings to be engendered. We desperately need new perspectives on growth as we enter a time of serious constraints; we need new perspectives as we enter an age of new opportunities and new obligations.

Our institutions must recognize that our world of work and of volunteer service is changing quite rapidly due to increasing world interdependence. Curricular discussions should reflect this change. The impact of our entrance into the information society is now only dimly perceived. Educators must find ways to deal with this within their own institutions. Our changed economy is another dimension to be considered by educators in many disciplines. The fact that our society can be labeled as an aging society has profound implications for our curricular thinking and planning. College and university graduates of today will enter their peak earning years as the Post World War II baby boom generation retires beginning in 2012. Think of the impact of life expectancy extending to age 90 and how that fact alone affects wage earners, retirement programs, recreation and leisure, continued learning, and so forth.

In light of these changes and trends, our educational institutions must expand their concepts of educational purpose. Our curricular offerings should include some redefinition or reorientation to absorb different concepts of growth, the changing world of work, changing human and community needs, new scholarship about women, and attitudes about the importance of nutrition and exercise. We also need to examine carefully what high technology will liberate us from and what it may chain us to. Finally, as stated by George Bonham, founding editor of *Change Magazine*, our institutions and curricular structures need to address what all this change means in terms of preservation of human creativity.

It is time for us, the faculty and administrators, to step forward with greater confidence and with a larger vision and concept of our roles as citizens and as educational leaders. We must continue to be teachers and learners, but we must also be leaders with a more humane outlook on life and with a willingness to speak to the values of lifelong learning and responsibility. As physical educators, you have such a broad educational and philosophical base and the advantage of working inside and outside the classroom. Why don't you take a lead in helping us develop new perspectives on the mission of higher education?

Higher Education And Physical Education: The Perspective Of Central Administration

Rosemary Schraer
Pennsylvania State University

Whatever our institutional alliances may be, we all live in an age of uncertainty imposed by the speed with which our human society is changing. Cognizant of the omnipresent pressures of change, I speak with the temerity that arises from full awareness of the academic condition. Most of what I have to say is embodied in the art of communicating who we are, what we have done, and why we are an integral and important part of the academic comminity.

Before turning to physical education in particular, it is important that we consider the coming decade and what is in store for American higher education. To speak without considering the forecast for the future would be foolhardy. Demographic studies illustrate conclusively that the numbers of students between the ages of 18 and 24 will fall by about 25% in the next 10 years. How much this demographic phenomenon will affect your particular institution depends upon your geographic location. The most severe drop in student numbers will occur in the northeastern part of the country, if the prognosticators are correct. Other areas of the country will experience varying patterns of decline in student numbers. Each of us should be aware of the demographic conditions surrounding our own institutions and recognize the pressures they impose.

Another area of primary concern is the fiscal climate that pervades higher education. Tuition is rising steadily in both public and private institutions. Indeed, increases have exceeded rates of inflation. Many of our institutions have become tuition driven. In most, if not all institutions, income from all sources has not kept pace with costs, and the result has been chronic financial strain. The dual threats of declining student enrollment and rising costs have led to strategic planning and retrenchment in most colleges and universities. These processes will continue. In such an environment it is essential that every sector of an academic community strive to optimize performance with every coping tool and skill available. Preserving strength depends on team effort. The wealth of scholarship, ingenuity, service, research, and teaching which have characterized the system of higher education in this country can be maintained in the face of the current pressures. The process will most assuredly be accompanied by change. Despite the difficulties of the times, change can be positive.

The nature of some of the approaching change is already predictable. For example, the percentage of minority students in the classrooms of the future will likely rise. Blacks and Hispanics in particular will be more equitably represented in the student bodies. Slowly, minorities and women will increase in numbers among academic faculties after the millennium. Such change will bring the strength of diversity.

Other problems of the future are already being seeded by policies of deferred maintenance of our institutions' physical facilities; this will have to be dealt with at some later date by massive capital investment. In like manner, we must also deal with the obsolescence of equipment for teaching and research, as well as the lagging acquisitions of our libraries. Astounding advancements in computer technology may assist us in recouping some of our accruing library deficiencies. The challenge of present and future dynamic change requires that each of us be adaptable.

In the light of the realities of today and the forecasts for the late 1980s and early 1990s, let us now turn to the communication lines between a functioning academic faculty such as physical education and its upper administrative officers. These lines build the perceptions that each party holds of the other. Size of institution, of course, is highly relevant in our discussion. Even if one does see and speak with the chief academic officer every day, which is not typical, a number of conditions and practices contribute to academic vigor and quality that deserve to be mentioned.

Since quality of the faculty is paramount to the strength and success of a field or discipline in any institution, a few remarks on that topic are pertinent here. The appointment and ultimately the granting of tenure to a faculty member represents an important resource investment in the future of any academic department. While the fiscal investment in a young faculty member can represent a multimillion dollar lifetime contract, what is of long-range importance to the academic community is the potential of that new faculty member to contribute strength to the academic mission of the institution. Thus, the elaborate process of a department's search, assessment, and ultimate recommendation of a new faculty colleague sends a forceful message to the upper administration about the quality of academic judgment in the faculty of the discipline, and serves as an explicit indicator of programmatic direction and development. Consequently the academic credentials of all new faculty members are an important consideration. Subsequent recommendations made on promotion and tenure are equally revealing.

In all personnel processes there should be a clear delineation by a faculty of its mission and objectives to provide stable foundations for personnel decisions. That foundation supplies an equitable and just framework for academic decision making. Any faculty that constructs a clear and realistic rationale for its recommended academic personnel actions communicates to the central administration a clear message of its academic identity and its strength of purpose. That message can be reinforced every time a new faculty member joins the unit. While in most instances the personnel decisions are recommended but not made by the faculty itself, the quality of faculty recommendations is repeatedly evident to the appointing authority.

Another function that is central to the academic well-being of a discipline centers around the skill and dedication with which a faculty imparts its knowledge to students in the classroom, the laboratory, in seminars, or in informal exchange outside of structured teaching. The reputation for quality teaching takes time to establish. Mastery of subject matter is foremost, but concern for teaching methods and genuine interest in the students separates the outstanding teacher from his or her less talented colleagues. Many departments harbor a single outstanding teacher, but few faculties hold a reputation for consistent excellence. When such excellence does exist, the message is clear to anyone who listens to students; and it is the students who speak forcefully to central administration. Excellence in teaching also serves to attract and sustain student interest and involvement in a discipline.

Closely coupled with excellence in teaching is the accompanying effort in research and scholarly work. Scholarship and research are essential to the growth of knowledge in both basic and applied disciplines. Scholarly research endeavors sustain both the growth and vigor of the discipline and the teaching function of the faculty member. Teaching in the absence of scholarly endeavor and/or research often becomes sterile and obsolescent. The two functions are inseparable. Collegiate faculty and administrators should guard against appointing to tenured contracts those who do not clearly demonstrate the ability to conduct meaningful research and scholarly work. Few professors can face the challenge of the college classroom for a lifetime without the renewal that comes from continued involvement in scholarly efforts. Wise central administrators monitor trends and activity in these areas closely.

Another area that sheds light on the quality and strength of a faculty refers to measures of performance. Perhaps the most important, as well as the most difficult to assess, is performance in teaching. Here student appraisals and judgments of collegial peers must serve as a basis for judgment. In fact, studies have shown considerable value in the assessments of students several years after a classroom experience. There is no doubt that it is difficult to assess the complex combinations of characteristics which make a teacher superior. Yet we must continue to study the factors that contribute to the phenomenon of the master teacher and be satisfied meanwhile with the somewhat subjective methodologies of assessment at hand.

Although teaching is difficult to assess, the faculty member's scholarly and creative works are somewhat easier to evaluate. Scholarly works in the various fields are a time-honored marker of a scholar's effort, originality, and creativity. Having studied and imposed interpretation and order on a body of knowledge, the working scholar encodes his or her findings in publications or other forms for both contemporary colleagues and posterity. Publication in print media is beset with problems that arise from the dramatic increase of human populations and the concomitant increase in the number of scholars. The power of modern computer technology may bring a high level of order and retrievability to libraries of the future to enable them to meet the challenge of increasing publication.

Another measure of faculty quality concerns the nature of the discoveries of the faculty researcher. Traditionally the researcher has published his or her methods, results, and conclusions in the scholarly and professional journals. Here, too, we find that research literature is growing exponentially in volume. (Yet the ability of technology to keep abreast of the librarian's archiving needs already exists; only capital investment in machines, systems, and skilled personnel to handle the challenge is problematic.)

The measure of teaching service to nonmajors in an academic community, while not universally applicable in every field, is certainly relevant in the field of physical education. In my own opinion, elective service courses to the nonmajor can be a much more effective educational approach than compulsory physical education credits. Any measure of how well a faculty serves its nonmajor students or how much a physical education unit contributes to the health and welfare of its larger academic community is a powerful indicator of performance.

Here one might wonder why I have spent so much time constructing a contemporary, even futuristic, academic scene and followed it with a discussion of quality in academic personnel decision making, and in assessment of teaching, scholarly works, research, and service. My thesis is that these *are* the fundamental issues which pass daily through a central academic office. Collectively, these issues define a field or discipline for a central administration. Of course each carries budgetary implications. Further, the requests and recommendations from very diverse disciplines, departments, and fields are remarkably similar. In handling the myriad of issues that arise, priorities for action and for access to limited resources must be established. The quality, scope, and importance of the requesting academic unit guides this establishment of priorities.

Before we focus on how an academic discipline or field can compete successfully in the larger institutional arena, let us pause to consider current societal attitudes, values and goals as they relate to the substantive academic pursuits in the applied field of physical education. Judging from our popular literature, our marketplace, and our lifestyle, perhaps there has never been a time in this country's history when so many were so deeply concerned about those multidisciplinary functions which comprise the field of physical education. A high value is placed on physical and mental well-being, active sport participation, and spectator interest in sports. Exercise and dance are more popular than ever. Commercial ventures offer a broad spectrum of services related to exercise, sport, body building, the dance, and behavior modification. Sales of sporting equipment increase phenomenally with each passing decade. The typical American is highly aware of and places great value in the multidisciplinary field we know as physical education. Few academic fields are so valued by the American public.

Physical educators need to recognize and respond to this high public sensitivity. In a collegiate environment they must act on the fact that some aspect of their broad field of endeavor is particularly important to each student. Moreover, exposing that student to activity and knowledge in selected areas can contribute to his or her future well-being and health in a unique way. No other discipline can do this. Why then, one might ask, may resources not be forthcoming when an academic request from physical education is judged?

The criteria for academic support are clear. If physical education seeks concurrence on an academic appointment, both faculty and unit administrators should consider the quality of the candidate and the relevance of his or her credentials to the mission and goals of that particular physical education unit. The most convincing requests are those that carry a clear and concise rationale relating need, academic quality, and specialization to the planned direction of program in the unit. The same principle applies to any rationale that accompanies recommendations for tenure and/or promotion. Strength of faculty is built on a foundational process that begins with faculty appointment. The process involves careful goal setting coupled with collegial mentoring and honest, periodic assessment of strengths and weaknesses by leadership. Each faculty member deserves an explicit description of departmental expectations at the time of appointment. A rational, goal-oriented process optimizes the opportunity of selecting the most suitable candidates for tenure.

In like manner, requests from physical education which involve teaching, scholarly efforts, or research endeavors should be made in the light of past records of accomplishment, goal fulfillment, and present student demand. The more frequently success has been enjoyed, the higher the probability of continued support. Students are quick to recognize quality instruction in physical education.

Success in communicating academic requests to central administrators is most assured when quality of faculty, teaching, research, and scholarly activity are well documented.

In a world where the products of the endeavors of physical educators are held in such high esteem, each of you should resolve to enhance the quality of the unit to which you belong. What you produce is important to and valued by society. Your academic endeavors contribute directly to the health and well-being of everyone. Your mandate is to strive for excellence. Excellence assures you the support of your central administration and promises academic integrity in the lean years ahead. Value yourselves and your discipline. The contributions physical education has made to generations of students in higher education is obvious. Your future role is even more important. You must adapt quickly to the changes ahead and teach your students how to do the same for a lifetime.

Corporate Athleticism:
An Inquiry Into The Political Economy
Of College Sports

Nand Hart-Nibbrig
West Virginia University

This paper focuses on the growing though often ignored penetration of corporate athleticism in universities and colleges. While the focus is on the larger universities—so-called Division I schools—smaller universities and colleges are by no means exempt from the problem (Naison, 1982). The concept of corporate athleticism used here involves the penetration of corporate values affecting the financial structure of institutions, as well as the political and moral structures of educational institutions. What is it that universities do to maintain their positions in the world of big-time college sports? As is repeatedly suggested in the press, athletic directors and coaches may distort institutional priorities to get additional resources for athletes in order to meet continuing competition from other athletic programs. The implication of being among the top football programs in the United States is fundamentally important. The longer a team holds its *positional rank* in a specific sport, the more predictable are the economic resources that that sport may bring. For example, a winning Notre Dame football (or basketball) team brings in additional television money for the following year.

Television has made it more possible, perhaps even necessary, for universities to ''market'' their products through communications. It is part of the corporate package. Television is one of the few means available to universities to market their products nationally. Therefore, television helps universities translate sports into an institutional ''product.'' In fact, the number of times a team appears on national or regional television is a prime indicator of positional rank (Hirsch, 1976).

Several factors indicate the magnitude and growth of corporate athleticism in the United States. When combined, these factors comprise a powerful force that affects universities and colleges. First is the growth and scale of the corporate-athletic complex itself. Indicative of this growth are the newly built sports stadia and supporting facilities so conspicuous on college and university campuses. They stand as symbolic monuments to this powerful network and serve as a reminder that the business of college sports is first and foremost a business.

Executive salaries for coaches are another conspicuous indicator of a corporate presence. The most glaring example of this is the recent move of Jackie Sherrill, former head football coach at the University of Pittsburgh, who reportedly signed a contract with Texas A&M for a yearly salary of over $250,000. While Sherill's salary may seem excessive, especially when compared with the low salaries of college professors, it really reflects a long-term trend toward executive salaries for leading football coaches.

The athlete as product constitutes the second factor in this corporate complex. Indicative of this pattern is the standard practice of isolating and sequestering college athletes from much that constitutes normal campus life. This contributes to a related problem of the athletic regimen: penetrating the private lives of athletes. Early recruitment and intensification of training amounts to year-round absorption of a young person's time and energy and furthers his or her encapsulation within the corporate athletic system.

Finally, there is an overlap of the amateur and professional status of college athletes. With increasing frequency, student athletes are using the financial hardship provisions in NCAA regulations and jumping to the professional leagues. This overlap in amateur and professional status also indicates the role of universities in semi-professional sports programs.

The concept of corporate athleticism is used here to interpret a unique process of institutional change now occurring in American universities. The thesis is that the financial aspects and institutional autonomy associated with big-time sports is more akin to the values of the modern corporation or professional sports than to the basic values and purposes of the university. As this process of institutional changes has progressed, university administrative officials frequently are unable to regulate the administrative behaviors of their own athletic departments. Alumni of these universities have come to expect their teams to win, and athletic departments have intensified their time demands on the student athletes of those teams. It is this intensification of recruitment, payment, and training which constitutes the central core of athleticism as a quasi-professional training and financial regime, while the financial rewards of such massive sports programs define its emerging corporate structure.

ISSUES OF POLITICAL ECONOMY

The rise of television sports as an important leisure activity has transformed intercollegiate sports into a lucrative economic enterprise. Few universities recognize the possible immediate or long-term consequences of this change in the status of sports within the American university. Administrators are reluctant to face the fact that sports constitute a big business within the university itself.

The struggle to control the increasingly large amounts of money paid to televise college football games has now moved into the courts. In a lawsuit aimed at stripping the National Collegiate Athletic Association of its exclusive control over televised football, the universities of Georgia and Oklahoma accused the NCAA of violating the Sherman Antitrust Act and depriving them of their property rights (Board of Regents, 1982). Briefly, the NCAA contracted for $263.5 million with ABC and CBS to televise up to 14 games each year for the next 2 years. While the dollar amounts vary under the contracts, the major networks indicated they would pay about $1.1 million in fees for each nationally televised game. However, there were limitations on the number of times a team can appear on television: no more than three times during each season. The limits on the number of appearances, the exclusivity of NCAA contracts, and the implied threat of sanctions against institutions that attempt to make their own deals were all grounds for initiating the suit.

According to Andrew Coats, the attorney for the two universities, the real issue was not football per se but how universities would continue nonrevenue producing sports given the financial burdens faced by athletic departments. Coats' argument signifies the boundaries between politics and economics in corporate athleticism. Essentially, he argued that external NCAA regulations impinge politically on the universities' capacity to allocate resources to nonrevenue producing sports if they are unable to maximize their income from the more financially lucrative sports. In this respect, the legal actions of the universities of Georgia and Oklahoma tacitly confirm the shifting boundaries of the political economy of college sports.

Ironically, while the recent proliferation of legal actions are indicative of the growing commercialization of college sports, the university argument against external regulation is justified in the name of noncommercial sports (now the traditional noncommercial sector of sports as salutary of the development of character), or the so-called nonrevenue producing sports.

On June 27, 1984, the United States Supreme Court fundamentally altered the corporate athletic nexus between American universities and the business system. The Court decided in the major antitrust action brought by the universities of Oklahoma and Georgia that the NCAA could no longer represent itself as the sole distributor of football games to the television networks. The Court's action not only curbed the role of the NCAA as a distributor of football games, but it ushered in a helter skelter scramble among the nation's athletic powers for prime time exposure. The major beneficiaries of this new unregulated market are likely to be the perennial football powers and, of course, the television networks. Not much stands in the way of television as it secures its position as the prime producer of intercollegiate athletics.

The recent decision of the University of San Francisco to end its men's intercollegiate program in basketball because, as its president said, misconduct on the part of alumni "boosters" and players threatened the institution's "integrity and reputation," illustrates the political hypothesis being developed here (*New York Times*, 1982). Slack regulation by the NCAA makes it possible for sports departments to use illegal means to attract first-rate athletes. Important questions concerning the regulatory capacity of the NCAA must be raised here. Who regulates the NCAA? What interests are in fact regulated or protected? If regulation by the NCAA is slack and ineffective, it seems evident that university administrators exercise little control over powerful athletic departments and their boosters. In spite of two warnings by the NCAA and the firing of one coach, the University of San Francisco was still unable to effectively control the practices of its basketball team. It was unable to influence the behavior of powerful alumni working in conjunction with basketball coaches. In this case, constituency interests did not operate to maximize the university's academic integrity. Rather, these external/internal constituency relations operated in ways that publicly embarrassed the university.

Legal cases, public exposures, and strengthened NCAA regulations are all working to shift the boundaries of the political economy of corporate athleticism. On the face of it, NCAA procedures are intended to regulate institutional competition and to enforce amateurism and fair play. But several recent legal cases have recognized the commercial, employer/employee relations involved in the commercialization of college sports.

The following pages deal with boundary maintenance in the face of the development of corporate athleticism. Growth, control, trade-offs, and the presumed costs and benefits are cited as consequences associated with the more prominent institutional place of sports within the university. The argument here is that the commercialization of sports does not fit easily, as the court cases and scandals indicate, into the university's academic structure.

In testimony before the court, Fred C. Davison, president of the University of Georgia, asserted that NCAA restrictions prevented his university from generating new money. The university further argued that it is constrained from pursuing new, financially attractive options from cable networks and pay TV because of NCAA restrictions, and asked that the court address the question of how the antitrust law applies to TV contracts. This trial, in the U.S. District Court for the Western District of Oklahoma, may develop as a landmark case fundamentally altering the relationship between college sports and the marketplace. Meanwhile it highlights the penetration of telecommunications into the financial structure of universities and colleges.

One would expect trade-offs, given a future of increased financial uncertainties for many institutions of higher education as they grope for some measure of administrative or political control over escalating athletic costs and semi-autonomous athletic departments. A highly successful sports team or athletic program may alleviate some of the financial uncertainty. Having a position in the structure of the market allows a college or university to reap considerable financial returns—returns which can be shared by the nonrevenue producing sports, the noncommercial sector. A strong team builds public support for the university by promoting its name and therefore its identity. This is especially true if the university has less than a distinguished academic program.

In too many instances these much heralded benefits result in increasingly unforeseen costs. These costs are often difficult to document but they are recognized nevertheless. In brief, the growing prevalance of market values in university sports programs not only erodes administrative procedures and academic standards but also compromises the educational mission in the name of marketplace competition. The increasingly frequent athletic scandals should be warning enough.

While not new, athletic scandals are but the most recent expression of corporate competition through fair and foul means and, moreover, they perhaps also indicate the rise of corporate athleticism. This rise is a function of the generalization of the market model as student athletes become a scarce commodity. Indeed, the recent rash of sports scandals is probably associated with the expansion of corporate athleticism within the universities. As university athletic programs have become increasingly commercialized, the competition for highly proclaimed and numerically scarce student athletes has resulted in a series of sports scandals within several universities. The notion of the student athlete may soon be a thing of the past. In what may become a landmark decision in a recent Indiana court of appeals, the court ruled that an Indiana State University football player who was seriously injured in practice was entitled to workmen's compensation payments because he held a football scholarship. It is believed to be the first time a court has ruled that merely receiving a scholarship entitles a player to workmen's compensation.

Issues raised in the Indiana case may have enormous financial implications for higher education. In the court's opinion, the rights and benefits received by the football player were conditioned upon his athletic ability and team participation. Consequently, the scholarship constituted a contract for hire and created an employer/employee relationship.

Although the decision was not sustained in the Indiana Supreme Court, the implications of this case are crucial. For example, one important issue has to do with the amateur status of student athletes. If scholarships are viewed as payment, then athletes are being paid to perform. One should expect an explosion of similar cases in state courts across the country, laying the direct financial burden on universities and colleges. In any event, with the expansion of television markets and increasing competition for scarce athletic talent, colleges and universities face perhaps more financial and legal uncertainties than previously imagined.

ATHLETIC DEPARTMENTS
AND ADMINISTRATIVE CONTROL

The semi-autonomy of Division I athletic departments to run their programs as they see fit with little effective control by central administration adds to the difficulty of immediate change. This pattern is likely to deepen given the financial crisis that more and more universities are facing. Pushed by the momentum to proceed, they will attempt newer, more prosperous markets. Recently, some universities that have large money-making sports programs have attempted to establish their own elite club of the most marketable teams in anticipation of increased revenues. Evidently, in the sports-business-university world, it is position in the market which guarantees the highest returns. This fact is relevant even though the competition is keen and few will dominate. The very uncertainty about who will dominate helps to explain and generate the initiative that maintains such a system.

Many who have dealt with the problems of control and accountability of athletic programs have little confidence in current attempts to get rid of the often stated abuses. This is especially true given the pressures from Title IX which mandates sports equality for women, and the fact that expanded television dollars promise relief from economic pressures (Hanford, 1979). One can readily understand why university administrators, facing the most profound series of crises in the last 30 years, tend to avoid antagonizing this powerful complex unnecessarily.

Their perspectives must be appreciated and understood before suggestions for change can be developed. First of all, college presidents are not free agents. Like all administrative decision makers, they are limited in their capacity to make and implement policy. They must persuade powerful and often conflicting groups (faculties, boards of regents, the local community) which are those segments of the economic community constituting the business/athletic power structure. Presidents find little incentive within this kind of a system to stir controversy. Rather, the strategies are to get along with those who can exert political and financial pressures.

In a sense, one might argue that corporate athleticism results mainly from the growing activities of the business based, corporate alumni lobby which seeks to replicate its model of aggressive sports competition within the university structure. To an important extent, the sports/business lobby is the political mechanism of corporate athleticism. Against the political influence of the sports/business lobby few university presidents have the political influence to advocate—much less implement—serious institutional reform.

There are indeed practical limits on the decision-making capacities of presidents and those who serve in their behalf, but there are also opportunities for policy change. The real question has as much to do with the values of the decision maker, the estimation of what can be accomplished (always less than anticipated before acquiring office), and the opportunity costs of taking on strong, organized clientele that athletic departments have developed in the largest and most competitive sports markets.

THE POLITICAL ECONOMY
OF CORPORATE ATHLETICISM

State legislatures typically are more familiar with the win-loss records of football and basketball teams than with who runs the university. This underscores the power of such programs and presumes a tacit recognition that college administrators have either abandoned or mollified academic interests in exchange for political support from government officials. Honesty dictates a quick skepticism about the ability, nay the willingness, of those who face crushing pressures at the university to meet this problem head on.

One must not underestimate the force and power of the marketplace in the guise of sports entertainment. Corporations that own professional football and basketball teams have the capacity to survive even when spectator turnout is low. This is due primarily to more complex corporate and financial transactions and enlarged home video markets (Halberstam, 1981). The bottom line is that corporate athleticism comes in the guise of a miltifaceted entity whose future and capacities to generate markets have increased profoundly. Few will be able to resist these forces. Most will find accommodation easier and more profitable.

A dramatic and often tragic outcome of this power becomes evident when we look closely at how minorities are socialized and recruited into an exceedingly narrow band of opportunity for which there may be one chance in a million to make it. Questioning the morality of this process is hardly sufficient to effect a change in outcome. Likewise, ignoring the situation achieves little and betrays the presence of racism's long shadow.

Unfortunately, the fact that football and basketball often overrepresent black players makes it easier to ignore the many wrongs done in the spirit of competition (Behey, 1974; Edwards, 1969). The point of view that there ought to be a place for the D student at the university, to the outright belief that these students are hardly more than hired hands, undergirds the elaborate accommodation which takes place.

University officials may be forced to make stronger commitments to those athletes who serve as their goodwill ambassadors to business clientele. Emerging from the ranks of athletes and former athletes almost imperceptibly are organizations directed primarily at reaching young men before as well as during their involvement in big-time sports programs.

The history of college sports reveals some interesting facts that help put today's realities into perspective, one being the rapidity and ease with which college football came to dominate the scene (Rudolph, 1962). The general public seized upon college football as a "subject of enthusiasm and identification (aided and abetted by the proliferation of mass circulation newspapers) which university presidents, operating in a climate not always conductive to intellectual concerns, began consciously to use as a vehicle for attracting financial and political support, whether from alumni, state legislators or prospective students and contributors'' (Naison, 1982, p. 3).

One is immediately struck by the contemporary flavor of the connection between sports as recreation and sports as business with the university. Private colleges, especially elite ones, while not devoid of the tendency to exploit public interest in college football, were somewhat restrained by the clientele and students who were equally interested in developing respected research faculties and graduate schools (Naison, 1982). On the other hand, public universities, especially land-grant schools located in the Midwest, West, South, and Southwest, having more comprehensive educational and training missions, and tied more immediately to specialized technical education for local and state business, farm, and technical interests were much more sensitive to pressures. Few college administrators failed to see that ''athletic victories were more important than anything else in convincing reluctant legislators to open the public purse'' (Rudolph, 1962, p. 385).

A paradox has been duly noted in that the most democratic features of state institutions (i.e., their responsiveness to public opinion; their deeper penetration into lower ranks of society to include racial minorities previously excluded from both the university and sports programs; their wider mission and scope of community interests) led many state universities and colleges to assume major responsibility for providing sports entertainment for their state and community (Naison, 1982).

It is clear that university officials and interested pressure groups wishing to make policy changes in this area must contend not only with the history of sports programming but also with the weight of decisions made to maintain community support for the university, especially in states and communities where support for the educational mission is either weak or nonexistent. When it is the only game in town, the problem is exacerbated.

The marriage of college sports to a political clientele, as noted, was established with astonishing speed and depth to the point that, by 1900, football and university public relations had become synonymous (Rudolf, 1982). It was only a matter of time before the full encapsulation of university sports programs with changing corporate interests was to be complete. As professionalization of sports achieved full recognition after World War II, its effects both in the marketplace and on university programs were to be profound and would, for the time being, dominate the now relatively simple public relations aim for competitors for what many euphemistically call the sports market.

If anyone doubts the significance of this point, he or she need only imagine what would happen if the NFL and the NBA suddenly declared bankruptcy, disposing of the professional football and basketball franchises across the country. Among the effects would be a crash in the college market. The pool of cheap labor recruited largely with the hope of big-professional pay would likely dry up. The elaborate justification for program maintenance would collapse under the weight of an infrastructure no longer necessary or useful to universities. The college game would not be totally destroyed, only its corporate character. Of course, this argument assumes that big-time college sports does not yet completely substitute for professional sports, a distinction increasingly more difficult to make. Stretching the point further, the necessity for exorbitant salaries for winning coaches would go by the boards. Illegal, unethical recruitment of professional prospects would evaporate. Under-the-table payments, fictional class attendance, and other conspiracies by university officials and clientele of athletic departments would become questionable and would be clearly seen as a less profitable use of scarce resources.

POLICY OPTIONS

It may be fantasy to assume the demise of corporate athletics at least in the near future. However, it is not fantasy to come to grips with the problem as a matter of policy and to make responsible changes, changes which would benefit those for whom the university defines its basic mission, not those whose primary interests are to fatten profit margins at great human cost. It is clear that this relationship, which is not confined to sports, represents a long-term problem: How will universities and colleges be able to influence transactions with corporate and political interests, especially during periods of economic and financial downturn in American higher education?

Attempts have been made to stem the tide of dominance by a corporate athletic complex. A few faculties have initiated successful struggles to change the climate, reduce the involvement, and upgrade the status at universities and colleges. Dr. Kenneth Clark, famous for his pioneering work on school desegregation, suggested recently that more black faculty on various university and college campuses were especially concerned about the status of athletes. In many cases, according to Clark, black athletes make up a significant percentage of the black males on predominantly white college campuses. As a result, some black faculty feel compelled to focus their efforts where numbers are significant (Clark, personal interview, June 1982).

By the 1950s and 1960s, some universities had greatly de-emphasized big-time sports and placed their athletic programs under tighter supervision. It is clear that the larger, more competitive universities did quite the opposite. Under the guise of greater control of university sports, the big athletic powers developed semi-professionalism to the point it is today.

Interestingly, the emergence of current athletic powers presents an uneven pattern of development. One is struck by the huge market success of schools such as USC and UCLA, whose competition has given rise to a particularly strong form of corporate athleticism. In contrast to these schools in southern California is the University of California at Berkeley, which has not developed as strong a sports program. Berkeley's academic prominence lies at the heart of the difference in sports programming. Partly as a result, the jewel in California's educational crown seems more concerned about educational excellence than sports dominance.

Racial desegregation has altered the sports power structure in very striking terms. The primary beneficiaries of black athletes in football and basketball programs have been southern, southwestern, and western schools. Colleges and universities such as Army and Navy, yesterday's collegiate powers, have for all practical purposes dropped from football prominence, as have many other football and basketball powers in the northeast. For the most part they have not been able to compete effectively for athletes whose entrance into colleges and universities is due to athletic prowess rather than academic promise.

One glance at the racial makeup of teams in the National Football League and the National Basketball Association, as well as the makeup of the big powers in college football and basketball, should tell us that not only has the black athlete arrived on the sports scene, but that this arrival occurs within the larger economic and financial realities of expanding capacities to market college sports for massive entertainment.

CONCLUSION

The argument has been presented that the evolution of college sports, especially those that generate strong revenue, is best understood by considering the political and economic factors that have shaped the broad contours of the changing structure of sports. This approach focuses on the systemic problems associated with this internal and external evolution. The implications of this approach are quite profound, particularly with regards to the weak institutional controls in the governance of college sports.

Since its founding in 1906, the NCAA did much to define the new sports system. University presidents, despite their concern for maintaining academic values, have not developed ways to contain the commercial aspects of sports. Moreover, it is not entirely true that the growth of sports erodes the authority of universities committed to truth and academic integrity. Indeed, one tentative conclusion here is that sports seems to be part of the general modernizing trend, which in effect reduces the gap between the university and society.

As used here, the term *corporate* refers to the influence of the business system as the predominant paradigm for the new sports system. The emphasis, above all on being number one, on securing gate receipts and television appearances, and on hiring the right coaches, attaches athletic values to the corporate structures of the American economy.

The capacity of college sports programs to muster resources for advanced training infrastructure, to adopt higher performance standards, and to recruit and train athletic talent are the functional outcomes of athleticism. The utility of these two variables is that they facilitate the more rigorously systemic interpretation of college sports offered here. It concentrates on persistent anomalies that other writers have also noted, and thrives for a deeper, more encompassing interpretation of the basic structure of college sports.

With the emergence of the athlete as *commodity*, we have seen the end of amateurism as the dominant concept for the organization of sports activity. At the contemporary American university, sports—not just basketball and football—are not just a way to enhance individual character. On the contrary, a deep structure exists, defining sports as a dynamic, economically-based system of corporate organization.

REFERENCES

BEHEY, J. (1974). *Hail to the victors: Black athletes at the University of Michigan.* Ann Arbor: Ulrich's Books.

BOARD of Regents of the University of Oklahoma and the University of Georgia v. NCAA. (1982). *The Chronicle of Higher Education*, **21**(16), 10.

EDWARDS, H. (1969). *The revolt of the black athlete.* New York: The Free Press.

HALBERSTAM, D. (1981). *The breaks of the game.* New York: Alfred A. Knopf.

HANFORD, G.H. (1979). Controversies in college sports. *Educational Record*, **60**(4), 365.

HIRSCH, F. (1976). The material economy and the positional economy. In *The social limits to growth* (pp. 27-53). Cambridge: Harvard University Press.

NAISON, M. (1982). *Sports in the political economy of higher education: Scenario for scandal; Protecting the educational opportunities of black college athletes: A case study based on experiences at Fordham University.* Unpublished manuscripts.

NEW YORK TIMES. (1982). July 30, p. A 15.

RUDOLPH, F. (1962). *The American college and university: A history,* New York: Alfred A. Knopf.

Section 2

Physical Education:
Is It Central To The Mission
Of Higher Education?

Physical Education: Is It Central To The Mission Of Higher Education? The Teacher's Perspective

Pearl Berlin
University of North Carolina—Greensboro

The processes of perceiving are highly complex. Our senses, intelligence, emotions, and values are involved in the perceptions we have of the world. Moreover, perceiving is considered to be an individual phenomenon. Because I regard the task of addressing the centrality of physical education to the mission of higher education largely as a matter of perception, the meanings I assign to the key concepts of the question warrant identification. I begin, then, with some definitions.

DEFINITIONS

Jan Felshin provides a definition of physical education to which I strongly subscribe. She states that "physical education is the study of movement as an art, a science, and a significant human process" (Felshin, 1967, p. 179). In her rich discussion of the promises of purpose, she also calls attention to the premises upon which the definition is based—scientific, social, human. As a teacher of physical education, her definitions and ideas about our discipline fit well the view I have of my own role in the university.

Henderson and Henderson (1975) explain numerous models delineating the central purpose of higher education. They begin with Cardinal Newman's well known ideal. And after discussing John Dewey, Robert Hutchins, and Mark Van Doren, they lead the reader to the idea of what they call a liberating education. I offer their summary as the framework for interpreting my comments about the mission of higher education.

> A liberating education liberates people from ignorance, superstition, fear, prejudice, unnecessary physical handicaps, and the need to use force in trying to solve recurring crises. More positively, it is the education that helps produce people who, because of their perspective of human experience, their sensitivity to the limiting forces of the time, and their knowledge of social dynamics, can aid in the further evaluation of man and society. (Henderson & Henderson, 1975, p. 27)

With regard to a definition of *the teacher*, let me rely on the familiar explanation of the teacher as one who guides and/or directs the learnings of others, that is, a facilitator.

THE QUESTION AND ANSWER

Teaching research methods courses over the years has markedly influenced the way in which I approach the answering of questions. I think about the structure of the question and the strategies that may be invoked in providing a response. Contemplating the "question" again? Have we not been over this ground before?

Were Wood and Cassidy not talking about this very same issue in 1927 when they first used the phrase "The New Physical Education" and related physical education to general education? They focused on the interdependence of human faculties in fulfilling the main function of education, that of developing efficiency "as an instrument of self-expression with reference to the various responsibilities and opportunities of life" (p. 3). Seven years later Steinhaus (1934) wrote about the physiological, psychological, and sociological outcomes of exercise and the vitality and outlook on life they add. Are these not also germane to the definitions of physical education and purposes of higher education addressed by the above definitions?

I recall Mendell's (1959) comments in his article entitled, "Vile Bodies." He spoke for physical education in the *Yale Alumni Magazine* in 1959 when he expressed the belief that the duty of American colleges involved not only equipping graduates to think effectively and to live in the complex world of the era with understanding and tolerance but that in order to do so, a "competent and coordinated body" was essential.

From my vantage point on the campus of Wayne State University at the time, the entire issue of *Quest I*, the monograph entitled *Quo Vadis/Physical Education*, pointed directly to the centrality of physical education within higher education. Furthermore, the ideas expressed in the editorial about the underlying philosophy of physical education seem to be as appropriate for today's NAPEHE meetings as they were in 1963.

Is there not a fundamental connection between Metheny's (1964) ideas about learning to play tennis as a dignified endeavor and Henderson and Henderson's liberating education? For some it may involve a global leap. For me, the experience is one that the Hendersons address when they refer to free people becoming masters of themselves. This occurs "when they have learned to utilize harmoniously their own individual abilities—intellectual, physical, and emotional" (p. 24). Metheny's connotation was that it is as significant to learn to play tennis as it is to learn biology or literature. All of those, in her judgment, are inherently human endeavors.

How can one ask the question of centrality after reading Huelster's (1982) discussion of the social relevance of our field of study? Dr. Huelster's statements about compassion, peace, and the human condition give me cause to see the objectives of physical education as extending far beyond the gymnasium, the playfield, or the classroom, into the larger arenas in which people live.

My answer to the question of centrality, considering the exact way in which it was asked, is then an unqualified *yes*. *Physical education is central to the mission of higher education*. Were the planners of the conference to have asked "why?" I would have answered that it is because I perceive it to be so. And given the preceding references, I feel that I am in quite good company!

THE RATIONALE

It would not do for me to be so cavalier and indicate that my answer is all a matter of perception. I wish to elaborate that perception by describing how physical education fits into the general scheme of the university. I will explain *how* I see my role as teacher of physical education fitting into the context of higher education. To accomplish this I borrow the ideas of Hagman (1966), who wrote a guest editorial in *Quest VII*, the monograph entitled "The Physical Educator as Professor." Hagman addressed the question "Of What is a Professor a Professor?" He underscored the notion that, first and foremost, a professor is a member of the university community. Extending Hagman's theme, I argue that one is primarily a teacher in her or his college or university, then a faculty member of a given college or school, and within that a member of a department. By virtue of the latter, the teacher is a "specialist" in a given field of knowledge. As such, she or he directs students' learnings in the classroom. Presented graphically, I see us, the teachers, as a drop in the bucket.

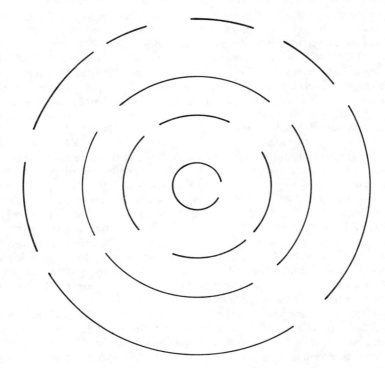

Figure 1. The context of the teacher of physical education in higher education.

It is the university, the largest concentric ring above, that my perceptual processing reveals to me as the boundary of my role. It is little wonder that I consider myself and my subject matter as "central" to the university. What appears to have occurred—and not without cause—is the tendency of many college professors to perceive these concentric circles from the opposite perspective. Whereas I perceive the circles from the outside in, their perceptions are from the inside out. Such teachers are big in their classrooms. They feel confident, secure, in control—when they have a captured audience of students before them. Within the department or school they are slightly more guarded. In the broader arena of the university they become much more timid and sometimes retiring to the point of nonparticipation. Teachers/professors of this type look to the university to provide important supports such as an account at the computer center, good library holdings, a monthly paycheck, and appropriate merit adjustments in salary for three or four more publications this year as compared to last.

I do not condemn these physical educators alone for what I regard as their distorted or flawed perspective of the university. This sort of tunnel vision is a malady in many other sectors of the institution, for example, departments of chemistry, economics, and English. It is not difficult to understand why these persons are continually trying to figure out how they fit into the mainstream of higher education; alas, they see no further than the walls of their own classrooms.

Carrying the ''drop in the bucket'' analogy just a few steps further, we read and hear about troubled times in higher education. The ivory tower and the marketplace, the individual and society, the humanities vis-à-vis technological knowledges—these are all issues that relate to our perceptions of the university. Consider the context of the university within the larger order of things.

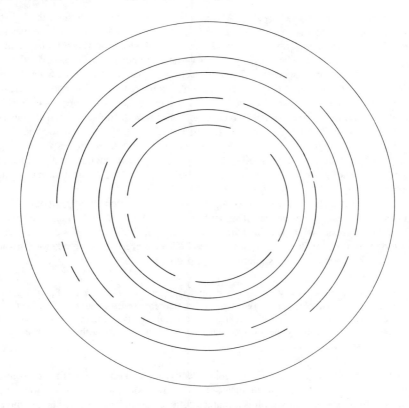

Figure 2. The context of the university in the communities of the world/humankind.

We have long used the phrase *town and gown*. Like many others, I have spoken with legislators in an attempt to "educate" them about the university. After all, in public institutions, they approve the budget which provides the financial sustenance that in the end makes it possible for us to teach. From my perspective of the university, the new degree programs we seek to establish and the curricula and courses we develop are just as much determined in the state legislature as they are by the university curriculum committee. Undoubtedly that is why Brademas, in his 1982 presentation to the American Educational Research Association, emphasized the need to be mindful of the politics of education. He called for professors as "citizens of a free and open society" (p. 13) to make the important connections between research and problem solving and between thinking and doing—the fundamental tools of institutions of higher education. In his own way, Hutchins (1936) nearly 50 years ago offered the same admonition when he spoke of isolation.

THE NEXT QUESTION

Taking a note from Getzels (1974), who argued that the distinctive role of the university in society is to find problems, that is, to raise critical questions, it behooves me to ask an important question. If I believe that physical education is central to the mission of higher education, and if I am a teacher—one who guides the thinking of others—*how* do I convince those with differing perceptions to adopt my view of the teacher as a drop in the bucket of the university, the geographic and political community, the American society, the world? Is there a way to help teachers see beyond the confines of their disciplines and classrooms to the outer reaches of the university? In all honesty I do not know. But that does not mean that I shall not try to be convincing.

Inasmuch as there are those who are well qualified to convey this message to colleagues and graduate students alike, I offer the following guidelines for interpreting a perspective of physical education that is central to the mission of institutions of higher education.

1. Accentuate the positive. For example, consider Thompson's (1981) findings about values and lifestyle preferences of students attending American universities today and how they compare with those of students 30 years ago. The results give cause for considerable optimism! Both males and females indicate a greater preference for outward activity that uses the body's energy. Thompson states:

> The finding is remarkably consistent with the rapid growth in recent years of participant activities. . . .university students enjoy getting together for exercises involving the expenditure of large amounts of physical energy, but also for ones where the emphasis is more on simple participation rather than on intense competition involved in winning some game or contest. (p. 515)

The responses were generated by students identifying the kind of lives they personally would like to live. As physical educators, we know about the benefits and joys to be derived from physical activity. It is a characteristic to be emphasized in the larger university context.

2. Be open and honest about what we are and what we do. We study human movement as artistic, scientific, and human processes. According to Renshaw (1973), in colleges and universities such studies take three forms:

> The academic study of the different kinds of theoretical and practical knowledge. . . .actual engagement in the language of symbolic movement; and the applied study of Human Movement. (p. 82)

Why do we need to invent quasi-sophisticated names and titles for what we do? Who are we trying to impress? My plea is to maintain the integrity of the field of study.

3. Behave like a scholar in the community of scholars. Be a skeptic. Nagai (1975) refers to the "organized skeptic." He alleges that skepticism improves the relationship between education and society. "Skepticism. . .helps entertain a liberal and a rich culture, the only basis from which. . .to comtemplate the possible directions in which human society could be moving" (p. 39). Dare, in the assembly of colleagues, to question, to argue, to take the unpopular position *if* the commitments you have and the rationale for them is sound—in your judgment. Nothing is more disappointing to me than to have a colleague say after a committee meeting, "I certainly do agree with everything you said." Where was the agreement in the previous assembled forum? To be a professor is to behave like one outside of the office and classroom.

4. Strive for excellence and the highest standards but do not forget that average or between -1 and $+1$ standard deviation encompasses 66 ⅔% of the population. In other words, acknowledge that excellence does not exclude mediocrity. In fact, there would be no excellence if there were not mediocrity. Within the framework of what I have been trying to convey are many other drops in the bucket.

In sum, we are creatures of a complex world who are committed to helping young people and one another fulfill their human potential through understanding and application of human movement. We use the college or university as the stage for our activities—intellectual, social, physical, emotional, and so forth. We recognize that the university and its purposes extend far beyond geographic boundaries. We belong to a universal community of scholars.

Such is my perspective of physical education and the mission of higher education. For more than 35 years, the perspective has stood me in good stead. I invite you to share a similar point of view.

REFERENCES

BRADEMAS, J. (1982). Higher education and the nation's future. *Educational Researcher*, **11**, 6-13.

FELSHIN, J. (1967). *Perspectives and principles for physical education*. New York: Wiley.

GETZELS, J.W. (174). Problem finding: The distinctive role of the university *Educational Researcher*, **3**, 5-6.

HAGMAN, H. (1966). Guest editorial: Of what is a professor a professor? *Quest VII*, 67-69.

HENDERSON, A.D., & Henderson, J.G. (1975). *Higher education in America*. San Francisco: Jossey-Bass.

HUELSTER, L.J. (1982). Social relevance perspective for sport and physical education. In E.F. Zeigler (Ed.), *Physical education and sport. An introduction*. Philadelphia: Lea & Febiger.

HUTCHINS, R.M. (1936). *The higher learning in America*. New Haven: Yale.

MENDELL, C.W. (1959). Vile bodies. *Yale Alumni Magazine*.

METHENY, E. (1965). Anyone for tennis? *Connotations of movement in sport and dance*. Dubuque, IA: Brown.

NAGAI, M. (1975). *An owl before dusk*. Berkeley: Carnegie Commission.

QUEST I, 1963.

RENSHAW, P. (1973). The nature of human movement studies and its relationship with physical education. *Quest*, **20**, 79-86.

STEINHAUS, A.H. (1934). Why exercise? *The Journal of Health and Physical Education*, **5**, 5-7, 42-43.

THOMPSON, K.S. (1981). Changes in the values and life-style preferences of university students. *Journal of Higher Education*, **52**, 506-518.

WOOD, T.D., & Cassidy, R.F. (1927). *The new physical education*. New York: Macmillan.

Self-Help

William Harper
Purdue University

General Maxwell Taylor is reported to have said "Don't fight the question. Answer it!" However much I enjoy the spirit of General Taylor's advice in regard to answering questions straight away, some questions by their nature do not serve to be so crisply dispensed with. "Is physical education central to the mission of higher education?" is just such a question.

Some questions, I think, are somewhat permanent. They are to be asked again and again. Their purpose is to generate conversations which in turn sometimes generate action. They are asked in order to call attention to something or other, to put into question a certain state of affairs, or to announce a willingness, in the words of that courageous creature Winnie-the-Pooh, "to go on an explore." In other words, some questions are so permanent that not to ask them is a certain sign of individual or professional death. So we might agree at the outset that our very willingness to ask again and again this particular question about physical education's centrality to higher education is life-giving, not life-threatening. Of this we should be proud.

On the other hand, we should be no less proud of maintaining a healthy skepticism toward the way in which these more enduring—if not particularly endearing—questions are put. For instance, regarding the question before us, consider the variety of assumptions already clinging to the question: (a) that there is something called higher education which can be understood apart from the diverse kinds of particular institutions which are said to compose it; (b) that there is something resembling a mission proper to higher education; (c) that this mission, generally speaking, is intelligible; (d) that this theoretical intelligibility is practically understood and carried out; (e) that even if we discern a mission (or missions), we understand the criteria for assessing the relative centrality of any field of inquiry to that mission (whether FTEs, the scholarly tradition, marketplace demands, extramural funding success, competency development, or whatever); and (f) that being central to the mission of higher education in whatever sense and in any or every particular moment is even desirable.

THE GREAT WALL OF CHINA

All in all, this present moment in higher education, at least from the perspective of a teacher, is uncomfortably reminiscent of Kafka's parable, "The Great Wall of China."

That parable told of how the wall was built over generations of labor. At one time, in the early years of the building of the wall, the people knew what they were doing. They were trying to keep the nomads out and thereby preserve their civilization. But in time the wall came to be built in piecemeal sections. Those working on one section were not in contact with those building another section. Most of all, they had gradually lost contact with the central capital. They did not even know if the capital was intact, who was ruling, or whether the empire itself still stood. Yet they continued to carry on their rather meaningless labor. They built even though they no longer knew what their purpose was in doing what they did.

Let us hope that the ongoing efforts to build the great walls of the academy are somewhat less desperate than the 1,200 years of Chinese history which Kafka abbreviated for us. Even so, we can still draw a useful lesson from this parable. There must be some living center somewhere in higher education in order for the labors on our section to make any sense. That's one obvious lesson. Even more obvious is the implicit warning Kafka gave about wall building in general, piecemeal or otherwise. But for our purposes—and freely acknowledging that wall building is *not* the best metaphor for the ongoing business of higher education—this parable at least hints that the part must embody the whole or forever lose its meaning; and furthermore, it is the responsibility of those partisans to find out for themselves, by studying their part, the whole their part is part of. In the end, Kafka wrote, there was "a certain feebleness of faith and imaginative power on the part of the people," that prevented them from "raising the empire out of its stagnation in Peking and clasping it in all its palpable living reality to their own breasts" (Kafka, 1936, p. 97). We aren't so feeble and unimaginative as that, are we?

A DIGRESSION—SELF-HELP

Let me digress briefly here. In 1859, the year Darwin's *Origin of the Species* and Mill's *Essay on Liberty* were published, the Englishman, Samuel Smiles, finished a book that sold 20,000 copies in the first year, 150,000 by 1889, and nearly 250,000 by the end of the 19th century. The book was called *Self-Help*. It celebrated the power of perseverance through a lengthy series of short biographies about the conduct, character, and successes of ordinary people—businessmen, inventors, artists, lawyers, engineers, and others. The general idea of the book was that most of the world's good works and deeds were achieved not so much by individuals of extraordinary genius and intelligence but instead through the energy, cheerfulness, prudence, and industry that all people are capable of. Although it was one example of the widely popular "success" literature genre of the mid-Victorian years, *Self-Help* was more than merely an inspirational guide for making one's way in the world. It was a forceful, sustained statement for strong, energetic individualism: the powers of self-respect, attention, application, purpose, observation, patience, and integrity. "The spirit of self-help," wrote Smiles, "is the root of all genuine growth in the individual; and exhibited in the lives of many, it constitutes the true source of national vigor and strength." He went on to say:

> Help from without is often enfeebling in its effects, but help from within invariably invigorates. Whatever is done *for* men or classes to a certain extent takes away the stimulus

and necessity of doing for themselves; and where men are subjected to over-guidance and over-government, the inevitable tendency is to render them comparatively helpless. (1859, 1866, p. 35)

HELPING OURSELVES

Returning now to the lesson from Kafka's parable, we can help best in raising the empire of higher education by helping ourselves. We help ourselves by centering ourselves. And we center ourselves by thinking for ourselves.

It should be clear from the short description of the overall spirit of self-help as Smiles described it, and when extended to partisans such as ourselves, that being agents of our own well-doing and well-being is not to be confused with either promoting ourselves (common to many of our AAHPERD and President's Council projects) or imitating others (common to many of our scholarly subdiscipline research projects). Self-help, then, does not mean self-promotion or helping ourselves to the work of others. Self-help is not another way of rationalizing self-serving in the pejorative meaning of that phrase.

Rather, being our own best helpers demands that we carry this invigorating spirit directly into our teaching, research, and service contributions. Each of us, each individual partisan, has the power, the will, the force of purpose of which Smiles spoke. "Whatever theoretical conclusions logicians may have formed as the freedom of the will," Smiles argued, "each individual feels that practically he is free to choose between good and evil—that he is not as a mere straw thrown upon the water to mark the direction of the current, but that he has within him the power of a strong swimmer, and is capable of striking out for himself, of buffeting with the waves, and directing to a great extent his own independent course" (1866, p. 231).

Consider two brief but concrete examples of what this power of self-help obliges us to do. If we are ever to control our own course in higher education, then as strong swimmers, so to speak, we will sometimes find ourselves fighting the current. There are at least two strong currents in higher education in which our thinking has presumably been done for us: sport and health. That is, insofar as the large themes of sport and health are concerned, we appear to be drifting with the current when perhaps self-help demands that we swim against it.

Truth and Sport

Our first example comes from the world of sport. Most of us, at one time or another and with varying degrees of skill, have banged a tennis ball back and forth across the net. Now popular opinion has it that playing tennis, however enjoyable it may be, is far from the truth. That is, whatever we should expect to encounter in playing tennis, we should not expect to encounter truth. Brand Blanshard, a philosopher, put it this way in the opening sentences of his study titled *The Nature of Thought*:

> Thought is that activity of mind which aims directly at truth. There are many activities of mind that aim at truth indirectly, such as learning to read or to use instruments of research.

There are many others that do not aim at it at all, such as sleeping, chopping wood, and playing tennis. But when and so far as we are seeking truth directly, we are thinking. (1939, p. 51)

Given the enthusiasm with which some physical education departments are willing to abandon their sport skills programs, many of us apparently agree with Blanshard. But, and as others in our field have argued (e.g., Kretchmar in the *Journal of the Philosophy of Sport*) genuine thinking is not limited to Blanshard's version of it. Indeed, if such other thinkers as Dewey, Heidegger, Jaspers, Earle, and Rorty are correct, the correspondence theory of truth (which is substantially what Blanshard's claim implies) falls short of accounting for the ways in which the human being experiences truths. That truths are lived, not merely taught, points to particular modes of being in truth which are based on performance or action and not exclusively on cognitive apprehensions. In a way, much of our movement-based literature, especially our dance literature, has already anticipated this notion of living truths.

Harold Taylor (1959), another philosopher, argued that most educators are unjustifiably narrow in their very understanding of what constitutes the intellect. To them, thinking is an activity which takes place in a separate faculty called the intellect; if our aim in education is to teach people to think, then such educators would naturally train the intellect through the so-called academic disciplines. But, Taylor pointed out, few philosophers and even fewer educators understand that the various performing and movement-based arts "are forms of knowledge even though they do not express themselves in words" (p. 11). Although we can help students learn *about* these various arts in conventional intellectual ways (such as in history and appreciation courses), more significantly we need to introduce students to the discipline of experiencing the forms themselves. "The important thing," wrote Taylor, "is the experience, the discipline and joy they give to those who engage in them and learn to value them" (p. 11). Developing such sensibilities is the key to teaching people to think for themselves and to organize for themselves the knowledge and understandings that begin with these direct, first-hand undergoings, enthusiasms, and meanings.

Self-help in this case simply demands that we attend carefully to the lived experiences of these movement forms. Rather than taking for granted what others would have us believe about the truth-giving abilities (or inabilities) of sport, dance, and movement forms, self-help means that we look at them directly ourselves and tell the world what we find. After all, and as Blanshard elsewhere urges us, "If one would learn to think well, the best way is to think with a determined regard for truth in one's field, whatever it may be" (Blandshard, 1973, p. xiii).

Hygeia

Our second example, which almost naturally follows as the consequence of the prevailing currents of our first example, comes from the world of health. Probably at no time since the age of the Victorian pursuits of rational recreations—indeed since the age in which Smiles himself wrote—has any age approached ours in the pursuit of maintaining and improving upon personal levels of physical health or what has come to be called wellness, holistic health, and prospective medicine. There is no need to trot out all the instances of this preoccupation, for today one cannot walk through a bookstore, browse magazine racks, turn on television and radio, or read or hear commercial advertisements and *not* be struck by our worship of Hygeia. The current is strong.

But is the current deep? Aren't we really letting others do our thinking for us? After all, if we accept the relative bankrupt truth status of such activities as tennis—our first example—then instead of trying to look for sources of intrinsic value and meaning in such activities, we settle instead for taking them simply as health-giving diversions. We take them as having only instrumental value. We reduce ourselves to scientifically authorized and professionally glorified cheerleaders for health. Accordingly, we then exclusively busy ourselves with such practices as preparing future corporate fitness directors, promoting the "scientific" approach to exercise and human performance, pushing hard for the marriage of sport and medicine, trying to win grants from the National Institute of Health, doing contract research for commercial health-related corporations, planning health fairs, managing hospital wellness centers, organizing 10-kilometer runs and triathalons, or training our youth to jump rope for our collective hearts.

However admirable those activities are, we should not let this current fascination with health exclusively represent the heart of our interests (both literally and figuratively). Sooner or later it will occur to some administrators of academic programs that these affairs of the heart can be better done outside the walls of the academy. After all the sweat is worked out of our subjects, after all the fitness programs are conducted, and after all our jump- or run-a-thon money is collected, a truly skeptical soul is going to ask us: "But what is all this good health for?"

The question is apt to shock us. We will discover that we have dreadfully confused our ends and our means. We will take as an end good health; we will take as the means to it the variety of movement, training, and sport arts and crafts. Even if there is some short-term advantage in identifying so exclusively with the health and therapy of it all, surely nothing could be worse for our long-term contribution to the ends of education—at least a liberal education.

Our proper contribution in regard to this healthful living example is to celebrate the potential for the intrinsic value of these various crafts and arts as the end toward which such experiences point, and on the other hand to understand that the means which makes these experiences possible resides in reasonable degrees of preparedness or healthfulness. Self-help, then, would call for us to swim against the general current of the variety of popular health movements. Buffeting the waves will require us to rigorously continue to explore these movement experiences not so much for what health-giving benefits they might incidentally provide but instead to explore them for the unique elemental and intrinsic meanings they might hold.

CONCLUSION

These two illustrative examples of currents worth swimming against—the bankrupt truth status of sports and the elevating of good health to an end in itself—are important of course. But we should remember that these sorts of examples chiefly illustrate the kinds of help we could do without. They have in common what Peter Berger, a sociologist, has called the triumph of triviality. Berger's example was our treatment of death. He argued that in our approach to death, we have sealed up the more philosophical questions in practice. Furthermore, he wrote, the questions about it are even "theoretically liquidated by regulating them to meaninglessness" (1970, p. 75). He associated this denial, practically and theoretically, to the triumph of triviality in which we shrink the scope of human experience.

Higher education exists (or ought to) primarily in order to expand the scope of human experience, not shrink it. It serves to legitimize the human search for answers to those three eternal questions: Where did we come from? What are we to do here? Where are we going? It serves to liberate the questioner from prejudice, dogmatism, and ignorance. It serves to free the individual for learning to learn. It serves to help the lifelong learner to understand the need to think and act reasonably. It serves to perpetuate through the learner the ideas of justice and duty, quality and taste, courage and truth. It serves to provide opportunities to assist the student of life find what interests, what talents and gifts, are unique to his or her expressive life. By way of this expressive life, it serves to multiply opportunities for occupation and originality, surprise and serendipity, peace and poetry, laughter and love, promise and playfulness—all of which can be reduced to Socrates' overworked but still apt dictum: "Know thyself."

We *do* have a part to play in this life-creating process. That others do not always understand this part is just as much our fault, or more so, than theirs. We perhaps do not often enough, persistently enough, or patiently enough help ourselves by thinking for ourselves. When we don't, we deserve the trivializing results, for we, as they, have failed to see in our part the whole; we drift even more as we and they become more feeble and unimaginative still. But when we do help ourselves, when we do think for ourselves, when we do let truths reveal themselves to us and celebrate them with others, we will be on center. We will be as the child in us is in this passage from Wordsworth's, "The Excursion"

> I have seen
> A curious child, who dwelt upon a tract
> Of inland ground, applying to his ear
> The convolutions of a smooth-lipped shell;
> To which, in silence hushed, his very soul
> Listened intensely; and his countenance soon
> Brightened with joy; for from within were heard
> Mummerings, whereby the monitor expressed
> Mysterious union with its native sea.
> Even such a shell the universe itself
> Is to the ear of Faith; and there are times,
> I doubt not, when to you it doth impart
> Authentic tidings of invisible things;
> Of ebb and flow, and ever-during power;
> And central peace, subsisting at the heart
> Of endless agitation.

(cited in Richards, 1962, pp. 116-117)

REFERENCES

BERGER, P. (1970). *A rumor of angels.* New York: Doubleday Anchor.

BLANCHARD, B. (1939). *The nature of thought* (2 Vols.). London: George Allen & Unwin, Ltd.

BLANSHARD, B. (1973). *The uses of a liberal education*. LaSalle, IL: Open Court Publ.

KAFKA, F. (1970 [1936]). *The great wall of China*. New York: Schocken Books.

RICHARDS, M.C. (1962). *Centering*. Middletown, CT: Wesleyan University Press.

SMILES, S. (1859, 1866). *Self-help*. London: John Murray, LTD.

TAYLOR, H. (1959). *Art and intellect*. New York: Doubleday.

An Alternate Perspective Of Physical Education In Higher Education

Thomas Sheehan
University of Connecticut

Many years ago, my first professor of physical education in my first course in physical education informed the class that we were entering a field of study that we would be defending for the duration of our occupational lives. At the time I thought the statement was sensationalistic and designed only for motivational purposes. Not so! Now, 30 years later, we are involved in what is ostensibly a defense of our field. We are again reacting to another crisis.

What problem produced this crisis? One need not be an astute logician to conclude that the theme of this conference reflects the problem and that the theme was precipitated by the newest crisis facing us in the 1980s: the systematic elimination of the alleged academic side of physical education programs in some institutions of higher learning. In spite of our beliefs to the contrary, we must conclude from the evidence that some people in higher education do not think we contribute to the ordained knowledge-based mission of the institution for which they are responsible. This most recent difficulty cannot be ignored with the hope that the eradication decisions will be reversed or that the threat will simply disappear. A precedent has been established, and precedents have a way of rapidly becoming normative procedure.

Given the financial constraints imposed upon the administrators of colleges and universities, it is easy to understand and to agree that academic departments or schools on campuses that cannot justify their academic integrity should be phased out of existence. The elimination of physical education in a few institutions will provide a rationale for other administrators to continue the purge. We must know the crisis is real and that the contamination will soon increase to pandemic proportions.

As a member of a department of physical education, I am concerned about my field of study's identification as an integral part of the central mission of my university narrowly and higher education broadly. At this point I am not ready to extirpate the academic study of physical education and somehow argue that we can only facilitate the mission indirectly by physically exercising students. I do perceive this external threat as a challenge—one that could stimulate the entire physical education family to work as a cohesive group with a single purpose. I am reminded of Dr. Samuel Johnson's remark about the threat of execution: "Depend on it, sir, when a man knows he is to be hanged in a fortnight it concentrates his mind wonderfully."

However excited I am about concentrating on this threat, as a person in the academic trenches I am also extremely anxious about how the challenge is going to be met. How the collective membership of physical education responds to this issue affects us all intimately. A significant portion of our identification and self-esteem is inextricably woven into our field of study. We have provided knowledge and behavioral experiences that have made a difference in how countless numbers of people live their lives. I want this to continue. The anxiety I harbor about the physical education community's meeting and satisfying this challenge is rooted in the relative ineffectiveness of our addressing previous questions about the credibility of physical education.

The question, ''Is physical education central to the mission of higher education?'' may be answered by simply outlining the mission of physical education and substituting the phrase ''higher education'' wherever the words ''physical education'' occur. Comparing this interpolated list to a list of the mission of higher education will demonstrate, at least in a qualitative sense, the degree of association between the two functions. Thus we may conclude whether physical education is central or peripheral to the mission of higher education.

As simplistic as this suggested comparative analysis sounds, it does have some construct validity and could answer the question. Following my documentation of both general and specific higher education mission statements, I concluded that a workable synthesis of these statements must, out of structural necessity, relate to knowledge—its discovery, extension, refinement, and dissemination. Regardless of the education prescriptions for development of the person, the maintenance and growth of technology, and the advancement of culture, the variable common to each of these goals can be identified and related to the input and output of knowledge. We in higher education are really in the knowledge business.

As I began to extract from our literature the mission of physical education with respect to fundamental knowledge specific to the field, I was confronted with conflicting messages, and thus the whole process became personally frustrating. The futility of this venture reminded me again of what I believe to be a very basic cause of the problem we face today. That is, we must be able to delineate clearly, and in a uniform voice, *what* we do when we do what we do. The absence of this delineation makes it impossible to enumerate the functions of physical education and provide evidence that these functions are reciprocal to the mission of higher education.

In my frustration I was overcome with a feeling of déjà vu. We have been here before. All of us over 40 years of age faced a strikingly similar situation a generation ago. In 1963 the emergency had to do with our survival vis-à-vis the scathing criticism of physical education by Conant, Rickover, Coleman, and Lieberman, to mention a few. We addressed this issue by trying to prove that the field of physical education conformed to the criteria of an academic discipline and, as such, should become a legitimate study in all schools and colleges. The real question we were asked to answer, however, was ''What do we study?'' It is unfortunate that we forgot the lessons learned in that traumatic time, because today our administrators and boards of trustees are asking ''Does your field of study complement the mission of higher education in general and our institution's goals in particular?'' For me, there is no real difference between these two questions.

Have we been able to reply to this query in a convincing manner? Apparently not. If we had or could have, we might merely analyze the knowledge of the field and determine where there is mutual accord or disagreement with the knowlege implied in the mission of higher education.

In spite of the fact that for 20 years we have been asked to define exactly what we do, we have not responded with acceptable, definitive efforts. Quite frankly, if we maintain our existing structure I doubt we shall be able to respond appropriately, due to our inability to isolate an object of study.

Such statements infuriate physical educators. Certainly we study something, and certainly we have worthwhile knowledge about compartments of reality. The truth is that we have too many objects of study and that they are related to each other only incidentally. A consequence of this is that we do not concentrate our efforts on one focus and expand our knowledge to a level that is in keeping with other scholarly units in higher education.

Do we have too many foci, and are they unrelated? It was once written, "there seems to be a very general misapprehension, even among intelligent men, as to the nature of the work in which we are engaged. By many it is regarded simply as a speciality in medicine, others think it merely a department in athletics; others still, with more gross ideas, regard us as men who devote our time and energy to the building up of muscular tissue." Luther Gulick wrote this in 1890. Then, 93 years later, Harold VanderZwaag wrote, "In essence, physical educators have an identity problem. They might well ask questions such as who we are, or what do we do?. . .The net result of the situation today is that physical education has evolved as an umbrella-like field with no real focus" (1983, pp. 68-69). Between the time of these two testaments, we have attempted to isolate this elusive focus. Lawrence Rarick (1967, p. 51) said "Physical education does, however, have a focus: namely, human movement. . . .This aspect of man's experience is our domain." Concurring with Rarick, Camille Brown stated "There seems to be agreement, however, that physical education deals with the study of human movement" (1967, p. 53).

In 1982 Charles Bucher concluded that future physical educators must "provide themselves with the proper credentials in order to establish jurisdiction over their domain." They must "help people to become responsible for their health and fitness," and they "must recognize that people will live longer and be more fit and active in the years to come." In the summer of 1983, AAHPERD published a functional handbook designed to acquaint its members with how physical educators can apprise their governmental officials about the advantages of their offering. For example the question, "What is physical education?" is answered with, "The study of how and why people move." The response to "Why do we need physical education?" is "We need to be taught how to use our bodies effectively and become physically fit for life."

These citations are but a few of the many statements of the past 20 years which designate either human movement or physical fitness as our focus. Add to this list the impact that the study of sport or sport science has had on college physical education curricula, literature, and national organizations, and we might conclude that we have enveloped three fields of study into one. This conclusion can be substantiated by an account of the major foci of these concepts. Although fraught with the error of reduction, human movement concerns the quality and quantity of how and why people locomote themselves in *all* life experiences. Limiting human movement study to those movements accommodated only in selected activities is not logically defensible. Physical fitness relates to the efficiency of the organism when performing work.

Contemporary fitness practitioners are expanding their sphere to include "wellness," a concept that is easily subsumed under the more general heading of health. Sport is a social institution structured for the express purpose of providing the individual a symbolic social experience through which he or she can reduce anxiety over nonachievement and cognitively assimilate achievement processes. These three areas of study are related only incidentally. Further confirmation of the secondary interaction among these areas is established when variables particular to each area are compared.

For example, sport people focus on sport as the dependent variable and *may* use human movement and fitness as independent variables. Contrary to popular interpretation, the primary object of sport is not fitness. Movement advocates use effective movement as the dependent variable and *may* use sport and fitness as independent variables. People who study fitness focus on physical health and *may* use sport and movement as independent variables. Each scholar and practitioner may, of course, use an infinite variety of causative variables to determine their demonstrative effect on the object of focus.

Members of traditional academic disciplines employ their study focus as the dependent variable in an attempt to describe and predict its function. Fields of study that are central to the knowledge mission of higher education can tolerate only one focus. Alleged fields of study espousing two or more foci—for example physical education—are doomed to extinction because of the inability to clearly demonstrate what is studied. I submit, and generalize, that every problem or survival emergency that physical educators have faced for the past 70 years has been caused by the lack of a clear object of study, one that is sufficiently important to know and does not infringe on or duplicate the academic territory of another field of study.

It could be argued that physical education is an emerging or evolving field of study. Thomas Kuhn (1970), a noted philosopher of science, maintains that lack of harmony on significant issues, the inability to define the field, and debates about basic theoretical concepts are the earmarks of preparadigm science or crisis science. Since the preeminent function of a science or a field of study is to discover cause and effect, it is tautological to conclude that at least in a general sense the field must determine its effect before the discovery process can begin. This effect is nothing more than a field's focus. The causes of this effect constitute the body of knowledge about a focus.

As we in physical education search for academic responsibility and respectability, we cannot at this time in our history even be viewed as a preparadigm or crisis field of study. To be eligible for this dubious distinction would necessitate a mutually accepted effect or focus, which would allow us to develop a body of knowledge. The futility we have always experienced in formulating a body of knowledge is a consequence of our not defining the focus. If physical education is anything presently, it is, in a manner of speaking, a postcrisis field. It is as if we have a bag of sticks—after being physically threatened we grab one stick to ward off our assailant.

What is the typical fate of pre- or postcrisis fields? The membership becomes frustrated, assumes a part of the field as its focus, and begins to legitimate its efforts. The members splinter from the main body. This has happened in physical education. However, most of our authors have misinterpreted our splinter groups and, as a result, have evaded a deeper and more meaningful issue. Sport psychologists, sport sociologists, sport historians, and others have formed associations and been labeled "splinter groups."

These are not our splinter groups—they indeed represent legitimate subdisciplines of sport science. Our splinter groups during the last 25 years have been those advocating human movement and sport science. They were groups in quest of a singular academic focus that was not the domain of another avowed academic focus. As these groups and their foci were being formed, the members could not predict that eventually they would become dissident factions within physical education. It is important to point out that these groups intended to replace the extant focus of physical education. They were protest/revolutionary groups that were dissatisfied with the field's current status. When it became obvious that the members of the field were not going to adopt their focus permanently, the groups did not rescind their substitute motion and they are still with us.

If these arguments have merit, can physical education be considered as central to the mission of higher education? The solution concerns our fierce resistance to the proliferation of more areas within the field. Rather we must divide physical education into three fields.

To accomplish this division in a manner that will protect the integrity of all of the foci in physical education, as well as to the satisfaction of our members' needs, I must agree with Harold VanderZwaag's (1983) suggestions in our own publication, *Quest*, with slight modification. Within the structure of a university, the area of fitness/wellness would become identified as health or health education and thus become a viable unit in a larger division or school of allied health professions. Movement people may transfer to departments of dance, or perhaps departments of educational psychology. This will give departments of educational psychology an opportunity to become involved in motor learning as well as verbal learning. The sport science area should assume departmental status within schools of fine and applied arts, where the members of this newly formed department will be able to interact with others who share the same cognitive and behavioral basis for their existence (in the Piagetian sense). It might be added, parenthetically, that our organizations also might begin to reconceptualize their structure.

It would be extremely difficult to deny the knowledge produced and disseminated from each of these reconstituted fields of study. Each would certainly be central to the academic mission of higher education. These areas can stand tall independently—they probably will not survive as interdependent entities because they are not truly interdependent.

The academic-related problems we face as department members are a microcosm of the larger problems in the field. The goals of the individuals within departments of physical education too frequently are not central to the mission of the department. At the departmental level, I want to interact with people who are interested in the same dependent variable. In the physical education departments I know, however, there is very little sharing between the groups in movement, sport science, and fitness. I also do not enjoy having to justify our legitimacy on campus every decade or so. I think it is time to put our house in order.

REFERENCES

AAHPERD. (1983). Questions and answers about physical education. In *Shaping the body politic*. Washington, DC: Author.

BROWN, C. (1967). The structure of knowledge of physical education. *Quest*, **9**, 53-67.

BUCHER, C.A. (1982). The future of physical education and sport. *Journal of Physical Education, Recreation and Dance*, **53**, 12-14.

KUHN, T.S. (1970). *The structure of scientific revolutions*. Chicago: University of Chicago Press.

RARICK, G.L. (1967). The domain of physical education as a discipline. *Quest*, **9**, 49-52.

VANDERZWAAG, H.J. (1983). Coming out of the maze: Sport management, dance management and exercise science—programs with a future. *Quest*, **35**, 66-73.

Physical Education: Is It Central To The Mission Of Higher Education? An Administrator's Perspective

Muriel R. Sloan
University of Maryland

To be asked to take a somewhat dim view of the question, "Is physical education central to the mission of higher education?—from an administrator's perspective—and to do so before an audience of friends and colleagues in physical education, seems foolhardy if not dangerous. College and university physical educators have continuously agonized over the field and have analyzed and reanalyzed its unique mission, its scholarly and educational contributions, its curriculum, its role in higher education. We have reconceptualized it, restructured it, and sometimes renamed it. Yet the question "What is it?" is still with us. Even more unfortunate for the determination of its centrality, our academic colleagues and much of the public either are as unsure of the field as we are or are quite sure of what it is but do not think of it in a complimentary way.

A simple though unsatisfactory answer to the question can be, "it depends." It depends, for one, on why the question of centrality is being asked and for what purposes the answers are intended. It is obvious that higher education is a nongrowth enterprise. As the resources diminish or reach crisis proportions, the responses range from automatic across-the-board cuts, to reallocations based upon head count and natural attrition, to, most traumatically, retrenchment involving tenured positions. I submit that a significant key to the concept of centrality and the degree to which any academic area is perceived as being "central" to the mission of higher education depends on the responses chosen by given institutions or the response choices available to them. The less stringent the response required or chosen, the broader the centrality band width.

Secondly, determination of centrality obviously depends on the mission of higher education. Just as the term "physical education" represents different meanings, so does the term "mission of higher education." Common to most institutions of higher education is a commitment to preserving and advancing knowledge and transmitting that knowledge for the benefit of society. Obviously the measure of centrality would shift for a number of fields, academic and professional, in institutions whose mission emphasizes the advancement of knowledge, usually through a graduate and research focus, as compared to those with strong professional and service goals.

In spite of their diminishing resources, all institutions of higher education strive for excellence in what they do. Mission statements are noted not only for broad generalizations but also for the repeated use of the word "excellence." As Peter Drucker (1983) said in "Making Room in No-Growth Firms," if a nongrowth business cannot grow bigger, it has to become better. He also remarked that nongrowth is even more tied to performance in nonbusinesses such as schools, universities, and hospitals. It requires the members to find their strengths and the opportunities to apply them productively. Therefore, the concept of centrality in higher education is a qualitative one, as well as a financial and quantitative one. The qualitative criteria chosen by given institutions will reflect their mission. Considering the ambiguity of the field of physical education and the continuing quest to identify the mission of higher education, centrality between the two is not a given.

Speaking somewhat generally, then, I would offer several contentions which speak to a lack of centrality for physical education in higher education. First, physical education has *never* been considered central to the basic mission of most institutions of higher education and particularly not to those emphasizing graduate and research goals or, for that matter, traditional liberal education. At institutions in which a professional school mission was stated—or tolerated—the physical education preparation program was accepted, particularly when it involved large numbers of students and therefore tuition. But the quality was not always perceived as high. Remember, for example, the notion that all intercollegiate athletes were "dumb jocks" and got through school only because they majored in physical education. In the late 1950s and early 1960s, the Sputnik era, the term "centrality" was not yet in vogue, but physical education was put on the defensive as universities were pressed to give more time to "real" subjects rather than to recreation and games. In most instances, physical education programs were saved by equally fearsome data on the shocking physical fitness levels of children, and by the nationally orchestrated campaigns which suggested total defeat by the enemy if physical education for the general college program was eliminated.

Second, the current or recurrent "crisis" in public school education will alter missions of higher education and may positively affect selected areas of teacher preparation at the university level. This will be less true, however, for physical education. Criticisms are aimed primarily at the public schools and the teachers at that level rather than at higher education. But the push for "back to basics," for more science, math, and computer literacy to meet the demands of an information society, are enabling universities to influence the public schools. They are doing so by upgrading admission standards, by increasing entrance course requirements in math, science, and languages—moves that reflect higher education's concepts of the disciplines central to contemporary undergraduate education. We see the reinforcing effect of higher education's demands and that of multitudinous panels, boards, and commissions making recommendations to the public schools about education in science and technology. What are the suggested solutions? Substantial lengthening of the school day, week, year; placing earlier emphasis in grades K-6 on increased and more effective interaction in math, science, and technology—a truly vertical curriculum.

Where is physical education in this? With regard to the public school debate, rarely if ever does one hear physical education mentioned as a basic subject that merits attention. We might call that the crisis of omission facing physical education. For example, the National Science Board's 1983 Report on Education in Science and Technology adheres to its charge of emphasizing only those teaching particular learning areas, but it recognizes that they cannot be separated from the teaching and learning of many other *important* subjects such as English, foreign languages, and history, where glaring deficiencies are also recognized. The National Science Board's report outlines the kinds of problem-solving insight and skills to be provided for the new pattern of education that must come to be.

What role would physical education serve in this vertical curriculum? What does it have to offer by way of understanding the science of movement through its instruction? Can physical educators articulate about the cognitive and affective components of motor performance? Or, is their own view limited to movement as an auxiliary tool for the learning of mathematics by having students move to numbered squares? Do physical educators see movement experience as a significant way of knowing—about ourselves and the world around us?

Physical education is not always ignored in recommendations for reform. For example, American University President Richard Berendzen (*Washington Post*, 1983) believes that high schools should turn nonacademic courses such as driver training and sex education into after-school programs to allow more time for more traditional academic subjects such as history, languages, and math. Although he believes that some of these things may be quite worthwhile, he also believes that the school day simply isn't long enough for everything. His suggestions were rebutted by another analyst who responded that driver education is already offered after school in many places, and that in many others the driver education teachers are now coaching football after school. The courses mentioned are often in physical education departments or in their related disciplines within colleges of health, recreation, and physical education.

The Maryland Commission on Education wants to make overall course loads more stringent than the current requirements of 4 years of English, 3 years of social studies, 2 years of science, and 1 year of physical education. They recommend a 3rd year of mathematics and 1 year of fine arts which can include dance. No further mention is made of physical education.

What effect on teacher preparation do some of these recommendations have? Over the past several years many colleges of education, which often include departments of physical education, have become shadows of their former selves. Student-teacher enrollment has dropped by 40% or more in many instances. Even though education has tried to adopt the academic discipline model espoused in higher education, its faculty members have not been recognized as peers by their colleagues in the more traditional disciplines. Further, the price they paid was a separation of theory from practice and a barrage of criticisms from the public schools for whom they provided the teachers.

But the crisis in the public schools may partially restore the losses sustained by colleges of education, particularly in the preparation of science and math teachers. Although there is great debate on university campuses about the role of colleges or schools of education versus the disciplines preparing future teachers, teacher preparation is beginning to be seen as more central to the mission of many universities. Therefore, what are viewed as subject deficiencies in the schools, such as in science and math, will influence the degree of centrality attributed to programs in higher education which will help to overcome these deficiencies. On the other hand, required teaching certification met by taking courses in education is coming under fire. The *Wall Street Journal* (Inman, 1984) headlined a battle which is stirring in many states because top-notch science and math graduates are not permitted to teach in those critical areas if they lack education courses. This battle has significant implications for the future of teacher preparation models.

What effect does all of this have on the preparation of physical education teachers? There has been no lament about physical education in the schools and no suggestions to enhance it or to give it more time. There already are vocational disincentives such as a lower pay scale, lower esteem, and little opportunity for advancement for women particularly; these may be sufficient to further decrease enrollment in physical education professional preparation programs.

Decisions of centrality at the university level will also be affected. For example, the University of Maryland has embarked on a program of academic planning to accomplish selective growth, or to become better rather than bigger. We are in the process of identifying programs to be targeted for enhancement with centrality as one of the criteria. University of Maryland Chancellor Slaughter, who is a former director of the National Science Foundation, said recently that in 1983 some 7,000 physical education majors were graduated as compared to 400 science and math teaching graduates nationwide. I believe selection of that fact by a university administrator has potential significance for the perceived centrality of the program areas mentioned.

A third factor operating against the centrality of physical education involves the continued necessity to defend physical education at all levels of education; this reflects an expectancy hypothesis in the field which may become a self-fulfilling prophecy. The front page of the October 1983 issue of *NASPE NEWS*, for example, contained an article entitled "NASPE Physical Education Justification Project Gets Under Way—Vern Seefeldt to Direct." Identified as NASPE's highest priority, the physical education justification repository is being developed cooperatively by NASPE and the President's Council on Physical Fitness and Sports. The contention is that the physical education justification packet will help to save physical education programs at all levels. This campaign is reminiscent of others to which I have referred. In the Sputnik era the same justifications for fitness came to the fore and, although there may be others today, obviously the professionals believe, and rightly so, that little has changed in the past 30 years. A second headline on the front page of that same issue, in even larger print, revealed continued support by one of physical education's staunchest advocates. It read "Department of Defense Supports Physical Education as Essential." The main thrust was physical fitness. I submit that although we all recognize the basic importance of physical fitness, headlining it as the unique mission of physical education will not enhance its centrality in the world of education. And what message do administrators get from the barricades set up in expectation of attack? Rosemary Shraer rightfully pointed out the importance of positive and continuing communication with administrators.

Yet another internal item which can have an adverse effect on the centrality question is the relatively recent "scientism" of physical education, recent in a long-range historical sense, which has brought mixed blessings to the field. The discipline approach in physical education initiated in the 1960s has emulated and glorified the academic discipline model in higher education. Its practitioners are being rewarded through promotion and tenure at the university level, but their separation from the instructional practices in physical education classes is almost complete. The emphasis on scientific reductionism has created separate camps within departments professing physical education, regardless of what they are called. There are the scientist-scholars, the preparers of teachers of physical education, and the teachers of activity classes. The latter two groups have a relatively low percentage of tenure. Time does not permit discussing the substantive implications of this condition on the concept of centrality, but it can put physical education in jeopardy simply from an administrative point of view. Nontenured lines are easier for administrators to recapture, either for reallocation to more central areas or for retrenchment. Perhaps the most striking blow to the centrality of all aspects of physical education is that little seems to have changed in the teaching of physical education at all levels of education.

There is still an emphasis on the "how to" rather than the "why," an emphasis which is not conducive to scholarly inquiry by teachers or to creative problem-solving by students. The sorrow is that as the science of movement becomes more sophisticated in the academic sense, and as we discover more about our subject matter, that knowlege is less and less available to teachers and students in physical education.

And what has happened to the art of movement which used to be mentioned as part of this new discipline whose subject matter was human movement? What has happened to the art and humanistic aspects of human movement since dance has left physical education for greener fields?

It seems paradoxical that at a time of tremendous public interest in self-development, creativity, and wellness through movement activities that physical education is not perceived as contributing significantly to these goals. Our colleagues in health education have adopted a more holistic concept of wellness which goes beyond physical fitness. For example, they are active in teaching eager students and faculty the causes and cures of stress—a national malady. And what do physical educators do? They test stress. Lost from the body of knowledge of human movement is the fact that skilled movement is based upon muscular tension and relaxation, the control of which can be learned, a skill which can be the underpinnings of self-directed techniques of stress reduction or reduction of hypertension. The public flocks to private classes and studios in which such work is done because it is rarely found in physical education.

Related to the double-edged sword of discipline status is the fifth problem—the still-unresolved quest for the unique subject matter or body of knowledge for physical education. The terms *exercise, sport,* and *human movement* further cloud the issue of centrality for both physical educators and administrators. As several have already said, fitness—through exercise and sport (or athletics) has been the main element of what physical education is all about for the American public. To add the term *science* to exercise or sport does not necessarily change what goes on in it, and it does not necessarily persuade administrators or the public that reform has taken place. It could simply represent a new label on an old bottle!

I subscribe to the argument for specifying a subject matter more narrowly than physical education, namely, that we cannot be all things to all people. But as an educator, a physical educator, and an administrator, I know that we can be more things to children and adults than only sport and exercise, and we should be. Even though the worship of sport has reached extraordinary heights, much of it is in a spectator context. Even though the public is enthusiastic about fitness, there are broader and narrower concepts of "fitness" and a number of routes for accomplishing it. Perhaps greater attention to "fitness" practices stemming from Eastern cultures appear more relevant to many than jumping rope, jogging, or otherwise grunting and groaning. Perhaps the fitness techniques used by dancers—and dancers have been shown to have very high levels of overall fitness—would appeal to many.

Perhaps the very popularity of sport, and the fine job that sport scientists have done to bring it under academic scrutiny, may give budget-cutting administrators (from department chair and up) some ideas. One way to economize and at the same time increase the band width of centrality is to look at overlap within an institution; do away with redundancy. Why don't the disciplines upon which some sport scientists in physical education departments today base their study—psychology, sociology, history—study that area themselves? Certainly some of those sport scientists would be qualfied for appointment in the traditional disciplines, and the result could be more palatable: realloca- tion rather than retrenchment of tenured academicians. At best they could be set aside from those other programs in the physical education departments which are not as central.

Finally, when all of the required centrality data are submitted to the final decision makers, conclusions about the centrality of physical education may still rest on (a) the point made earlier about the band width of centrality relative to response choice and (b) to personal experience with a field, ignorance of changes in the field and its corol- lary, and reliance upon traditional stereotypes on the part of administrators, parents, and taxpayers.

As I mentioned earlier, each division of the University of Maryland's College Park campus has been asked to target program areas for enhancement. My division has ap- proximately 100 programs within it, depending upon how a program is defined. Each college within the division submitted enhancement justifications for five or six of its programs. My staff and I had to then choose six from approximately 24 programs sub- mitted. Let me reveal some of the inner-sanction discussion among administrators.

The College of PERH proposed enhancement for *all* of its departments. The college is generally highly regarded on the College Park campus; all departments are rated in the top 10, even though not by the National Academy of Sciences. Of all three depart- ments, one made the division staff's final list. Some comments made during the delib- erations were:

- Well, it would be pretty hard to justify physical education as a top priority of the College Park campus. What would President Toll do with that?
- Even though health education has one of the highest WCH/FTE [weighted credit hour/full-time equivalence] quotients on campus, it all comes from sex education!

To help prepare for this presentation, I asked other administrators at the Maryland Campus about their 'gut' feelings on the centrality of physical education to higher education.

The chancellor, a scientist-engineer, replied he had not given much thought to physical education or schools of education. From his experience at Washington State he knew that the School of Education (which included the Department of Physical Education) was not seen as a peer among equals, that the department chair was very capable, but often had to defend her department, and that physical education was low on that already low totem pole.

For this part, the vice-chancellor of academic affairs knew more about the physical education graduate areas in the sciences. He felt they were doing good work, he praised the undergraduate kinesiology program and, of the service program, he said it would be hard to imagine a university without one.

The assistant provost, a retired associate dean of the school of Education at Wiscon- sin, indicated that his view of the centrality of physical education had probably covered the scale from zero to nearly 10. His reasons for shifting his perspective included: (a) his coming to know and respect the work of some physical educators; (b) the fact that AAPHER became AAHPER*D* in recognition of dance; (c) his acquaintance with a bright young woman, a recent graduate of the University of Maryland who had majored in kinesiology and who he thought would bring credit to any physics or philosophy department. He concluded that the judgment of the contribution of discipline to a university's purpose rests on knowing the people in that discipline and coming to understand their research and teaching programs.

In conclusion, I would strike a tone of optimism mixed with the pessimism. I strongly believe in what physical education can contribute to all levels of education, and I believe it can do more than it is doing. I believe that university faculty and administrators are receptive to broader concepts of physical education for the university community. Martha Church is, and so is Rosemary Schraer. Perhaps the ones who need the most persuasion are those in physical education!

REFERENCES

DRUCKER, P. (1983, December). Making room in no-growth firms. *Wall Street Journal*.

INMAN, V. (1984, January). Certification of teachers lacking courses in education stirs battles in several states. *Wall Street Journal*.

NASPE News. (1983, October). No. 8.

WASHINGTON Post. (1983, December). High schools should shove aside nonacademic fare, AU president says.

Physical Education: Is It Central To The Mission Of Higher Education?

Margaret Robb
University of Rhode Island

Is physical education central to the mission of higher education? Of course it is! However, conference planners purposely ask questions that cannot be answered with a simple yes or no, so I will detail my rationale for answering yes.

How can the answer be yes when many physical education departments have diminished in size and stature? How can it be yes when fewer students are pursuing a major in physical education, and fewer are availing themselves of the elective program? Quite simply, the answer is yes because physical education is unique. It is the only subject area that stresses an understanding and appreciation for sport and human movement. It is the only subject matter which contributes to the physical well-being of people through movement. It is the only discipline whose professionals believe that quality living and professional success in life involves much more than the important verbal, mathematical, and communication skills. It is a field with a rich heritage. What would Gulick, McCloy, Williams, Homans, Metheny, Broer, Ley, Nash and a host of others say to us if we forgot our heritage? How could we answer them if we gave in by default?

Physical education is not the only subject area being examined or questioned in higher education. There is no field or discipline that does not continually undergo self-examination, a justification of its existence, a questioning of its worth. The humanities are going through it. They perceive themselves as being attacked by those who believe only in practical outcomes and by those who believe that the only subject worth studying is one that ensures survival in the job market. The professionals in the humanities sometimes have as difficult a time defining their subject area as do physical educators. The historians went through a process of self-examination when history of western civilization courses were no longer required. The English professors are questioning why they have to teach writing and composition. All fields must constantly reexamine and reestablish their rightful place in higher education. Physical education is no exception.

I wish I could say that the centrality of physical education to higher education is so well recognized and accepted that we are exempted from this go-around. But that would not be true. Instead, we must reaffirm and reestablish the rightful place of physical education in higher education. The reaffirmation of the centrality of physical education will take place in many arenas. The debate, discussion, and argument will take various forms. Yet, underlying the debate in whatever arena will be the knowledge that physical education is the only discipline that deals primarily with the phenomenon of sport and human movement. It is the only discipline that understands and studies motor development. Sport has existed in our society since the beginning of time. It will continue to exist. All of these concepts are worthy of study in higher education. But let's examine the arenas in which the debate will take place.

One important arena will be the associations other than the Alliance. For example, the Association of American Colleges has established a project to redefine the meaning and purpose of baccalaureate degrees. Since more than 500 different baccalaureate degrees can be awarded by colleges and universities, this association is concerned with the quality of an undergraduate degree. A statement will be released concerning the criteria and standards for evaluating undergraduate programs in instruction at the association's January 1985 annual meeting.

The only reference to physical education in the booklet "A Search for Quality and Coherence in Baccalaureate Education" was found in the section entitled "Extracurricular Contributions to Undergraduate Education." This reference was in the form of sports, recreational facilities, and intramurals. This is very distressing and implies that the committee is only interested in recreational sports, not the discipline of physical education. Ultimately these committees and the association will greatly influence the direction of higher education. We all know that physical education is not just an extracurricular activity, that while recreational facilities are important, physical education involves much more than leisure activities. We must make sure the associations also know this.

Another important arena will concern curriculum committees, both institutional and national. The curriculum remains the heart of education, representing the centrality and mission of particular institutions. Since World War II curricular change has resulted in a proliferation of various departmental offerings. In the 1960s relevance and student demands guided the curriculum. In the desire to meet student demands, many departments including physical education relabeled their courses. In the desire to become acceptable to the scientific community, physical education has tried different names, such as human kinetics. A declining enrollment and negative economic factors have increased this scramble to be all things to all people. In the desire to keep up with the scientific emphasis some programs have neglected the basic philosophy of sport, the joy of movement, the thrill of sport, and the appreciation of movement. In a desire to keep up with fitness some physical education programs have become so scientific in nature that the courses dealing with values and ethics appear to have been totally neglected.

In some schools, other disciplines have begun to include in their curriculum subjects that were once taught in physical education. The history department may offer a course in racism in sport; the psychology department may offer a course in perceptual motor learning; the sociology department is interested in the sociology of sport. As physical educators, we have always had knowledges in these areas, areas that in the past were generally reserved for our major students. Curriculum committees today are interested in interdisciplinary courses. Thus, perhaps this is one answer: an interdisciplinary course offered to all students. Physical educators know more about sport and about human movement than do other disciplines. Other disciplines can add their knowledges to enhance the content of the course, but it is the physical educators who must take the initiative to plan these interdisciplinary courses.

Some chairs and faculty maintain membership on curriculum committees just to make sure their major survives. Others are not as subtle; they actually say they don't care what is done to the curriculum so long as their major is saved. Still others firmly believe that a college curriculum must ultimately serve the higher purpose of perpetuating whatever it is in civilization that is worth perpetuating. If this is to be the direction of academic affairs committees then I find it difficult to accept that the knowledges about aesthetics of movement and the joy of movement are not worth perpetuating. I find it hard to believe that the relevance of studying sport and human motor performance is being questioned.

There are others who influence institutions and curriculum decisions: boards of governors, trustees, taxpayers, and society in general. Much of society sees value in subjects that specifically prepare one for a job. Taxpayers, boards of trustees, and boards of governors look for pragmatic ends, thus the demand for business education, computer science, and engineering. When there is no longer a need for those jobs or when the fields become saturated, those fields will also be questioned. Along this line, it appears that society has viewed physical education as either a field that trains people to teach or a subject that provides play/recreational experiences. Somehow along the way, the value of understanding the sport and movement experience and the importance of exploring the human fascination with sport, dance, and aquatics were lost. These aims must again be spoken, discussed, and debated with society. We must somehow reestablish the base of our discipline. The only ones who seem to know what physical education is all about are the physical educators themselves. How about forming advisory committees similar to those for the arts? How about inviting the boards and the trustees over for a look at our enterprises?

Another arena in which centrality must be reaffirmed is maintained by the administration. Today, administrators are held captive by talk of declining enrollments, budget crunches, the lack of federal research and development funds, and the belief that high tech and strategic long-range planning offer salvation. The quest for accountability has driven administrators to neglect the important aspects of higher education; they have become formula driven and might as well be called accountants. They have forgotten the main purpose of why they exist. Administrators exist to facilitate our job of teaching, our research mission, and our service responsibilities. Today many administrators are so interested in the credit hours produced that they do not really know what is happening to the student. Many administrators are so involved in evangelistic long-range planning that they are unable to react to the rapid change and fresh expectations of today's students.

The need for academic reform is crucial. The need to discuss the centrality of all subjects, including physical education, is of utmost importance. The need for quality control and leaders with vision has never been greater. Without this context, physical educators have a unique opportunity: We know game strategy; we know the difference between offense and defense; we know how to analyze. Our next step is to identify the persons within each institution who are best able to market and sell the important concepts of physical education to the administration, the curriculum committees, the taxpayers. Key people should be placed on key committees. A national effort is needed. Key people should be identified for every area, on every committee on our campuses. We also must identify new young people (we're all getting tired!), dynamic young leaders to be nurtured for a fresh approach. We know that we're in the only business of understanding sport and human movement. No other subject involves totality of the mind and body as does physical education. Administrators and others may forget these important things, but we can help remind them.

Thus, my answer is yes. Yes, physical education has a body of knowledge worthy of research and transmission. Will others in various arenas automatically accept this? Of course not. Do we once again have to justify our existence? Of course we do, just like everyone else. Will administrators listen to us? Probably not at first, but when planning returns to the important agenda item of quality education we will have an opportune moment to make our case. We can once again remind others that people not only work—they also move; people not only function in a cognitive manner—they also have perceptual motor abilities; people are not just minds for thinking—they are moving entities capable of great accomplishments. We can remind educators that there are no limits to the possibilities of learning. As higher education moves forward in a quest for quality—quality of teaching, quality of living, and quality of learning—physical educators can be at the forefront. Physical education can make a difference in the education of our students.

Perhaps the first step has been taken by someone asking the question. The next step is to examine the issues and to reaffirm and reassert our uniqueness, our contributions, our wonderful heritage, and our belief and faith in the value of sport and human movement.

Section 3

Social Science
And Physical Education:
Theoretical
And Practical Issues

Applying Sociology To Physical Education: Who Needs It?

C. Roger Rees
Adelphi University

The motivation for this paper stems from my perception that sociology of sport in particular and social science in general is not perceived by physical education administrators in higher education to be as important as it should be. This perception is developed from subjective experience and objective evidence. On the subjective level we have recently witnessed the dissolution and/or redirection of several programs in physical education which have a strong social science component. Those of us who read the *Chronicle of Higher Education* have noticed a reduction in the number of jobs for PhDs with specialized knowledge in sociology or psychology. On a more objective level, several in-house reviews of the status of sociology of sport have noted the peripheral value of this area of research to physical education (Greendorfer, 1977; Loy, 1980; Loy, McPherson, & Kenyon, 1978; Melnick, 1975, 1981). Finally, recent evidence from a national survey suggests that physical education curricula that concentrate on teacher preparation do not generally offer sociology of sport, let alone require it (Southard, 1982). Yet, sociology of sport is central to the mission of programs designed to develop teachers of physical education, is essential for physical education teachers or anyone else who wants to coach, and is an integral part of sport studies curricula at the undergraduate and graduate levels.

THE EMERGENCE OF SOCIOLOGY OF SPORT

The most developed link between sociology and physical education has been through the subdiscipline called sociology of sport. In order to understand why physical education has tended to eschew sociology it is necessary to understand how this subdiscipline developed. Sociology of sport is the most recent subfield to be developed within physical education, and perhaps because of its recency it has not yet achieved respectability in the eyes of physical education administrators in higher education. This may be part of a larger problem concerning the academic status of sociology in science, but it is also related to the fact that the subdiscipline is sociology of sport and not sociology of physical education. This point has been the subject of several critiques of the field (Greendorfer, 1977; Melnick, 1975, 1981; Ulrich, 1979) which have questioned the relevance of sociology of sport to physical education. These may have been read by administrators of physical education and used as justification for not including sociology of sport in their programs.

A detailed review of the emergence of sociology of sport has been provided by Loy and his associates (Loy, 1980; Loy, McPherson, & Kenyon, 1978). Loy (1980) concluded that the subdiscipline was stuck in an academic no-man's land; shunned by sociology for being nonserious and atheoretical, and rejected by physical education for not being applied enough or concerned with problems in physical education (as opposed to sport). Critiques of sociology of sport written by scholars from the field of physical education tend to support Loy's contention. This discussion focuses on two points. The first is that research in sociology of sport has tended to be basic rather than applied (Melnick, 1975, 1981) and, as such, is more interested in describing social reality in sport (from a functionalist perspective) than in trying to change that social reality. The second point is that research tends to be about sport, not physical education (Greendorfer, 1977; Hanson, 1982; Melnick, 1981), and done on top-class athletes rather than less skilled performers (Hanson, 1982; Ulrich, 1979).

It has been suggested (Gruneau, 1978) that the basic or value-free approach to sociology of sport reflected a desire for academic legitimation by early sport sociologists at a time when sociologists considered basic research to be somehow better than applied research (Rossi, 1980). Recently, Rossi and Whyte (1983) have noted that the line between applied and basic research is fuzzy. They cite several examples of basic research being applied over time. Because of its subject matter all sociology of sport can be thought of as applied, and there have already been examples in the subfield of what Rossi and White were talking about (Braddock, 1980). Although the subfield is young, the potential for developing an applied sociology of sport has been recognized (Melnick, 1981). However, the potential may not yet have been realized by administrators of physical education in higher education. I suggest that these administrators develop applied programs at the graduate level in conjunction with schools of business and departments such as social work and psychology. There is great potential for expanding graduate education in physical education by this method. Furthermore, it is a better approach than discouraging graduate students from studying sociology of sport because the present job market for PhDs with a specialization in sociology of sport is so bleak.

THE NONTEACHING OPTION

To some extent, the use of sociology of sport in conjunction with other subjects has already been developed at the undergraduate level. Sociology of sport is an integral part of the sport studies curricula that have been developed for physical education students who are not interested in teaching. This option has grown at the undergraduate level as teaching positions in physical education become more scarce. Programs such as sports management, sports administration, and sports counseling all use knowledge developed by sport sociologists. Courses in sociology of sport can serve a dual purpose in such programs. In addition to serving physical education students in the nonteaching option, they also provide interesting courses for nonphysical education majors, especially if recognized by the university as fulfilling a social science requirement (see VanderVelden, 1982, for an example of one such course). In this way they can help recruit students to physical education who have no declared major or are not strongly committed to another major. Innovative planning can lead to such courses being offered as part of a double major that would give the student more marketability (Fowler, 1982).

To summarize, it is suggested that research in sociology of sport, like research in sociology, is both basic and applied. The original dichotomy no longer accurately reflects the state of research in sociology (Rossi & Whyte, 1983), and consequently should not be applied to sociology of sport. Sociology of sport can be offered at the graduate and undergraduate level by departments of physical education in programs that incorporate courses from outside the department.

THE EDUCATION OF THE PHYSICAL EDUCATION TEACHER

If the pure versus applied dichotomy is being made redundant, the claim that sociology of sport is not important to physical education remains to be discussed. The contention is that the subject matter is sport, not physical education, and consequently the knowledge generated by sociology of sport is not useful to teachers of physical education (Hanson, 1982). I find this argument very puzzling. Sport, or more specifically organized sport (athletics), is central to physical education. It is the main component of what is taught in classes, and it occupies much of the time of physical education teachers (in their teaching and coaching roles) and their students. It is also the medium through which physical education is supposed to teach affective values such as fair play, leadership, self-discipline, and so forth. Therefore it is quite logical for prospective physical education teachers to study the sociology of sport: They will be intimately concerned with the effect of organized sport on the children they will teach.

Further support for the centrality of sport to physical education comes from an analysis of the course content for physical education curricula at the university level (Southard, 1982; 1983). A significant component of this content, both from the perspective of course work offered and the importance attached to the subject matter, was the teaching of team, lifetime, and individual and coaching sports. Southard reported that this content was considered by university administrators to be as important as any other area of the curriculum. Given the time allotted to organized sport in the physical education curriculum, it is disturbing to note that 42% of the 536 schools polled in Southard's study did not offer a course in sociology of sport. When the data were analyzed on a state by state basis, "none of the 50 states had a status mean (for sociology of sport) greater than the elective level" (Southard, 1982, p. 371).

Since physical education teachers spend so much time with organized sports, the argument that sociology of sport is irrelevant to physical education is untenable. While there is a need for research in sociology of sport to concentrate on ordinary athletes as well as elite performers (Coakley, 1983), it also seems unfair to condemn sociology of sport because it has concentrated on elite athletes in the past (Hanson, 1982). The same criticism could be leveled at all the subdisciplines within physical education (with the possible exception of curriculum analysis).

While there is not enough space to review here the substantive knowledge developed by sociology of sport, the generalization is made that the main thrust of the field has been to debunk or demythologize sport (Coakley, 1983; Loy, 1980). It is important to include the results of this endeavor in the curriculum of physical education majors so that they do not perpetuate these myths during their professional careers (Greendorfer, 1983). Furthermore, as part of the debunking process, the belief that participation in organized sport automatically leads to the development of social values such as fair play, self-discipline, leadership, and so forth, has been refuted (Sage, 1980). In the quest to find which conditions in organized sport lead to such positive social values, the discipline of sociology becomes even more important. Sociology and social psychology contain theories that suggest how conditions of interaction in social groups, of which sports teams are an example, affect the development of social values. These theories are being tested in the context of sport (Rees, 1984; Rees & Miracle, 1984) and will provide information to physical education teachers and coaches who feel social development is an important part of their curriculum.

In summary, I am suggesting that sociology of sport contains valuable knowledge for both potential and practicing physical education teachers and coaches. The value of the subfield to physical education is growing as more knowledge is developed. Sociology of sport should be included as a required course in the curriculum of teachers of physical education. According to Southard's (1982) study, only 7% of the teacher preparation programs require sociology of sport and another 19% require it in combination with some other subject.

PHYSICAL EDUCATION ADMINISTRATORS NEED
SOCIOLOGY OF SPORT

I have argued that the subject matter of sociology of sport is important in training physical education teachers and essential if these teachers become involved in coaching (which they invariably do). Sociology of sport courses can also be used as part of a nonteaching option which can increase the weighted credit hours of the department. If this function is not performed by a specialist in sociology of sport in a physical education department, it probably will be developed by a sociologist in a sociology department. At both the graduate and undergraduate levels, programs in sociology of sport can be developed to cater to physical education students who do not wish to teach and to non-physical education majors interested in the academic study of sport. Thus I have suggested both instrumental and expressive reasons for physical education administrators to use sociology of sport.

Although administrators may agree with some of what has been said, they may not be able to introduce courses in the sociology of sport and employ faculty with a specialized knowledge in this area. Because of the present trend toward contraction rather than expansion in higher education, administrators find it difficult to keep existing faculty lines, let alone obtain new ones. On the other hand it may be that, as Loy (1980) suggests, physical education administrators are somewhat prejudiced against sociology in general and sociology of sport in particular. Since many of them have been trained in subdisciplines such as physiology, biomechanics, and motor learning which have their roots in the natural sciences, they may not see much value in the social sciences. Of interest here is a publication of the American Academy of Physical Education in which leaders of the various subdisciplines in physical education were asked to summarize the most significant research of the past decade (*The Academy Papers*, 1982). The areas of knowledge they identified were physiology of exercise, biomechanics, motor learning and control, motor development, physical activity and emotional health, sociocultural aspects of physical activity, and pedagogical research. While sociology (and psychology) of sport were not chosen as full-fledged subdisciplines, at least topics from within these areas were chosen as relevant for physical education. However, sudisciplines from the natural sciences predominated. Perhaps administrators of physical education feel that sociology is a "soft" rather than a "hard" science and therefore not worthy of study.

However, we should remember that teachers deal with people and the behavior of people is the province of social science. To those physical education administrators who are biased against the social sciences, I suggest that you throw off your cloak of ignorance, reserve your soft/hard classification for more appropriate phenomenon such as ice cream and pornography, and accept the importance of sociology of sport at the graduate and undergraduate level for both the teaching and nonteaching option. In short, you should hire sociologists of sport at every available opportunity.

REFERENCES

ACADEMY Papers, No. 16 (1982). *Synthesizing and transmitting knowledge: Research and its application.* Reston, VA: AAHPERD.

BRADDOCK, J. (1980). *Institutional discrimination: A study of managerial recruitment in professional football.* Washington, DC: National Football League Players Association.

COAKLEY, J.J. (1983). From elites to everybody. A changing agenda for sport sociological study. *Journal of Physical Education, Recreation and Dance, 54*(3), 21-23.

FOWLER, E.M. (1982, September 1). Careers: Selecting marketable courses. *The New York Times.*

GREENDORFER, S.L. (1977). Sociology of sport: Knowledge for what? *Quest, 28,* 58-65.

GREENDORFER, S.L. (1983). A challenge for sociocultural sport studies. *Journal of Physical Education, Recreation and Dance, 54*(3), 18-20.

GRUNEAU, R.S. (1978). Conflicting standards and problems of personal action in the sociology of sport. *Quest, 30,* 80-90.

HANSON, D. (1982). Applications. In *The Academy Papers, No. 16.* Reston, VA: AAHPERD.

LOY, J.W. (1980). The emergence and development of the sociology of sport as an academic specialty. *Research Quarterly, 51*(1), 91-109.

LOY, J.W., McPherson, B.D., & Kenyon, G.S. (1978). *The sociology of sport as an academic specialty: An episodic essay on the development and emergence of an hybrid sub-field in North America.* Ottawa: CAHPER.

MELNICK, M.J. (1975). A critical look at sociology of sport. *Quest, 25,* 34-47.

MELNICK, M.J. (1981). Towards an applied sociology of sport. *Journal of Sport and Social Issues, 5*(1), 1-12.

REES, C.R. (1984, March). Expressive and instrumental roles of international sport: Application of the contact hypothesis. Paper presented at the Annual AAHPERD Conference, Anaheim, CA.

REES, C.R., & Miracle, A.W. (1984). Participation in sport and the reduction of racial prejudice: Contact theory, superordinate goals hypothesis or wishful thinking? In N. Theberge & P. Donnelly (Eds.) *Sport and the sociological imagination*. Fort Worth, TX: TCU Press.

ROSSI, P.H. (1980). The presidential address: The challenge and opportunities of applied social research. *American Sociological Review*, **45**, 889-904.

ROSSI, P.H., & Whyte, W.F. (1983). The applied side of sociology. In H.E. Freeman et al. (Eds.), *Applied Sociology* (pp. 5-31). San Francisco: Jossey-Bass.

SAGE, G. (1980). Growth of sport sociology. In *The Academy Papers*, No. 14 (pp. 24-30). Reston, VA: AAHPERD.

SOUTHARD, D. (1982). A national survey: Sociology of sport within American college and university physical education professional preparation programs. In A.O. Dunleavy, A.W. Miracle, & C.R. Rees (Eds.), *Studies in the sociology of sport* pp. 365-372). Fort Worth, TX: TCU Press.

SOUTHARD, D. (1983). Importance of selected competencies and relationship to corresponding coursework in programs of teacher preparation, *Research Quarterly for Exercise and Sport*, **54**(4), 383-388.

ULRICH, C. (1979). The significance of sport sociology to the profession. In M.L. Krotee (Ed.). *The dimensions of sport sociology*, (pp. 11-19). West Point, NY: Leisure Press.

VANDERVELDEN, L. (1982). Sport and American society: A course for kinesiological science majors and general university students. In A.O. Dunleavy, A.W. Miracle, & C.R. Rees (Eds.), *Studies in the sociology of sport* (pp. 385-391). Fort Worth, TX: TCU Press.

Psychological Knowledge And Its Emerging Role In The Physical Education Curriculum

Brad D. Hatfield
University of Maryland

Psychological knowledge within the undergraduate degree programs of physical education and kinesiological science has typically been attained in two ways—both from within and outside of the department. Many programs offer specialized courses in sport psychology or the psychology of coaching, either supplementing or supplanting these courses with prescribed offerings from the psychology department. However, the focus here deals with the concerns and development of formalized sport psychology courses as conducted within physical education departments; the subdiscipline of sport psychology is viewed as an emerging field which is both distinct and unique from the parent discipline.

In terms of the role of sport psychology knowledge within these degree programs, I believe it has achieved less of an impact than have some of the other subdisciplines. This occurrence is somewhat understandable since sport psychology is a relatively young emphasis as a formal discipline of study, but it appears that youth is not the sole reason for its slow acceptance among coaches and curriculum planners (Landers, 1981). Be that as it may, the important issue is whether sport psychology can contribute meaningfully to the knowledge base and skills required for physical educators and coaches to effectively perform their jobs. Are developments occurring that would persuade degree program planners to incorporate sport psychology coursework in the curriculums? Before examining this issue, let us consider several factors that have been problematic for the field of sport psychology.

FACTORS RETARDING THE EMERGENCE
OF SPORT PSYCHOLOGY

Landers (1981) has observed that much of the research direction in sport psychology has been too theoretical and laboratory-oriented to be useful to coaches and athletes. Additionally, Landers (1983) has stated that the field's major emphasis from the mid-1960s through the late 1970s was on the assessment of social psychological theories and their applicability for physical activity environments. This development fostered a gap between the kinds of questions being answered by sport psychology researchers and the needs of the practicing coach, athlete, and physical educator.

In spite of Landers' (1981) concern over the lack of practical information available to the practitioner, I do not believe he is advocating a shift in focus to the professional or applied dimension but, rather, that more needs to be done in this area *in conjunction with* basic research (Landers, 1981; 1983). In fact, Landers has cautioned against the demise of theory-testing studies within sport psychology because of the lack of generalizability and disjointed knowledge promoted by atheoretical work. It would seem that the field has an obligation to derive the general relationships (i.e., theories) between such variables as stress and performance, arousal and attention, cognitions and performance, observational learning and performance, and the underlying mechanisms; but this often necessitates the control of the artificial laboratory situation.

Because sport psychology is a young field, the effort used to establish much of this basic knowledge (from which applied knowledge eventually derives) has created a gap between the scientist and the practitioner. Unfortunately, some individuals, either well-intentioned or otherwise, have responded to the coaches' and the athletes' needs before a strong base of valid applied knowledge has been developed. Dishman (1983) has voiced concern over the developments within applied or professional sport psychology, cautioning that the product being delivered to the athlete has not yet been established in terms of its limitations and applicability. In other words, sport psychology has not yet matured to the point at which it is both systematically investigating the problems of athletes in the field and testing their problems within a theoretical framework. For example, Landers (1981) has mentioned the recent emergence of cognitive intervention strategies (Mahoney, 1974; Meichenbaum & Cameron, 1974) within psychology and the rapid acceptance of these techniques by sport psychologists in terms of their applicability to athletes. But even with the rapid acceptance of cognitive restructuring techniques (e.g., modifying what athletes say to themselves and helping them to think rationally), there is a lag in the documentation of its effects on sport performance.

In essence, the temptation to meet the needs of the coach/practitioner in order to gain credibility has prompted many to try to put the cart before the horse—to implement psychological training with the athlete before the facts are in. There is a danger in this approach, and the emergence of practical guidelines should accompany systematic research (Dishman, 1983; Landers, 1983).

Martens (1979) has also addressed this issue in his article ''About Smocks and Jocks'' which called for a greater emphasis upon field research conducted with athletes in the field, on the court, and in the water, with less reliance upon the laboratory environment. In essence, Martens called for an abandonment of the lab but not at the expense of research. I believe that he sees the gradual emergence of theory from sport performance observations within athletic environments which will be distinct from the social psychological theories borrowed from the parent discipline.

For some time sport psychologists have borrowed theoretical propositions from general psychology (e.g., social facilitation, the Yerkes-Dodson Law) and then applied them to motor performance situations to determine whether they fit. Such an approach seems limited. A program of research conducted in the field à la Martens (1979) with elite-level marksmen by Landers, Christina, Hatfield, Daniels, Wilkinson, and Doyle (1980) determined that traditional notions of the arousal-performance relationship do not always hold with individuals in a sport performance setting. Similarly, Tharp and Gallimore (1976) observed some time ago that the reinforcement contingencies in a skill learning situation practiced by former UCLA basketball coach John Wooden most certainly did not conform to traditional learning theory. Wooden used criticism much more often than praise with his students, which again raises the issue about the psychological uniqueness of the sport environment.

I believe that both Landers (1981) and Martens (1979) in a sense are advocating the same concept: We now need to conduct research in the field with the sport participant. This approach will help to overcome the theorist-practitioner gap but without doing it too hastily. In order for sport psychology to attain and maintain respectability within the sport sciences, it must show relevancy to practical concerns and factual validity for its proposed guidelines. This knowledge will take time to achieve. The indiscriminate and unsubstantiated use of psychological training programs with athletes and teams will hinder the development of the field in the long run. Even though individuals may wish to appease the need for psychological training and guidelines required by coaches and athletes, and may be quite successful in doing so, several problems could emerge from such a nonresearch approach.

Therefore, it is argued that one of the perceived limitations in the popular emergence of sport psychology has been its focus on theoretical laboratory research. As already noted, there are developments to bridge the gap with the practitioner, but this must be done carefully and with field research to ascertain whether the laboratory knowledge applies to the gymnasium. With the emergence of such an approach I believe that sport psychology will evidence itself as a unique body of knowledge (distinct from psychology) and will make progress toward its professional and research functions.

In addition to the above, sport psychology has traditionally been associated with a rather limited scope of personality and social psychology issues. Although Morgan (1969, 1973, 1979) had conducted prior investigations in the area of exercise and mental health, the primary focus until the late 1970s was upon social psychological influences of motor behavior (Landers, 1983). Only recently have the clinical and psychophysiological emphases been added. It appears that both of these directions will enhance the field's ability to provide psychological training guidelines for the coach and the athlete. For example, a recent study by Daniels and Landers (1981) has demonstrated the efficacy of establishing a psychophysiological profile of elite marksmen (e.g., examining their heart rate and ventilatory parameters in relation to shooting performance) and then using the identified performance-relevant parameters for biofeedback purposes. In this manner, Daniels and Landers were able to contribute meaningfully to the performance levels of the marksmen while testing a theoretical perspective proposed by Schwartz (1979). Besides expanding the body of knowledge in sport, it would seem that psychophysiological research (e.g., the effects of cardiovascular arousal upon EEG processes, the determinants of perceived exertion ratings) would enhance the degree of involvement with other sport science areas and promote the visibility of the field.

From a professional perspective, Dishman (1983) has questioned the sport psychology community's lack of involvement with the American College of Sports Medicine, one of the world's largest and most influential sport science organizations. Apart from the interdisciplinary research efforts mentioned above, perhaps a more visible presence of sport psychologists within the ACSM would promote a greater spirit of collegiality and cooperative research efforts.

To elaborate further, it would be shortsighted for scholars within the field not to have an appreciation for both the physical and mental factors involved in sport. The clinician may adopt a narrow perspective when diagnosing a performance problem;

the biomechanician may see the athlete's problem only from a mechanical perspective; the psychologist may see it only as a mental problem. I believe that such points of view are restrictive and that an additional factor which contributes to the uniqueness of sport psychology (as compared to psychology) is the understanding required of physiological/biomechanical limitations. The sport psychologist should have knowledges distinct from the psychologist since his or her domain concerns physical performance.

Many topical areas of investigation do not need to address specific concerns of performance limitations (e.g., social cohesion research), yet a greater spirit of cooperation between biophysical and behavioral researchers would benefit the research process and, more importantly, the athlete. For example, Landers (1981) told of a collegiate female rifle shooter who was having trouble with the consistency of her score, to which she attributed an attentional problem. The heart rate and the breath pattern psychophysiological measures being gathered on her revealed that her score covaried with her breathing activity during the trigger pull. When she was made aware of this, her accuracy improved significantly. In essence, a perceived psychological problem was nothing more than a simple correctable physical problem.

Athletes need these kinds of clear diagnoses of their problems, but in general there has been a lack of clear definitive statements from sport psychology for coaches, teachers, and athletes. This is not to deny the valuable work being conducted with athletes at institutions around the country, but in general the field has not progressed to the stage at which a healthy supply of guidelines and summary statements can be found in the literature. A recent exception to this was the general statistical review or meta-analysis of the literature on mental practice conducted by Feltz and Landers (1983). Instead of calling for more research in this area, these authors called for a resolution of the diverse findings already produced by numerous investigators. From their reexamination, four general conclusions were drawn about mental practice and its effects on motor performance.

In addition to this recent development, Smoll and Smith (1979) empirically developed a set of behavioral guidelines to help coaches conduct effective practices. Coaches and teachers generally have knowledge about physical training methods and coaching strategies (although they don't agree on strength and conditioning guidelines) but the psychology of coaching seems vague. The coaching guidelines established by Smoll and Smith help to define this vagueness with statements on the proper way to point out errors, the proper way to model a skill, how often to use general encouragement, and so forth. Their coach effectiveness program was based upon the observation of thousands of discrete coaching actions. As such, definitive statements or summaries of prior literature are surfacing to help the student of sport psychology sort out the maze of experimental findings.

From a pedagogical perspective, some additional problems seem to have limited the development of the field. First, there is a notable absence of strong pedagogically oriented textbooks in the area, a need felt at both the graduate and undergraduate levels. Many of the texts in sport psychology are anthologies of several works written by several authors. This approach to textbook writing allows each expert to write a chapter on his or her area of expertise, but there is a danger that such joint ventures may in fact be disjointed. Finally, it appears that much of today's graduate training in sport psychology is devoid of clinical experiences, a situation that tends to divide the researchers from the clinicians. More programs should emphasize the development of scholarly research capabilities along with practical internship experiences so that the student can effectively operate within both areas (Landers, 1981).

While all these factors have caused problems for the growth of sport psychology, I do not mean to portray a pessimistic picture for the field. Many of the problems are probably due to growing pains. Certainly efforts are being made to compensate for these weaknesses. However, I believe that in limiting the development of the field these problems have subsequently limited the strength of the program at the undergraduate level at which students gain their first impressions. Although undergraduates may not be deriving a positive experience from current offerings, matters will improve as courses based upon a broader, more sport-specific frame of knowledge are offered.

In order to ensure the continued development of the field and its place in professional degree programs, the concerns raised above must continue to be addressed. In spite of these stated shortcomings, the field of sport psychology is perceived both by curriculum planners and athletic coaches as an important dimension within physical education. The results of a national survey of 546 college physical education administrators (Southard, 1983) regarding the status and importance of various courses of study within undergraduate programs illustrates this. The study examined the perceived importance of each of 20 areas within physical education such as motor learning, physiology of exercise, anatomy, coaching theory, and psychology of sport on a 5-point semantic differential scale; a score of "1" was equal to no importance and a score "5" indicated it was very important for majors to acquire. Psychology of sport was ranked 12th of the 20 areas examined, with a mean ranking of 4.0. This ranking would indicate a relatively favorable attitude toward the field. However, the current status of these courses within the curricula was also assessed and a disappointing profile emerged. In general, the mean status of sport psychology was assessed a "2.3" (on a 1-5 scale), which indicated that it tends to be offered as an elective, but in combination with other subject matter. This ranking placed sport psychology near the bottom of the offerings as it was ranked 18th out of 20 areas.[1]

According to Southard, the results of the study imply that administrators personally hold a positive view of sport psychology but the actual program implementation does not reflect this. Perhaps there is a degree of faith regarding the importance of sport psychology, but it may be that some problems discussed earlier are restricting its status.

Gowan, Botterill, and Blimkie (1979) summarized a survey conducted by the Coaching Association of Canada regarding the perceived importance of the various sport sciences for coaching effectiveness. The results of this Canadian national survey among volunteer coaches and the administrators of various national sport governing bodies showed sport psychology to be the highest ranking area of scientific knowledge. Specifically, the respondents indicated motivation, peaking, and stress management as their areas of greatest concern within sport psychology. The successive rankings were then ascribed to physiology, biomechanics, sports medicine, motor learning, growth and development, and the sociology of sport.

The results of these two surveys indicate that sport psychology is deemed an important area of competency for the professionally oriented individual, but also that this perceived importance is partly based on faith as the field has not yet attained the level

---

[1]In order to assess the current status, the survey designated "not offered" as a score of "1," "offered as an elective in conjunction with other work" was designated as a "2," "offered as an elective" was scored as a "3," "required in conjunction with other work" was designated as a "4," and "required" was scored as a "5."

of expectation that is held for it. I believe that optimism is warranted for the future of sport psychology, however, because of some of the previously mentioned concerns with which the field is wrestling.

REASONS FOR OPTIMISM FOR THE GROWTH OF SPORT PSYCHOLOGY

A significant development for sport psychology has been the emergence of recommendations by the U.S. Olympic Committee for the certification of sport psychologists who wish to render professional and research services to amateur athletes. These guidelines were formulated by the sport psychology committee of the USOC Sports Medicine Council. The committee views three broad activities of sport psychologists and has identified these roles as the clinical sport psychologist, the educational sport psychologist, and the research sport psychologist. Thus, the USOC is attempting to formally recognize the role of the sport psychologist, and this represents a step in the right direction.

An article appearing in the Newsline section of the November 1982 issue of *Psychology Today* indicated the potential role that sport psychology may play in the near future in the Olympic movement.

> In competition, Olympic teams can have only 20 official medical staff members; Kenneth Clarke, the health educator who is director of sports medicine for the USOC, has little hope that any of the 20 will be psychologists in 1984. "We're aiming for 1988," Clarke says. "By then, I hope that more of the stigma against sports psychology will have been overcome. (1982, p. 22)

The combined acceptance and emergence of sport psychology within the formal Olympic movement should increase the opportunities to work with elite performers and enhance the knowledge base of the field while offering clinical and educational services. Hopefully, this future development will benefit both the athlete and sport psychology. I believe that the new knowledge attained and the increased public visibility gained from such a venture will eventually enhance the quality of offerings in undergraduate physical education curriculums.

In addition to the developments occurring at the Olympic level of competition, several colleges and universites are establishing athletic counseling programs for their varsity athletes. Lanning (1979) and Spinelli and Barrios (1980) have described the basic concerns that such programs are involved with—from stress management for the improvement of athletic performance, to career counseling, to psychologically dealing with injury recovery. The establishment of these centers within intercollegiate athletic departments should also promote greater awareness and acceptance of sport psychology by the athletic administration and staff. This would be a healthy development for sport psychology.

It should also be noted that in addition to the formal units of athletic counseling on the college campuses, several athletic programs benefit from the consulting services of individual faculty members within sport psychology, psychology, and psychiatry. In fact, the intercollegiate athletics department at the University of Illinois has recently hired a full-time sport psychologist to devote his efforts to the program. This is certainly a landmark development for the field, and something that was only a remote possibility a few years ago.

Another factor underscoring the growth of sport psychology has been the relative stability achieved by its associated professional organizations: the International Society for Sport Psychology, the North American Society for the Psychology of Sport and Physical Activity, and the Sport Psychology Academy within the structure of the American Alliance of Health, Physical Education, Recreation, and Dance. In conjunction with these organizations has been the arrival of the *Journal of Sport Psychology* in 1979 which serves as a major outlet for scholarly activity exclusively concerned with sport psychology. This journal is strengthened by the availability of several other sport science publications such as the *Research Quarterly for Exercise and Sport*, the *Journal of Motor Behavior*, and *Medicine and Science in Sports and Exercise*, (which of course are not exclusively organs for sport psychology). I believe that the research results published in these journals will continue to find their way into textbooks available to undergraduates. Some of the older texts within the field did not have the benefit of this literature; however, future texts will be based largely on this empirical, sport-specific knowledge. Indeed, this is already occurring.

Finally, although some may see it in a negative light, the current debate over the role and future direction of sport psychology may simply be a sign of growing pains (Brown, 1982; Danish & Hale, 1982; Nideffer, DuFresne, Nesvig, & Selder, 1980). In essence, this argument centers on the future of professional sport psychology, that is, the aspect of the field dealing with the delivery of services to the athlete as opposed to the disciplinary research dimension. Even though problems are perceived in this regard (Dishman, 1983), the concern with such issues was not heavily publicized until recently. An article on the professional concerns of sport psychology appeared in the fall edition of the American Psychological Association Monitor in 1982 which (in spite of certain limitations stated by Landers, 1983) at least increased the visibility of the field.

SUMMARY AND DISCUSSION

What does all of this rhetoric mean for sport psychology and its role within the professional college curriculum? The optimistic view is that sport psychology is well perceived and gaining public attention (whether one perceives this as good or bad). Certainly a number of professional developments are taking place such that sport psychology is actually working with and reaching more athletes. I am sure that the concerns for sport performance associated with the 1984 Summer Olympics are helping to promote some of this acceptance with the athletic community. So, we are delivering our services.

But I also believe the warnings raised about the professionalization of sport psychology (Dishman, 1983; Landers, 1981) should be heeded. The matter simply boils down to the possibility of the field hurting itself by failing to recognize the complexities and individual differences interacting with sport psychology services. We must not proceed too quickly or all of the positive development previously mentioned may be set back. To be more specific, I endorse the opinion of others that the research dimension of our field must come first because our services are limited by our knowledge, and our knowledge itself is limited. Sport psychology should extend its services in balance with the growth of theoretical knowledge in the field. If this knowledge grows quickly, then we can extend our services; if this growth is slow then we should be cautious. With this kind of approach, I believe that the field will demonstrate a balanced growth.

If sport psychology does progress in such a manner, this would seem to justify its inclusion in future curricula and perhaps enhance its present status. As the field develops and demonstrates its worthiness in the sport sciences, only then will it increase its standing in college curricula.

REFERENCES

BROWN, J.M. (1982). Are sport psychologists really psychologists? *Journal of Sport Psychology*, **4**, 13-18.

DANIELS, F.S., & Landers, D.M. (1981). Biofeedback and shooting performance: A test of disregulation and systems theory. *Journal of Sport Psychology*, **3**, 271-282.

DANISH, S.J., & Hale, B.D. (1981). Toward an understanding of the practice of sport psychology. *Journal of Sport Psychology*, **3**, 90-99.

DANISH, S.J., & Hale, B.D. (1982). Let the discussions continue: Further considerations on the practice of sport psychology. *Journal of Sport Psychology*, **4**, 10-12.

DISHMAN, R.K. (1983). Identity crises in North American sport psychology: Academics in professional issues. *Journal of Sport Psychology*, **5**, 123-134.

FELTZ, D.L., & Landers, D.M. (1983). The effects of mental practice on motor skill learning and performance: A meta-analysis. *Journal of Sport Psychology*, **5**, 25-57.

GOWAN, G.R., Botterill, C.B., & Blimkie, C.J. (1979). Bridging the gap between sport science and sport practice. In P. Klavora & J.V. Daniel (Eds.), *Coach, athlete, and the sport psychologist*, Toronto: University of Toronto

LANDERS, D.M., Christina, R.W., Hatfield, B.D., Daniels, F.S., Wilkinson, M., & Doyle, L.A. (1980). Moving competitive shooting into the scientist's lab. *The American Rifleman*, April, pp. 36-37, 76-77.

LANDERS, D.M. (1981). Reflections on sport psychology and the Olympic athlete. In J. Segrave & D. Chu (Eds.), *Olympism*. Champaign, IL: Human Kinetics.

LANDERS, D.M. (1983). Whatever happened to theory testing in sport psychology? *Journal of Sport Psychology*, **5**, 135-151.

LANNING, W. (1979). Coach and athlete personality interaction: A critical variable in athletic success. *Journal of Sport Psychology*, **1**, 262-267.

MAHONEY, M.J. (1974). *Cognitive and Behavior Modification*. Cambridge, MA: Ballinger.

MARTENS, R. (1979). About smocks and jocks. *Journal of Sport Psychology*, **1**, 94-99.

MEICHENBAUM, D., & Cameron, R. (1974). The clinical potential of modifying what clients say to themselves. *Psychotherapy: Theory, Research and Practice*, **11**, 103-117.

MORGAN, W.P., (1969). A pilot investigation of physical working capacity in depressed and nondepressed psychiatric males. *Research Quarterly,* **40,** 859-861.

MORGAN, W.P. (1973). Influence of acute physical activity on state anxiety. *Proceedings of the National College Physical Education Meeting,* 113-112.

MORGAN, W.P. (1979). Anxiety reduction following acute physical activity. *Psychiatric Annals,* **9,** 141-147.

NIDEFFER, R.M., DuFresne, P., Nesvig, D., & Selder, D. (1980). The future of applied sport psychology. *Journal of Sport Psychology,* **2,** 170-174.

SCHWARTZ, G.E. (1979). Disregulation and systems theory: A biobehavioral framework for biofeedback and behavioral medicine. In N. Birbaumer & H.D. Kimmel (Eds.), *Biofeedback and self-regulation.* Hillsdale, NJ: Erlbaum.

SINGULAR, S. (1982, November). U.S. Olympians flirt with sport psychology. *Psychology Today,* pp. 21, 76.

SMOLL, F.L., & Smith, R.E. (1979). Psychologically-oriented coach training programs: Design, implementation, and assessment. In C. Nadeau, W. Halliwell, K. Newell, G. Roberts (Eds.), *Psychology of Motor Behavior and Sport—1979.* Champaign, IL: Human Kinetics.

SOUTHARD, D. (1983). Importance of competencies and status of coursework: A nationwide study. Unpublished manuscript, Texas Christian University.

SPINELLI, P.R., & Barrios, B.A. (1980). Psyching the college athlete: A comprehensive sports psychology training package. In R.M. Swinn (Ed.), *Psychology in Sports—Methods and Application.* Minneapolis: Burgess.

THARP, R.G., & Gallimore, R. (1976, January). What a coach can teach a teacher. *Psychology Today,* pp. 74-78.

UNITED States Olympic Committee Establishes Guidelines for Sport Psychology Services. (1983). *Journal of Sport Psychology,* **5,** 4-7.

Social Process And Traditional Physical Education

John D. Massengale
Eastern Washington University

Traditional American physical education is based upon many foundations, and one of those foundations, regardless of exact title or definition, always features a strong general relationship to social process. The successful integration of social science into physical education curriculum at all levels, especially as it relates to behavior and/or learning, remains paramount in the eyes of many physical educators. In all aspects of traditional physical education and at all levels, there is social reality. It is often observed, occasionally emphasized, sometimes evaluated, and almost never accurately documented. Social process in traditional physical education remains vague and ambiguous, but most important, it remains pervasive.

Although its pervasiveness has been noted by some of the most prominent scholars of the day from the fields of physical education and sociology (Coakley, 1982; Eitzen & Sage, 1982; Loy, McPherson, & Kenyon, 1978; Snyder & Spreitzer, 1983), the study of social process in traditional physical education still lacks serious significance and acceptance. Even within the subdiscipline of sport sociology the study of social process in traditional physical education remains incomplete and neglected. A casual review of scholarly efforts in sport sociology will reveal an overemphasis on those topics that tend to be exciting and sensational, namely competitive athletics and the protest of the status quo. Yet, traditional physical education with all of its components comes into contact with almost every student in America.

The purpose here is not to chastise those involved in physical education in higher education for contributing to this situation, or to scold sport sociologists for perpetuating "soft science" research conducted with "hard science" models that are often inappropriate for traditional physical education. Rather, the purpose is to present and discuss the common-sense practical significance of social process in physical education. What is being suggested is that social process in physical education is entirely credible and easily observable, can be analyzed, and continues to be highly desirable; the fact that it is seldom featured as accurately measurable scholarly research is nothing to be concerned about.

THE MEANING OF TRADITIONAL PHYSICAL EDUCATION

When the word *tradition* is used in association with physical education, it should not necessarily mean old-fashioned, conservative, or out-of-date. It should mean the transmission of culture, the passing of worthwhile elements to the next generation, and the utilization of time-honored well-established practices. The establishment of traditional physical education itself is a social process.

Traditional physical education is the whole big picture. It is everything that physical educators do that is professionally related to learning. Traditional physical education is a concept that is so complex that it defies exact description or agreement of definition. A simple description might resemble the table of contents of a typical textbook used for introductory professional physical education courses, such as those authored by Bucher (1983) or Nixon and Jewett (1980) which are currently in their ninth editions. The ninth edition of any physical education textbook cannot avoid being considered as traditional, and that understanding of traditional cannot be anything but complimentary.

THE MEANING OF SOCIAL PROCESS

Social process is a system of operations which results in the creation and production of acceptable values that are considered significant in the socialization and education of a society (Ulrich, 1968). It is person-to-person social exchange that creates action, requires adjustment, establishes power, features observable results, and has the potential to produce mutual satisfaction. It is usually progressive, continual, ongoing, functional, and has the inherent ability to bring about individual and collective changes in behavior. Social process is one of the components that allows American physical education to be perceived as traditional.

A principle that cannot be overlooked when analyzing social process is the amount of information that becomes available as the basis for selective actions or decisions (Buckley, 1967). This information may come by way of actions or interactions, closed or open systems, creative tension, feedback, reciprocal relations, exchange bargaining or negotiation, conformity or deviance, role strain, or through the challenging of legitimate authority. Any list of information systems is almost inexhaustible; however, such information systems are always evident in traditional physical education.

SOCIAL PROCESS IN ACTION

Traditional physical education depends upon social process for self-perpetuation and, by doing so, successfully presents itself as a microcosm of American society. Physical education as a microcosm of American society becomes a transmitter of tradition in many ways. One of those ways is through the language of games which becomes subtle description and reinforcement in the form of analogy, cliche, assumed fact, popular phrase, and slogan (Snyder & Spreitzer, 1983). The language of games has become so ingrained in American society that metaphors have gained acceptance, although they often represent partial truths or stereotypes. Games and the language of games, although relatively simple, have become acceptable models for a very complex society. This situation prevailed because games are small enough and simple enough to understand while still reflecting behaviors and attitudes that are common characteristics of American society.

Those games are the result of play, the kind of pure play (Huizinga, 1960; Caillois, 1961) which, because of social process, becomes an integral part of traditional physical education. Social process in a complex society takes pure play which is characterized by freedom, frivolity, make believe, pleasure, spontaneity, and a lack of structure, and then transforms it into a highly organized vehicle that functions for societal education and socialization. Play as a necessary element for games eventually becomes transformed into sport and then finally into athletics (Figler, 1981). That social process is perhaps the basic foundation of traditional physical education. It is the application of limits, restrictions, rules, authority, goals, motivation, structure, and the pursuit of excellence. It is part of the tradition of our culture, taught through social process, with physical education simply fulfilling its mission.

Traditional physical education prepares students by contributing to psychomotor development through such diverse activities as movement education on one hand and competitive athletics on the other, and then relating both to personality. Invention, creativity, and the pursuit of excellence can become top priorities in any of the activites being sponsored within a program of traditional physical education.

Consider American education's most recent preoccupation with the pursuit of excellence, which has been ignited by the "Gardner Report" (Gardner, 1983). It calls for more competition, more commitment, more risk, higher standards and, most important, more effort. Those requests can be met through educational settings provided in any facet of traditional physical education if physical educators themselves will begin to reemphasize traditional traits such as discipline, self-discipline, perseverance, or simple personal pride. Traditional physical education can become the arena in which students are allowed to try as hard as they can, attempt to accomplish everything that they can, and yet be allowed to fail because, ideally, American education should provide every student with the opportunity to find out just how good he or she can become. Failure can yield a realistic recognition of one's limitations and an evaluation of one's chances of success in selected ultimate goals. Such action becomes a social process that fosters the intention of doing one's best without creating fantasies, illusions, and expectations that border on the impossible.

Social process in traditional physical education also provides a means for establishing primary groups, secondary groups, significant others, peer groups, face-to-face encounter situations, and the all important functions of social sanction (Synder & Spreitzer 1983; Ulrich, 1968). Peer groups are normally structured along the lines of age, interests, values, purposes, identities, and a sense of belonging. Traditional physical education provides this process for education and society in all of its programs, with competitive athletics gaining additional importance due to its high peer-group visibility (Coleman, 1961).

The social sanction capabilities of peer groups, primary groups, or particular reference groups provide an important element to social process in physical education. These groups are a little tougher on their members than are typical family structures. They are often perceived to have little appreciation for individuality, to be uncaring, to be rigid, to control thoughts and behavior, to be unforgiving, and to have the power to punish. Although harsh at times, these groups reward conformity and membership by providing a sense of security. In addition, primary groups reward according to the standards, mores, and customs of society. Primary groups attempt to define what is "normal" and what is "deviant," doing so within the confines of contemporary society while at the same time providing acceptable parameters for uniqueness, self-identity, creativity, and the limits of personal space.

Traditional programs in physical education usually provide a method of mobility and transition into higher levels of organized sport, most often in the form of competitive athletics. In turn, competitive athletics is often perceived to supply a method of mobility and transition into higher levels of social status. Although upward social mobility is commonly believed to be a frequent result of athletic participation, the research that supports this perception is somewhat ambiguous (Snyder & Sprietzer, 1983).

Part of this misconception is due to that portion of social process in traditional physical education that promotes popular culture and folklore within the American athletic system. Rags-to-riches examples of sport hero role models are constantly presented to student/athletes by coaches, teachers, parents, and the media. When information on sport hero role models is overemphasized and then mixed with several years of work ethic mentality, the resulting image may be less than accurate.

The fact is that sport involvement and the meaning of sport is class-linked, with the working class less involved than either the middle or upper classes (Snyder & Spreitzer, 1983). However, there is documentable social mobility, which is far less than generally assumed, and the extent of that mobility varies depending on ethnic group, race, economic factors, and often the social climate of any society at any given time.

The use of sport hero role models in traditional physical education is certainly not undesirable, and is easily one of the most visible and most acceptable methods of socialization in American society. Cultural values are taught, reinforced, and then rewarded in our society with selected actions, behaviors, and traits of sports heroes used as examples. Some of the values commonly referred to are courage, integrity, stamina, composure, persistence, dependability, tenacity, toughness, sportsmanship, and dedication. Although there are numerous values of this type and any number of places where these types of values can be taught, traditional physical education because of its transitional process toward highly organized competitive athletics remains a highly worthwhile transmitter of values.

It is difficult to discuss sport hero role models without considering the concept of leadership. Much has been made of the development of leadership through social process in traditional physical education—some documented, some observed, and some imagined. However, it is a given that leadership does not exist separate and apart from social process (Cratty, 1967), and that process is fundamental to physical education. It is a group-related quality that results from certain personality traits which at least partly depend upon an individual's physical prowess. That physical prowess is often evident in the form of appearance or perception and may or may not be overt behavior. It is an aura of having the capacity for action by using traits such as intelligence, size, strength, or problem-solving abilities. It is charisma and the ability to manage intelligent risks successfully. It is the opportunity to display traits which establish physical prowess that makes social process in traditional physical education unique and significant.

Leadership also depends upon competitive and cooperative behavior, which are both encouraged in traditional physical education. Regardless of fad, fashion, or movement, it is important to teach acceptable competitive and cooperative behaviors since both are necessary for an accurate understanding of American culture. In American society, behaviors such as aggression are often described in complimentary terms. American society also uses other complimentary terms that really mean combat, terms that become completely acceptable when referred to as "approved conflict," "conflict resolution," "combatives," "combative activities," or "combative sport."

Through all of this social process, traditional physical education continues to stress sportsmanship by teaching, interpreting, and reinforcing specific behaviors that American society will find moral and ethical, even though those specific behaviors might really result from accommodation, manipulation, or intimidation. Hopefully, traditional physical education will gravitate to teaching sportsmanship through the social process of appropriate recognition and not by emphasizing blind obedience to certain specific behavior patterns that remain unchallenged.

SOCIAL PROCESS AND DYSFUNCTION

As mentioned earlier, traditional physical education should be a means of transmitting culture, or of passing worthwhile elements from one generation to the next, or of using time-honored, well-established practices. It should not be a means of transmitting those elements that tend to be dysfunctional and then simply accepting the premise that in order to honor tradition we must accept a few bad things along with the good things. It is true that dysfunction in American society is often considered traditional. However, that certainly is not a good reason to scrap traditional physical education but it may be an excellent reason to initiate reform.

Such a reform could begin by challenging some of the basic beliefs of traditional physical education. These beliefs include deterrence or rehabilitation theories in crime and delinquency that are associated with involvement in programs of traditional physical education. There is some evidence that delinquent students are often weeded out of traditional physical education programs or that they use these programs for association and camaraderie among lower socioeconomic groups, the same groups that produce most of the crime (Segrave, 1983). There is also mounting evidence of social dysfunction through subculture formation and the organizational deviance promoted through traditional physical education (Snyder & Sprietzer, 1983).

The literature contains numerous examples of dysfunction; yet traditional physical education remains content with the idea that we must accept the bad along with the good and that there is much more good than bad. Some of those examples are the internalization of false values, the effects of inflated egos, the result of undue pressures, the apparent loss of identity, the labeling of stigmas, the withdrawal due to repeated embarrassment, and the opportunity for frequent disapproval from one's peers.

When examining dysfunction that is more closely related to education, other examples surface. These include commitment to excellence that gathers such intensity that it becomes counterproductive and distorts real education, occupational failure due to one's acceptance of a greatly inflated athletic role, or the unequal opportunity that relegates many males and most females to a position of less importance.

Physical education has an important history, a significant role in American education, and deserves that label of "traditional" when it is placed in a cultural heritage context. However, like many other American traditions, physical education should initiate a program of progressive reform. This reform movement would make *traditional* physical education even more traditional, making that word more true to its real meaning especially when it is associated with the field of physical education.

REFERENCES

BUCHER, C.A. (1983). *Foundations of physical education*. St. Louis: Mosby.

BUCKLEY, W. (1967). *Sociology and modern systems theory.* Englewood Cliffs, NJ: Prentice-Hall.

CAILLOIS, R. (1961). *Man, play and games.* Glencoe, IL: Free Press.

COAKLEY, J.J. (1982). *Sport in society.* St. Louis: Mosby.

COLEMAN, J.S. (1961). *The adolescent society.* Glencoe, IL: Free Press.

CRATTY, B.J. (1967). *Social dimensions of physical activity.* Englewood Cliffs, NJ: Prentice-Hall.

EITZEN, D.S., & Sage, G.H. (1982). *Sociology of American sport.* Dubuque, IA: Brown.

FIGLER, S.K. (1981). *Sport and play in American life.* Philadelphia: Saunders.

GARDNER, D.P. (1983). *A nation at risk: The imperative for educational reform.* Washington, DC: U.S. Dept. of Education.

HUIZINGA, J. (1960). *Homo ludens.* Boston: Beacon.

LOY, J.W., McPherson, B.D., & Kenyon, G. (1978). *Sport and social systems.* Reading, MA: Addison-Wesley.

NIXON, J.E., & Jewett, A.E. (1980). *An introduction to physical education.* Philadelphia: Saunders.

SEGRAVE, J.O. (1983). Sport and juvenile delinquency. In R. Terjung (Ed.), *Exercise and Sport Science Reviews*, **11**. Philadelphia: Franklin Institute.

SNYDER, E.E., & Sprietzer, E.A. (1983). *Social aspects of sport.* Englewood Cliffs, NJ: Prentice-Hall.

ULRICH, C. (1969). *The social matrix of physical education.* Englewood Cliffs, NJ: Prentice-Hall.

Section 4

Physical Education:
To Save Or Not To Save?

Is Physical Education In American Schools Worth Saving? Evidence, Alternatives, Judgment

Patt Dodds and Lawrence F. Locke
University of Massachusetts

Physical education as it now exists in many American public schools is not worth saving. None at all would be better than what we have. That is the dismal premise of this paper. We can all answer, "Yes, but. . ." and continue with lively accounts of isolated pockets of excellence in programs, or teachers, or students' attitudes, drawn from our personal experience. Nevertheless, the general condition of our patient, in hospital terminology, remains critical. Our purpose, lest you think we will quickly run through a catalogue of symptoms and get on with learned professional diagnoses, prescriptions, or recommendations for radical surgery, is only to pull together a comprehensive listing of the symptoms to get the clearest possible view of the problem. Perhaps the reader's trained expertise can then generate some solutions (if any are available to halt further deterioration in the condition of the patient).

It is all too likely that a typical local newspaper of any given day will feature a story such as: "Local School Committee Slashes Budget by Cutting P.E. Programs: 12 Teachers Lose Jobs." In Massachusetts alone, the devastating effects of Proposition 2½ resulted in approximately 22% of physical educators losing their jobs across a 2-year period (Massachusetts Department of Education, 1983). There now exists considerable evidence for eliminating public school physical education. Data come from all sides, creeping inexorably into our consciousness in much the same way as the grit seeps into window cracks and under doors when a West Texas sandstorm passes through.

While most of the data are overwhelmingly discouraging, there is some encouragement to be found in the clear distinctions emerging between elementary and secondary physical education programs. The first appears to be more alive and reasonably well, but the second represents a terminal case. The viability of elementary physical education is demonstrated by the continued lively debate about organizing centers and conceptual frameworks appropriate for planning good programs (Gallahue, Werner, & Luedke, 1972; Graham, Holt-Hale, McEwen, & Parker, 1980; Hoffman, Young, & Klesius, 1981; Logsdon, Barrett, Broer, McGee, Ammons, Halverson, & Roberton, 1977; Siedentop, Herkowitz, & Rink, 1984), by the wide availability and diversity of curriculum texts and materials, and by frequent, stimulating professional interchanges such as the Orlando conference on professional preparation for elementary teachers.

Although surface features may present a less depressing picture, we all should be warned that there is trouble in every part of "River City" and some of our evidence certainly fits both elementary and secondary programs.

OPINION SOURCES

Warning signals come from all directions of public opinion, codified in a number of ways. Some 15 annual Gallup Polls of the Public's Attitudes Toward the Public Schools, (the most recent appearing in *Phi Delta Kappan*, September 1984) repeatedly affirm the low priority of physical education (eighth in a list of 11 required subjects for high schools). Recent reports of the national school reform movement (*A Nation At Risk*, the Twentieth Century Fund Report, *Action for Excellence*, the College Board's Education for Equality Project) only reiterate and confirm that physical education is a bastard child in American schools.

None of these reports recommends including our subject in the New Basics list, none calls for increased time allotments or specific hour requirements for physical education, and nowhere is it advocated that new curricula be developed or teaching skills be improved or teacher education programs be revised in order to upgrade physical education for children in schools. The repeated neglect or omission of physical education, except where mentioned pejoratively as a "frill" subject, sends us the powerful message that what we teach is not highly regarded by the general public or by those who make decisions about the education of American youth (e.g., school committees).

State-level responses to these national reports echo the gloom and doom flavor of the recommendations. In Massachusetts, for example, the commissioner of education recently issued guidelines for secondary school curricula to school committee chairpersons, superintendents, boards of education, and professional associations. These people, who represent the collective power to decide which subjects are maintained or dumped from the curriculum, found an innocuous two sentences about physical education (other subjects rated several paragraphs) listed in the eighth of 11 positions, even though it is the only subject mandated by explicit state regulations. The MAHPERD state organization has waged an ever more difficult battle in each of the last three state legislative sessions against those who want to repeal that mandate.

While the actual language of the school reform movement, as seen in the major reports to the public, very directly excludes physical education from proposed suggestions for improving schooling, the indirect messages are even stronger and more devastating: (a) physical education is simply not worth reforming; (b) if time, money, and energy are needed to upgrade essentials such as English, computer skills, and science, there is nothing left to expend on unworthy subjects such as physical education; (c) if the experts don't mention physical education, it can't possibly be important to anyone else; and (d) nobody who counts cares about gym classes, so why should I?

Actions at the local level regarding education are closely contingent on events in the wider contexts of national and state events. The Gallup Polls, the school reform reports, and state reactions to such negative criticism corroborate local horror stories all of us have heard from parents or kids about poor gym classes, once again reiterating that physical education is "subjecta non grata" in education. Competition for tax dollars is intense; there is no positive public support for either maintaining or revitalizing physical education in the general curriculum; and the people who sit on school committees or administer the schools are in the long run those who must be convinced that physical education is worth saving—not the teachers or students who live in the gym. It is too bad that these natives are the only ones who know what really goes on in the gym. Rarely do administrators, other teachers, parents, or interested members of the community visit the place in which we all live. The reality that physical educators face daily is not the actual quality of our programs but rather the public perceptions (from afar) of what happens when those double doors are closed.

Because schools are social institutions, the fate of any subject is responsive to the social, political, historical, and economic forces at work in the broader societal context. When these influences are not calling for increased time allotments, improvement in teacher training programs or better curricula in physical education, we have so much less leverage for convincing decision makers than do subject areas in which such outcry exists. The old squeeze play is on—no more dollars just to help kids play games. Perhaps because we've played elimination games for so long in our classes, we're now the ones being taken off the floor by concerned citizens for better schools.

IN-HOUSE CRITICISM

At least as disturbing as public inattention to physical education are the increasing volumes of protest from our own professional ranks against what happens in the majority of school gymnasia. More college-based physical educators are drawing attention, gently but persistently, to the perils of existing practice in physical education. Years ago, Guy Lewis (1969) raised the question of how long physical education could last in schools were it not tied so closely to athletics. To drive this point closer to home, how long would any of us in higher education last if there were no public school programs for which to prepare teachers?

It may have been hyperbole when one of us referred to physical education as the most poorly taught subject in the school curriculum (Locke, 1981), but we certainly are not alone in harboring grave doubts that the secondary school requirement will make it to the end of this decade, much less the 21st century. Just recently Vander-Zwaag (1983) characterized physical education as an outmoded ''umbrella program with no real focus.'' Metzler (1980) called attention to ''supervised recreation,'' which he believes is now gradually replacing instructional programs. In perhaps the strongest condemnation of present conditions, Siedentop (1981) stated:

> I have no trouble envisioning the rapid extinction of high school physical education in the next two decades. As it is currently programmed and currently taught in most places, it probably deserves to die out. . . .Too many students are apathetic about it. Too many students are disruptive within it. Too many students have already become cynical about it. The vast majority have learned to tolerate it, not to expect too much from it, and not to give too much to it. (p. 11)

One remaining contingent of experts about school physical education is, of course, the students themselves. Their testimony is as damaging, and even more despairing, than that of outsiders who never see what happens in gyms, or teachers who never experience the client point of view. Damning evidence converges once again to illustrate the plight of physical education.

In 1969 Clifford Wilson published a study that compared various viewpoints about the purposes of physical education. In addition to their formal responses, Wilson's student group expressed some revealing unsolicited comments. Examples include:

1. Physical education is a criminal waste of time.
2. The attitude about gym is bad. If gym was made more enjoyable, kids would like it more.
3. I feel that half the things we do in gym class are of no use at all.
4. The purpose seems not aimed at physical improvement personally but basic dabblings for a motley group.
5. Physical education is for people who don't exercise and have to be made to do it.

When students grow up, their feelings remain quite negative about their school-based physical education experiences. An in-depth interview study (Jackson, 1980) revealed that one very prominent reason why adults avoid participation in sport stems from their previous school physical education programs. A recent *Sports Illustrated* article (Kirshenbaum & Sullivan, 1983) analyzed the fitness craze, concluding that large segments of our youth and adult populations are not actively pursuing fitness. And *Athletic Purchasing and Facilities* business magazine ran a lead article (Ebel, 1983) about corporate fitness programs, including the interesting item that the dropout rate is phenomenally high. Why aren't adults continuing their participation patterns once established? Does the spectre of prior experiences in school gymnasia lurk behind such dropout behaviors?

Regardless of our personal reactions to any of these statements, the fact remains that some insiders now are willing to admit publicly that severe problems exist in the practice of physical education.

WHEN OUTSIDERS PEEK INTO THE GYM

A second major source of evidence about the worth-it-ness of physical education comes from inside the schools in the form of research data collected in actual classes. One perception shared by many researchers was expressed by McLeish when he said: "We were quite frankly bored in observing the majority of lessons. More importantly, it is possible that many of the students were bored as well" (cited in Siedentop, 1981). As the following examples show, other negative effects on students also result.

When researchers use qualitative methods of inquiry to move the level of observation down to the individual participant in physical education, the picture of life in the gym can look grim indeed. Both teachers and students can contribute to making class an unpleasant place and, for some, a place with ominous psychological hazards.

At the most fundamental level, the new "teacher watchers" have found some reason to question our comfortable assumption that, in schools, teachers intend for students to learn. In the abstract, we think of physical education teachers as working to help students acquire new motor skills, become physically fit, or improve their play skills. Yet Placek's (1982) qualitative study of teacher planning in physical education revealed that her subjects often did not seem to intend for their students to learn anything in particular but only to be busy, happy, and good while in class.

Placek's observation is not unrelated to the work of Jenkins and Bausell (1973), which revealed that neither teachers nor school administrators rate the ability to reproduce learning as a particularly significant factor in effective teaching. In contrast to the theoretical definition of effective teaching, there is good reason to believe that some physical education teachers simply do not define their own success in terms of whether or not their clients learn (Harootunian & Yarger, 1981; Placek, 1983). Given a more realistic assumption about the intentions of students and teachers in the gym, the quantitative research literature that is based on the use of systematic observation instruments would contain fewer laments about how little time is spent on learning in typical physical education classes. From the participants' perspective, if learning is not irrelevant at least it is not central to their intentions.

Another component of good physical education is that teachers treat students fairly and equitably, regardless of their particular characteristics. Templin (1981b) found that high school students socialize their student teachers to be more custodial and to treat "athletes" and "best classes" much more charitably than "motor morons" and "poorest classes." So much for fair and equal treatment by teachers at the beginning of their career. Martinek's work (1983) on Pygmalion and Galatea effects further substantiates observable teacher behavior differences toward students with various characteristics.

Two interim reports from a case study conducted by Griffin (1983; 1984) indicate that teachers unconsciously allow gender stereotyped student-to-student interaction patterns to occur as class norms. Both sexes self-limit their own opportunities to participate in sports by pejorative labeling (e.g., gymnastics is a girls' thing while football is only for boys). It is also clear that five of six identified girls' participation patterns (junior varsity athlete, cheerleader, femme fatale, system beater, lost soul) were counterproductive to learning anything positive about any aspect of motor play.

In the theoretical model of good physical education we assume that teacher and student agendas are fairly congruent, whether explicitly shared, covertly perpetrated, or implicitly carried out with no conscious intent by any participant. The final two citations from qualitative research show deleterious effects of noncongruent teacher and student-run curricula, particularly when teachers with consciously honorable intentions are caught sending out stronger, conflicting nonverbal messages through their unconscious actions. Some results from Kollen's (1981) study indicate that high school seniors learned many negative lessons about physical education that no teacher would acknowledge as part of her/his explicit intentions:

> The physical education environment. . .is characterized by embarrassing situations, public humiliation, not being believed, unrealistic expectations, rigid irrelevant movement activities, angry teacher put downs, discomfort, forced display of performance when the student feels incompetent, and feelings of vulnerability. . .Students respond. . .through minimal compliance, lack of involvement, manipulation of the teacher, false enthusiasm, rebellion, leaving, failing class, isolation, or giving up. (pp. 87-88)

In our final example, Wang's data (1977) revealed that teacher-directed explicit curriculum may directly conflict with a student-directed hidden curriculum, with the latter being far more powerful in shaping students' behaviors and determining learning outcomes. New students in the physical education class studied were quickly put in their places by the other students' emphasis on segregation and stratification by gender, race, socioeconomic status, skill level, and other traits, while the teacher simultaneously espoused the values of cooperation, mutual supportiveness, and democratic behavior.

Such qualitative analyses, because they provide intimate glimpses of students' experiences in the gym, emit clear signals of distress from school physical education. The situation is particularly invidious when we remember that these negative events happen not only in the worst classes but also in classes in which reasonably good teachers make noble attempts to do good things in their teaching. Tousignant and Siedentop (1983) blame the present sorry state of our subject partially on our failure to invent adequate accountability systems for teachers and students for instructional, managerial, and traditional tasks. When nobody cares what happens, teachers are not accountable for good teaching—nor are students accountable for good learning.

Taken singly, none of the preceding citations of trouble would be great cause for alarm but could be dismissed merely as isolated instances of minor dysfunctions in American physical education. Taken together, however, the cumulative effect of public opinion, expert testimony, the more intimate personal experiences of teacher-watching connoisseurs, and research evidence points to the gravity of the state of physical education in the schools and raises urgent questions about its potential longevity. When widely divergent data sources are triangulated toward the same inevitable conclusion, then we must, however reluctantly, accept the bad news.

HOW DID WE GET INTO THIS MESS?

The immediately available scapegoat of course is the teacher. As others already have pointed out (Locke, 1981; Siedentop, 1981) we are too quick to blame teachers for poor teaching, and we are too quick to assume that if only teachers would teach better, the problems of physical education would be solved. Casting aspersions on personal worth, or holding the unrealistic expectation that if teachers only would work harder things would improve, are nonanswers to the highly complex problems that we now confront.

Deeper analysis reveals that several factors contribute to our current dilemmas. Internal factors include failure to cope with systemic rather than individual domains of the problem, failure to realize the dominant value system operating in physical education, failure to consider the profound implications of teacher/coach role conflicts, and failure of curriculum experts to help practitioners in useful ways. External factors that impinge include growing public awareness of the gaps between our rhetoric and reality of student achievement in developing fitness, the proliferation of too many goals for physical education programs reasonably to achieve, the rising number of community activity programs offered on a cost basis, and the failure of society to understand the differences between the concepts of physical education, athletics, intramurals, play, and recess.

No solutions even can be contemplated unless we first acknowledge that what we really are facing are systemic problems that require systemic solutions. Schools are, above all, sociocultural settings in which the norms, values, and mores of the larger society are acted out *upon* teachers as much as *by* them. Teachers are bound by implicit and explicit assumptions made by others about their functions and roles, and it is difficult to break out of the norms for teaching behaviors in the gym, however hard any single individual might try. One could ask why more high school physical educators do not teach nontraditional activity units, or significantly revise their overall programs, or attempt to implement new teaching styles. Most teachers simply cannot overcome systemic level problems on the strength of their own isolated efforts. That a few remarkable individuals, whether by superhuman effort or exceptional ability, are able to do so is joyous testimony to human genius but entirely irrelevant to the situational dilemmas that entrap the vast majority of physical education teachers.

A related reason for the troubled state of physical education is that the predominant value system laid on students is masculine, athletic, and competitive (Kollen, 1983), a cluster that automatically eliminates many girls, low skilled youngsters, and nonaggressive/nonassertive students from full participation in learning. Both teachers and students find it difficult to hold or act upon any values other than those which constitute the perceived majority position in physical education experiences.

Too many physical educators in the past have fulfilled the dual role of teacher and coach, and many still contend with the pressures inherent in the simultaneous expectations of both roles. Role conflict (Bain, 1978, 1983; Bain & Wendt, 1983; Earls, 1981; Locke & Massengale, 1978; Templin, 1981a) involves the contradictory expectations of working with small numbers of elite, highly motivated athletes in the coaching environment juxtaposed with teaching large numbers of students exhibiting mixed skill levels and mixed motivation in the instructional setting. Further, teachers/coaches face role strain or overload because they simply don't have the time, energy, or commitment to both teach and coach as well as they would like. As a result, they must make choices—choices which often mean that teaching is neglected because one's win-loss record is ever so public while one's teaching is only too private. If nobody really cares what happens anyway, who can hold you accountable for an 8 a.m. volleyball class on a Thursday morning in January?

Given that most teachers want to be good but are bound by the sociocultural constraints of schools as institutions and by value systems that limit their options to perpetuating the prevailing view of the public toward physical education, and given that teachers all too often are further hampered by finite physical and mental energies from both teaching and coaching well, isn't there someone to whom teachers could turn for help in revitalizing physical education programs? Alas, the curriculum theorists one might natually approach in these circumstances are rather more of a hindrance than a help, and they constitute a fourth factor partially responsible for our present predicaments.

Physical education curriculum theorists can without exception be labeled as traditionalists (Pinar, 1975), their principal function being to guide practice by making recommendations and suggestions for improving school programs. One result of the way curriculum theorists in higher education have defined their work, however, is that there really are none who see their personal function to be that of giving immediately useful assistance to teachers responsible for motor play environments.

Most theorists engage in seemingly endless ethereal debates about purposes, processes, hermeneutics, and metaphorical analyses, paying little attention to the real problems of teachers and students in school gymnasia. It seems clear that at present no substantial assistance can realistically be expected from those who could be expert consultants on curriculum development (Dodds, 1983).

The gap between curriculum theorists and physical education teachers is so great that even simplistic interventions such as assistance with program design would not be adequate responses to complex problems. The recent work of conceptual empiricists and reconstructionists (Giroux & Purpel, 1983; Giroux, Penna, & Pinar, 1981) has expanded our thinking to include multiple levels and complex interweaving relationships among those levels in nonlinear models far distant from Tyler's four primordial questions about curriculum processes (Tyler, 1950). Curriculum is now much more than a program of study, including virtually all teacher and student activities that occur whenever they are interacting with each other. Thus, within this definition, curriculum redesign involves rearranging the contingencies (relationships among events) of the physical education environment for participants.

If functional curriculum is the bottom line of experiences from which students actually learn, then events must be arranged so that positive, pleasant behaviors and attitudes are maximized for students while negative, unpleasant learnings are reduced. There must be congruence among levels of curriculum, including teachers' explicitly stated and shared intentions and the related learning activities, teachers' covert intentions for student learning, hidden curricula operated by teachers and students without either party's awareness, and even the null curricula of experiences omitted from the learning environment.

The curriculum theorists could help teachers become acutely aware of all the curriculum levels operating when they teach, so that most behaviors and attitudes taught could be raised to conscious teacher intention, either explicitly or covertly. Only in this way can the functional curriculum be controlled to greater degree by the teachers responsible for arranging their students' learning conditions.

EXTERNAL CONDITIONS INFLUENCING PHYSICAL EDUCATION

In parallel with the kinds of in-school factors responsible for the state of American physical education, new factors external to the school also contribute to the problem. The increasingly sophisticated general public is now past the point of being lulled by our old, spurious arguments that one major purpose of public school physical education is to improve the fitness of American youth. Parents and other community members today generally know that programs meeting twice a week for 30 minutes of vigorous activity are simply not sufficient to increase fitness levels. Add to that the fact that few programs attempt any systematic record keeping to demonstrate student progress and we have an increasingly vulnerable rhetoric unsupported by reality.

Further, fitness is not the only avowed purpose of physical education in schools. No activity program even if meeting every school day could hope to accomplish the diverse goals frequently claimed for physical education. With so many goals, physical education has the flavor of trying to be all things to all people—to the point at which the public is suspicious, and rightly so, of any claims made for any accomplishments.

Community activity programs for fitness or the acquisition of motor play skills are increasingly available in a variety of sports, dance, and play activities. The advantage of built-in accountability through the business model makes such programs more and more attractive to those who can afford to participate (Siedentop, 1981). Disadvantages of community-based programming include the cost, geographical distance, and lack of availability of specific activities; thus not all Americans have equal access to these programs (Kirshenbaum & Sullivan, 1983).

A final factor contributing to the complexity of problems in school physical education is the public's confusion about the terms *physical education, athletics, intramurals, play*, and even *recess*. Bad publicity about grading scandals or recruitment violations in college athletic programs become associated somehow with poor physical education programs in the minds of consumers. In Massachusetts, public failure to differentiate free play from instruction about motor play skills or fitness— or to care about such differences—led to the common practice of counting recess activities toward the state requirement for physical education. The fact that physical educators persistently and clearly separate the two was of little consequence given this wider misunderstanding.

Additional confusion about the purpose and functions of physical education, upon which we cannot even agree among ourselves, further impedes communication between physical educators and the general public. A teacher who talks about motor skill acquisition goals to a community member thinking of fitness goals is guaranteed miscommunication, if not failure, at the outset of the conversation. By not unifying our goals within the profession, we present a fragmented front to the outside world of children and adults who consume our services. We do not argue that a single goal or purpose ought to be adopted uniformly, but simply that we must begin to communicate our intentions clearly and distinctly as we engage in dialogues about our subject.

To summarize thus far, several danger signals point to serious problems in school physical education. The messages range from public opinion polls reiterating the low status of physical education to school reform reports which ignore the subject entirely; they range from highly critical analyses by experts within our profession to research evidence graphically displaying the unhappy results of inadequate curriculum. The problems are immensely complicated by factors inherent in public schools. Those factors include a social system that exempts neither teachers nor students and that operates to transmit predominant cultural values of masculinity, athleticism, and competition to students. Also, consider that teachers perform the double duty of coaching and teaching, that they get minimal help in solving their problems from curriculum experts, and that the intricacies of functional curricula discourage easy or quick solutions. None of these factors should surprise those who think critically about our field. In addition, there is the increasing public awareness of glaring mismatches between the rhetoric of goals and purposes of physical education and the reality of actual practices, the tendency of non-physical educators to lump physical education with recreation, athletics, intramurals, and recess, and the bewildering profusion of purposes within our ranks. All imply strongly that if we cannot change from within, we may be cut from without.

Our patient has so many symptoms that nothing short of heroic life-support measures and intensive care could fully restore all functions. The scope of problems in physical education is so broad that large-scale actions, even if we believed that a sweeping reform could be mounted—and we don't—are just not feasible. Any solutions which can lead to substantial progress will come in tiny steps, over long periods of time, in the company of like-minded reformers content with small-scale assaults on specific local topics about which there is some reason for a group of people to believe that they can make a difference. No national efforts loom on this horizon, nor are any soon expected.

THE PROBLEM DETERMINES THE SOLUTION

Several possible solutions suggest themselves, depending on how one ultimately defines the problem. If the "real" problem is taken to be that *physical education programs generally are excellent but we just aren't communicating well with people* outside the gym about successes and positive accomplishments, then we could solve this problem by image management and improved public relations. If the problem were so simple, structures and mechanisms already exist for publicizing what we do. Using AAHPERD as an example, good publicity comes from various projects. The new Health-Related Fitness Tests, the Jump Rope for Heart program, the PEPI Project, the Teacher of the Year Award, the Profiles of Excellence Series for Elementary and Secondary Teachers in *JOPERD*, and similar efforts promote physical education as a worthwhile activity for kids in schools. NASPE (AAHPERD, 1983, published in NASPE NEWS) recently initiated the Physical Education Justification Project to collect a broad evidential base to support the continuation of physical education as a serious school project.

A second way of defining the "real" problem in physical education is to admit that *far too many schools not only fail to measure up to ideals, but they miseducate and are dangerous to their clients.* If that is the real problem, then publicity is at best an evasion and substantive reform is the only responsible action. Such solutions sadly require more than any of us can give in time, energy, or resources. Making educationally significant change soon enough to stave off cuts in local school committee budgets would involve such extensive reforms that the task is literally insurmountable. Individual teachers and the school systems within which they teach are highly resistant to change. The degree of change necessary to revitalize physical education involves coordinated mobilization not only for physical educators but also of administrators, students, parents, other teachers, and community members.

Even if the magnitude of combined effort could overcome inertia sufficiently to initiate change, continuing conditions for sustaining and supporting changes already instituted must be created or no change can persist. The literature of educational change hammers this point again and again (Bentzen, 1974; Chin & Downey, 1973; Giacquinta, 1973; Havelock, 1973; Sarason, 1982).

To contemplate any possibility of national reform for school physical education seems fruitless against the historical background of less than far-reaching results produced by previous innovations. The phenomena of movement education and the spectrum of teaching styles illustrate this point. Both entities were conceived and promoted with the underlying theme of replacing current practices in physical education, the first by introducing a tight conceptual framework of movement theory from Laban's work and the second by providing a wide array of possibilities for designing and carrying out instructional experiences. However, their ultimate impact has been lessened (neither was adopted widely in pure form), transfigured (each teacher implements her/his own conception of movement education or teaching styles), and diluted (some fragments of each are now included in many programs, but neither whole scheme ever substituted for current practice).

Discouraging though the litany of educational change in terms of national reform efforts may be, it certainly gives no cause for believing that individual attempts cannot or do not succeed. Wherever there are good programs and excellent teachers, school physical education has a fighting chance to survive. Wherever programs are poor and teaching is mediocre, physical education may die without anybody even missing it. To the extent that each teacher can make her/his gym a pleasant, supportive, exciting place where kids want to learn to play better or get stronger or take risks or engage in esthetic movement activities—to that extent will there be real evidence to preserve physical education in that public school. In the end, local school committees are the ones who must be convinced that physical education is valuable to students in their communities for they will decide whether physical education goes or stays.

If the "real" problem is that *physical education in schools is so bad that it ought to be deleted*, then the questions to ask are: Should kids learn motor skills? How and where? Is physical education in schools worth keeping if its central purpose is to provide a setting in which kids can learn motor skills? Developmental literature resoundingly affirms that much early learning takes place through movement and that vigorous movement contributes extensively to a healthy child's normal growth patterns. Fitness literature reiterates the importance of regular intensive exercise to enhance cardiovascular fitness. Psychological and social benefits or motor play activities are equally well documented. It seems logical to conclude that the more motor skills children learn well under humane conditions, the more likely they will engage in vigorous motor play for the rest of their lives and continue to enjoy the benefits. Yes, kids should learn motor skills of competitive and expressive play activities.

If they cannot learn motor skills through school physical education, how will they learn them? Backyard, after school, or weekend pickup games with friends and family teach some kids what they need. But not all children have good play spaces, more boys than girls are socialized to engage in these informal opportunities for physical self-education, and children tend not to tolerate their lesser-skilled peers, who in turn learn not to take the social risks of attempting to participate. A second opportunity arises from private commercial or community-sponsored offerings. Unfortunately, not all kids can afford to take advantage of such programs, not all localities offer many opportunities, and widely varying costs of different activities often preclude much real choice among things to learn. One remaining possibility is to have children wait until adulthood to learn motor play skills. But how realistic is it to assume that as adults they would build new habits such as active life-styles? Nonschool possibilities, then, just can't reach all potential consumers.

Yes, physical education is worth doing in schools, if only because all youngsters can be reached through free public education which guarantees a captive audience through compulsory attendance laws. But only physical education *done well* is acceptable. Our experience here suggests a categorical imperative: poor programs invariably are worse than no programs.

There are other ways of thinking about problems related to physical education in the schools, but no matter how one chooses to define the "real" problem, no solutions look very promising. Since local school committees hold the power to keep or cut physical education, we college physical educators have only as much influence as any other informed citizen. Our functions are to support good teaching and good programs where we find them and to provide whatever assistance we can. The realities of the situation dictate that this happens in useful ways only when requested by teachers who already want to make their programs better, and believe they can despite systemic constraints. It is axiomatic that while we can be most helpful to these teachers, they are the ones who least need our assistance. One way teacher educators can assist is to enourage small groups of teachers and teacher educators to work together to create an impact on physical education as it is taught in their local community schools. If enough small candles are lit together, the darkness will begin to recede.

In the final analysis, school physical education may be saved by the conservative institutional nature of schools. Failure to cut programs may be the path of least resistance for school committees—as long as the money holds out. Attractive as this may be at first glance, the problems of inferior programs, poor teaching, and negative student attitudes would remain. Those come to rest on us as teacher educators and on our public school colleagues. We have no easy medical solutions to suggest for helping our ailing patient. Those of us who care, however, must begin a consultation that leads to realistic therapy. Otherwise, the patient may leave the ICU through the morgue rather than the front door.

REFERENCES

AAHPERD. (1983). Department of Defense supports physical education as essential. *NASPE NEWS*, No. 8. Reston, VA: Author.

AAHPERD. (1983). *NASPE physical education justification project gets underway— Vern Seefeldt to direct. NASPE NEWS*, No. 8. Reston, VA: Author.

BAILEY, A. (1983). The education equality project: Focus on results. *Phi Delta Kappan*, **65**(1), 22-25.

BAIN, L. (1978). Differences in values implicit in teaching and coaching behaviors. *Research Quarterly*, **49**, 5-11.

BAIN, L. (1983). Teacher/coach role conflict: Factors influencing role performance. In T. Templin and J. Olson (Eds.), *Teaching in physical education: Big Ten body of knowledge symposium series, Vol. 14*. Champaign, IL: Human Kinetics.

BAIN, L., & Wendt, J. (1983). Undergraduate physical education majors' perceptions of the roles of teacher and coach. *Research Quarterly for Exercise and Sport*, **54**(2), 112-118.

BENTZEN, M. (1974). *Changing schools: The magic feather principle*. New York: McGraw-Hill.

CHIN, R., & Downey, L. (1973). Changing change: Innovating a discipline. In R. Travers (Ed.), *Second handbook of research on teaching*. Chicago: Rand McNally.

DODDS, P. (1983). Consciousness raising in curriculum: A teacher's model for analysis. In M. Carnes (Ed.), *Proceedings of the third curriculum theory conference*, Athens, GA: University of Georgia Press.

EARLS, N. (1981). Distinctive teachers' personal qualities, perceptions of teacher education and the realities of teaching. *Journal of Teaching in Physical Education*, **1**(1), 59-70.

EBEL, H. (1983). Corporate fitness programs need the personal touch. *Athletic Purchasing and Facilities*, **7**(12), 12-18.

GALLAHUE, D., Werner, P., & Luedke, G. (1972). *Moving and learning: A conceptual approach to the physical education of young children*. Dubuque, IA: Kendall/ Hunt.

GALLUP, G. (1983). The 16th annual Gallup poll of the public's attitudes toward the public schools. *Phi Delta Kappan*, **66**(1), 23-38.

GIACQUINTA, J. (1973). The process of organizational change in schools. In F. Kerlinger (Ed.), *Review of research in education, Vol. 1.* Itasca, IL: Peacock Publ.

GIROUX, H., Penna, A., & Pinar, W. (Eds.). (1981). *Curriculum & instruction: Alternatives in education.* Berkeley, CA: McCutchan.

GIROUX, H., & Purpel, D. (Eds.). (1983). *The hidden curriculum and moral education: Deception or discovery?* Berkeley, CA: McCutchan.

GOLDBERG, M., & Harvey, J. (1983). A nation at risk: The report of the national commission on excellence in education. *Phi Delta Kappan,* **65**(1), 14-18.

GRAHAM, G., Holt-Hale, S., McEwen, T., & Parker, M. (1980). *Children moving: A reflective approach to teaching physical education.* Palo Alto, CA: Mayfield.

GRAHAM, P. (1983). The twentieth century fund task force report on federal elementary and secondary education policy. *Phi Delta Kappan,* **65**(1), 19-21.

GRIFFIN, P. (1984). Girls' participation patterns in a middle school team sports unit. *Journal of Teaching in Physical Education,* **4**(1), 30-38.

GRIFFIN, P. (1983). "Gymnastics is a girls' thing": Student participation and interaction patterns in a middle school gymnastics unit. In T. Templin & J. Olson (Eds.), *Teaching in physical education: Big Ten body of knowledge symposium series, Vol. 14.* Champaign, IL: Human Kinetics.

HAROOTUNIAN, B., & Yarger, G. (1981). Teachers' conceptions of their own success. Washington, DC: ERIC Clearinghouse on Teacher Education. (ERIC Document Reproduction Service No. ED 200 518)

HAVELOCK, R. (1973). *The change agent's guide to innovation in education.* Englewood Cliffs, NJ: Educational Technology Publications.

HOFFMAN, H., Young, J., & Klesius, S. (1981). *Meaningful movement for children: A developmental theme approach to physical education.* Boston: Allyn & Bacon.

JACKSON, J. (1980). Sport rejection: An in-depth inquiry. University of Victoria, British Columbia.

JENKINS, J., & Bausell, R. (1973). How teachers view the effective teacher. University of Delaware. (ERIC Document Reproduction Service No. ED 075 364)

KIRSHENBAUM, J., & Sullivan, R. (1983, March). Hold on there, America. *Sports Illustrated.*

KOLLEN, P. (1983). Fragmentation and integration in human movement. In T. Templin & J. Olson (Eds.), *Teaching in physical education: Big Ten body of knowledge symposium series, Vol. 14.* Champaign, IL: Human Kinetics.

LAWSON, J. (1983). *The secondary school curriculum in Massachusetts: Recommendations of the commissioner of education.* Boston: State Department of Education.

LEWIS, G. (1969). Adoption of the sports program, 1906-39: The role of accommodation in the transformation of physical education. *Quest,* **12**, 34-46.

LOCKE, L. (1981). Prognosis: What can be predicted for the profession? Paper presented at the American Academy of Physical Education annual meeting, Boston.

LOCKE, L., & Massengale, J. (1978). Role conflict in teacher/coaches. *Research Quarterly*, **49**, 162-174.

LOGSDON, B., Barrett K., Broer, M., McGee, R., Ammons, M., Halverson, L., & Roberton, M. (1977). *Physical education for children: A focus on the teaching process.* Philadelphia: Lea & Febiger.

MARTINEK, T. (1983). Creating golem and galatea effects during physical education instruction: A social psychological perspective. In T. Templin & J. Olson (Eds.), *Teaching in physical education: Big Ten body of knowledge symposium series, Vol. 14.* Champaign, IL: Human Kinetics.

METZLER, M. (1980). Supervised recreation: How long can we live with it? Paper presented at the meeting of the Central Association for Physical Education in Higher Education, Hutchinson, KS.

NATIONAL Commission on Excellence in Education. (1983, May). *A nation at risk: The imperative for educational reform.* Washington, DC: *Congressional Record-Senate*, S6060-S6065.

PHI Delta Kappa. (1983). *Challenge & opportunity* (brochure). Bloomington, IN: Phi Delta Kappa's Ad Hoc Committee on Response to Reports on the State of Education.

PINAR, W. (Ed.). (1975). *Curriculum theorizing: The reconceptualists.* Berkeley, CA: McCutchan.

PLACEK, J. (1982). An observational study of teacher planning in physical education. *Dissertation Abstracts International*, **43**, 106A. (University Microfilms No. DA 8219838).

PLACEK, J. (1983). Conceptions of success in teaching: Busy, happy and good? In T. Templin & J. Olson (Eds.), *Teaching in physical education: Big Ten body of knowledge symposium series, Vol. 14.* Champaign, IL: Human Kinetics.

SARASON, S. (1982). *The culture of the school and the problem of change, second edition.* Boston: Allyn & Bacon.

SIEDENTOP, D. (1981). Secondary physical education: An endangered species. Paper presented at the meeting of the AAHPERD, Boston.

SIEDENTOP, D., Herkowitz, J., & Rink, J. (1984). *Elementary physical education methods.* Englewood Cliffs, NJ: Prentice-Hall.

TEMPLIN, T. (1981a). Teacher/coach role conflict and the high school principal. *NAPEHE Annual Conference Proceedings*, **2**, 70-81.

TEMPLIN, T. (1981b). Student as socializing agent. *Journal of Teaching in Physical Education*, introductory issue, pp. 71-79.

TOUSIGNANT, M., & Siedentop, D. (1983). A qualitative analysis of task structure in required secondary physical education classes. *Journal of Teaching in Physical Education*, **3**(1), 47-57.

TYLER, R. (1950). *Basic principles of curriculum development.* Chicago: University of Chicago Press.

VANDERZWAAG, H. (1983). Coming out of the maze: Sport management, dance management and exercise science—programs with a future. *Quest*, **35**(1), 66-73.

WANG, B. (1977). An ethnography of a physical education class: An experiment in integrated living. *Dissertation Abstracts International*, **38**, 1980A. (University Microfilms No. 77-21,750)

WILSON, C. (1969). Diversities in meanings of physical education. *Research Quarterly*, **40**(1), 211-214.

Is Physical Education Teacher Education In American Colleges Worth Saving? Evidence, Alternatives, Judgment

Lawrence F. Locke and Patt Dodds
University of Massachusetts

The impetus for this and the companion paper (preceding chapter) does not rest in the dialogue occasioned by *The Nation At Risk*. Neither have we been much inspired by the latest reflex of self-castigation (Howsam, 1981; Sykes, 1983) or journalistic muckraking (Lyons, 1980) over how we prepare teachers. Our motives are not so lofty that we have not been tempted to ride the latest professional hobby horse in which style triumphs over substance (this year school/college collaboration is in and teacher competencies are out), but we have lost some of the old zest for such recreations.

Our daily work involves trying to figure out what goes wrong in the business of teaching and teacher education—and how to fix it. As with many others who do the same work, this seemed an opportune time to share some of the information, questions, and insights we have acquired. Nothing more is intended, nothing more will be attempted.

For readers who would like to have our response to the rhetorical question posed in the title—without having to plow through all the evidence and reasoning—the conclusion is, given any reasonable alternative, "NO." The present model for preparing physical education teachers is entrapped in a web of systemic problems, ensconced in a hostile environment, and empowered with wholly inadequate supports.

Some other model might be better, but that is the catch. None of the alternatives presently being examined seems likely. Schools of pedagogy (Smith, Silverman, Borg, & Fry, 1980), extended preparation requirements (Denemark & Nutter, 1979; Howsam, Corrigan, & Denemark, 1976; Scannell & Guenther, 1981), or clinical training centers in the schools (Howey, Yarger, & Joyce, 1978) simply are not in the cards for the near term. We are left, then, with the task of doing better with what we have. That means, in equal parts, figuring out why things sometimes don't work and how to find replacements or make repairs. This paper deals exclusively with the first of those two equal parts.

THE PROBLEM OF TRAINING PHYSICAL EDUCATION TEACHERS

The central issues in teacher education remain now as they were 50 years ago: What values and skills do teachers need to do their work? What exactly is wrong with how we presently attempt to provide those values and skills? How do we stop doing teacher preparation one way and start doing it another? What is a more effective form of preparation? How can schools be transformed so that they will not press new teachers back into existing patterns of curriculum and instruction?

We hold the assumption that the condition of physical education in the public schools demonstrates the existence of serious problems in preparing teachers. If the physical education delivered in the school is inadequate, then the preparation of teachers must be inadequate. As one immediately will recognize, that is not the commonly accepted conclusion. It is more usual to assume that teachers beginning their careers are generally well prepared by the training institutions. In the ensuing scenario, however, the values, motives, and acquired skills of new graduates are overwhelmed by the press of socialization in the workplace. In turn, that stifles the execution of their best efforts and results in what teacher educators, at least, hold to be inferior levels of performance. As the public school workplace is beyond the control of anyone in higher education, accountability for these hypothesized events is neatly sidestepped. If the physical education that kids experience is less than ideal, it cannot possibly be our fault!

We are uncomfortable with that account of events for two reasons. First, there is the fact that the other party has an opposite and equally firm explanation which holds the incompetence of beginning teachers ("they don't know the subject matter, they don't know how to teach, they don't know how to handle students, and they don't know how to behave in a school") to be a major factor impeding the development of quality programs. Can that account be entirely without substance?

We also are struck by the fact that not a single physical education teacher of our acquaintance graduated from a preparation program on another planet. They all were produced by our own program, or ones like it. Distancing teacher education from what teachers do in the schools, as though all practitioners were imported from Mars, is a neat trick but not so convincing if one watches the pea rather than the walnut shells.

Occasionally we graduate subject matter illiterates and pedagogical incompetents from our program. Are we really alone in that sin? The oppressive effects of school socialization on some teachers during the entry years is a reality, and thereby ought to be a central problem for teacher educators as well as those who operate schools. Certainly it ought not be an escape hatch for evading responsibility. Just why are our graduates so vulnerable, and why are we not working with school personnel to devise more positive forms of professional induction? There are plenty of defects to discover, understand, catalogue, and remediate in teacher education. While we are not accountable for every failure of our graduates, we and the imperfections in our programs must shoulder some reasonable portion of responsibility.

What follows is divided into three parts: (a) external problems that frame and shape the internal problems of design and operation—the issues of money, time, talent, and environment, (b) internal problems that everyone knows about—the issues of designing and operating an effective preservice program, and (c) the problems nobody really knows about—the unthinkable possibilities that haunt the dark recesses of our intuition.

A WARNING

One caveat is essential. We will try to note useful articles and research reports at appropriate points, but the reader should not expect much of substance that deals directly with preservice physical education. That literature is thin, unreliable, and often uninformative. Teacher educators have remained remarkably incurious about what they do. Several years ago we began a laborious two-part review of research on preservice teacher preparation for physical education (Locke, 1983; Locke & Dodds, 1981b). If we had known at the start how little we would learn, we might not have made the effort. Here, as in those earlier reviews, we will have to make use of documents and studies from sources outside physical education, and far more use of personal judgment and best guess than we would wish for a topic of such importance.

FRAMING FACTORS:
THE PROBLEMS OF MONEY, TIME, AND TALENT

This first category of problems includes conditions external to the preparation program. B.O. Smith (1980) has called them "framing factors" because they shape and limit operation of all programs in a universal way, irrespective of how particular programs may be designed. From a larger set we have selected those with which physical educators will have had the most direct experience: money, time, and talent.

Money talks in teacher preparation programs no less than elsewhere on the campus, but mostly it speaks in a whisper. The average cost of instruction per undergraduate in teacher education in 1980 was $927, with the lower end of the range at $578 among institutions recently surveyed (Peseau & Orr, 1980). The equivalent figure for full-time students in higher education was $2,363 and the per-pupil expenditure in public schools averaged across all states was $1,400. If recent trends in federal legislation continue, teacher education will be even more seriously underfunded in the future (Howey, 1982). Quite simply put, we attempt to train teachers "on the cheap." Worse, and more tragic in the long run, we have come to accept starvation of our programs as a normal condition (Peseau, 1982).

No separate budget figures are available for programs in physical education. Because the credit generating capacity of general physical education programs is used in many institutions to maintain minimum funding for the preservice program, it is probable that most are no worse off than other teacher training programs on the campus. The balance between funding and commitments may again be shifting, however, and what was simply bad may soon get worse.

Teacher training in physical education evolved as a labor intensive operation. On the one hand we make little use of capital intensive technology such as CAI, videotapes, simulation games, programmed learning materials, or audiotape libraries. On the other hand, we do make it a common practice to have students sit in classrooms and hear us talk about teaching physical education—a cost-effective if questionable training strategy. The heavy costs of operating clinical training are largely avoided in the final practicum by allowing cooperating teachers to operate student teaching on a day-to-day basis as virtually cost-free volunteers.

The present push to employ earlier, more extensive and more truly clinical field experiences, a fad sanctified by legislation in some states, will require an enormous increase in labor just to administer, much less to conduct in some pedagogically defensible manner. At our institution we already are attempting to operate three 30-hour field pre-practica prior to student teaching without an increase in resources. The line between valor and foolishness is thin indeed. After an extensive study of fiscal support for teacher preparations, Peseau and Orr (1980) sadly observed that "perhaps the most distressing generalization one can make about professional educators, is that they tend to accept expanded responsibilities without having the resources to meet them (p. 100)."

If teacher training programs do not receive their fair share of the fiscal pie, they are positively starving with the slice of time served in undergraduate education. The preparation time required for entry into most professions and semi-professions has been extended over the past half century. The single exception has been education, where the time available to train teachers to cope with an increasingly complex role has not increased at all.

Trade schools not infrequently provide a year or more of intensive 40-hour-a-week training for artisans. In these same terms, 5 day weeks of 8-hour days, professional preparation for a lifelong career as a secondary school teacher now requires a national average of 6 weeks to complete (Joyce, Yarger, Howey, Harbeck, & Kluwin, 1977; Yarger, Howey, & Joyce, 1979). The preparation of elementary-level teachers requires just over 12 weeks, about 3 months of full-time study. For comparison, community colleges that employ full-time training models for technologists and nonprofessionals such as barbers, beauticians, dieticians, medical secretaries and childcare workers frequently require a full year or more (Howey, Yarger, & Joyce, 1978). In Florida, the Barbers' Board presently requires 1,500 hours of barber schooling before a person may take the certification examination. This substantially exceeds the hours of instruction required of a person in the professional component of a preparation program prior to certification as a teacher.

The question, of course, is not whether 20% of 190 quarter hours or 120 semester hours would or could serve other vocations. The question is whether it is adequate for training physical education teachers as well as we know how. The answer must come from what we know about teaching, and what teachers are required to do.

Since 1930 the expansion of coursework requirements in social science professions such as law, health science professions such as pharmacy, and hard science professions such as civil engineering was demanded by expansion of the knowledge required to provide adequate client services (Smith & Street, 1983). The teacher's role has undergone similar growth in complexity. The knowledge base that is relevant to effective teaching in physical education has doubled and doubled again in a few decades. Meanwhile, the time and credit package for teacher preparation has remained constant. Subject matter preparation in motoric play, foundational preparation in the academic disciplines, and pedagogical preparation for the work of teaching are all cheated by time constraints. Peter already has been robbed to pay Paul. From what essential area of preparation will we now steal hours for an expanded clinical training component?

While money and time determine what the program can do, it is the raw material, the input of talent brought by entering students, that determines the success of whatever training can be put into place. Although, in theory, admissions and selective retention are internal matters, the talent pool from which students must be drawn is not. With admissions and retention held constant (in most institutions they appear to have changed little in the last decade), qualitative changes in applicants have a magnified effect.

In a self-selection, nonrecruitment, semi-profession such as teaching, some simple axioms govern the impact of shifts in job market conditions. When demand for new graduates falls, the number of applicants entering preprofessional training will fall. Further, so long as graduates exceed the number of available openings, the quality of potential recruits in the applicant pool also will decline (Hopfengardner, Lashley, & Joseph, 1983). The operation of these axioms now is apparent in teacher education. It is an established fact that teaching attracts and retains a disproportionately high percentage of those with low academic ability and fails to attract or retain those with high ability (Vance & Schlechty, 1982).

Using SAT verbal and math scores of college-bound students as the measure, the scores for students entering education have declined steadily since 1972 (Weaver, 1981). The erosion is of considerable magnitude, about 30 points for both elementary and secondary-level majors. Although the rank order position for education has not changed, located as it is in an unchallenged spot at the bottom of the list, the rate of decline for future teachers has been twice as great as the national average (Weaver, 1977). The downslope, then, is not just a mirror of a wider national trend. It is uniquely linked to the circumstances of a soft job market and, perhaps, to a continuing decline in the attractiveness of careers in teaching (Sykes, 1983).

The sorting accomplished by transfers and attrition does not help. Education continues to be the only major in which there is not average gain in measures of academic ability over the 4 years of college (Weaver, 1979). The weakest students transfer in from other majors and the strongest transfer out at disproportionate rates. Education majors in the upper quartile of ability are twice as likely to transfer out of the program as students in the lowest quartile. In addition, GRE scores of education graduates have declined relative to college population means and, to add insult to injury, the NTE scores of graduating seniors have shown roughly the same pattern (Weaver, 1981).

There is no reason to believe that these depressing data have anything to do with an influx of minority students—not because their presence might not have influenced SAT, GRE, or NTE means, but because there has not been any such influx (Weaver, 1981). Further, declining indices of academic competence are not just a case of salvaging the best from a bad situation. Brubaker (1976) reported that even before the lean years were under way, teacher education programs rejected fewer than 10% of all applicants.

It is true, of course, that we are not sure what can be predicted from SAT scores or, for that matter, any academic measure including college grades. Certainly lower SAT scores have not presaged lower grade point averages for education majors. However, that may be a function of the fact that education professors continue to assign the highest percentages of A's among all undergraduate areas of study.

If the ties between SAT scores and teacher effectiveness are unclear, it does not follow that intelligence, academic ability, communication skills, or general information are irrelevant either to teaching or to teacher training. Many of the tasks in teacher preparation do require considerable cognitive capacity. Given any increase in the relative number of students with marginal thinking skills, one of three things must happen: (a) failure rates must rise as it becomes necessary to weed out more students unable to cope with training program demands, (b) standards of achievement must be lowered to accommodate more students who cannot meet minimum standards, or (c) a mastery model of learning must be instituted that provides more time to completion and more tutorial supports for more students.

Each program will have a unique history regarding the number and quality of entering students and the forms of response employed if and when detectable declines occur in student ability (Schlechty & Vance, 1983). Some programs have experienced declining applications and used the opportunity to raise the quality of admitted students. Others have seen almost no loss in numbers but have detected substantial erosion of quality. If any generalization can safely be made for physical education, it is that the ability of recruits constitutes a significant restriction on what can be achieved within the preservice training cycle.

Faced with the broadened academic demands in the disciplines of physical education, and higher expectations for use of cognitive skills in planning, executing, and evaluating modern versions of pedagogy, students in preservice programs often must meet rising expectations with underdeveloped study habits and impoverished verbal skills. The influence of underconsumption and oversupply in the job market only serves to make that a more serious problem. Unfortunately, impassioned calls for higher admission standards (Watts, 1980) overlook the fact that the costs of enhancing the status of the profession enough to attract and hold students in the upper half of the college population would be enormous. No school district or state legislature of our acquaintance is ready to deal with that.

INTERNAL FACTORS:
THE PROBLEMS OF DESIGN AND OPERATION

Teacher educators are familiar with many of the problems encountered in designing and operating preservice programs. Although few of us take the time to develop precise definitions or taxonomies, the list of difficulties is long, variegated, and perplexing. For anyone interested in reviewing these problems as a set of interrelated phenomena, we can recommend two excellent catalogues.

For teacher education in general consult the venerable article by Martin Haberman (1971), "Twenty-three Reasons Universities Can't Educate Teachers." The author refers to his collection of fatal flaws in university-based teacher preparation as "merely illustrative," which leaves most readers grateful that he never put his mind to producing a comprehensive list. Haberman's long residence in a large state university gives him an unerring instinct for what frustrates teacher educators most. In these days when college departments and public schools grope toward each other, his gloomy assessment of the possibilities for achieving genuine collaboration is painfully vivid. "Slow-witted, lumbering elephants circle each other for a century only to discover they are both males and incapable even of friendship (p. 134)."

Unlike others, this particular listing of problems in preservice education addresses the mismatch between the demands of teacher preparation and the missions, values, and traditions that shape institutions in higher education. From reward systems that punish rather than encourage faculty involvement in clinical field experiences to the dominant model of instruction that serves the university so well (lecture, read, discuss, and abstract), but which is so inappropriate when used in public schools, it is difficult to imagine a place more ill-suited to the preparation of teachers.

For a compendium of the special problems encountered in designing and operating preservice programs in physical education, we suggest consulting a volume edited by Hal Lawson (1981), *Undergraduate Physical Education Programs: Issues and Approaches*, published by AAHPERD. Surely one of the best kept secrets in Reston, Virginia, few people have seen, much less read this valuable resource (still available from AAHPERD Publication Sales under Stock No. 245-26905). In a chapter written by Locke, Mand, and Siedentop (1981), the authors develop a list of problems to be surmounted in preparing physical education teachers. However, their list is limited to problems having two characteristics: (a) importance—the problem must be serious enough when left unresolved to produce demonstrable negative impact on graduates, and (b) difficulty—each problem must be sufficiently complex to ensure that some teacher education faculties would have been unable to devise a satisfactory resolution.

There are 55 problems which meet the twin criteria of importance and difficulty. They are divided into familiar categories such as program design, program content, institutional supports, faculty, students, and practica. Each problem is defined by describing both the ideal condition and a typical deviation from the ideal as it occurs in real programs. The consequences of failing to resolve each problem, both in the lives of graduates and in their pupils, are described in behavioral detail.

For a thorough review and orderly catalogue of the problems already experienced by our colleagues, this AAHPERD publication is highly recommended. We think it is a far more logical basis for program accreditation than any of the models presently under consideration in our professional organizations.

THINKING THE UNTHINKABLE: THE PROBLEM OF CHIMERAS

We turn now from what everyone knows to what nobody knows. Like the ancient Greek concept of chimeras, which were fantastical creatures beyond the grasp of human intellect, these problems are unthinkable because the substance needed to contemplate them simply is not available. We offer here three quick sketches which, like those fuzzy photographs of supposed UFOs, are the only concrete traces we have. If you find yourself unconvinced, that is healthy skepticism. If you find yourself persuaded, that may be hypersuggestivity. If you find yourself interested but vaguely uneasy, then you share our own response.

The first chimera is buried, dead and gone with a wooden stake driven into its heart and a silver bullet in its entrails. Or so we are assured by people who must know these things. In 1964, W. James Popham at UCLA began a 4-year federally funded project to investigate the measurement of teacher competence. Because he had parallel interests in both CBTE and the use of behavioral objectives in teaching, one series of experiments (Popham, 1971a) included all three elements: a measure of teacher effectiveness, specified learning objectives, and subjects selected to illuminate the impact of traditional (non-CBTE) teacher preparation.

In brief, two groups of subjects, one consisting of certified, experienced subject-matter specialists from public schools and the other consisting of matched subjects who had subject-matter competence but no training, certification, or experience in teaching anything to anyone, were given a set of explicit learning objectives for a subject matter unit, an intact public school class, an array of instructional support materials, and nine

1-hour sessions in which to teach. In each subject area for which the experiment was performed (for example, auto mechanics, electronics, social studies), ordinary people—tradespeople, housewives, college sophomores—produced as much learning as certified teachers (Popham, 1971a; 1971b). When objectives are specified and clear, when a valid and reliable measure of student learning is the test of effectiveness, and when classroom conditions are such as to eliminate most of the noninstructional role demands, then there appeared to be no inherent advantage to having received formal teacher preparation.

The limitations of such an investigation are obvious and have been subject to extensive critique (Glass, 1974; Good, Biddle, & Brophy, 1975; Turner, 1973). In both the technical report (Popham, 1971a) and accounts appearing in professional magazines (Popham, 1971b), Popham was restrained in his interpretation of the results, suggesting only that the certified teachers in those experiments seemed not to have been provided with any particularly powerful strategies for producing learning. At least they had not acquired anything which an intelligent and well intentioned layperson would not spontaneously employ, given a clear idea of the learning goals to be accomplished.

Despite Popham's caution, a nasty public debate ensued in professional circles (Bausell & Moody, 1973; Turner, 1973). Others, less restrained than Popham, suggested that the data demonstrated the irrelevance or at least the impotence of teacher training programs. All this would have disappeared had not other investigators been so industrious as to attempt similar investigations, taking care to address some of the limitations in the original version (mainly length of treatment, age of subjects, and the confounding of teacher experience with teacher training) (Bausell, 1976; Bausell & Moody, 1972; Dembo & Jennings, 1973; Jennings, Dembo, & Swensen, 1971; Moody & Bausell, 1971).

The main finding replicated perfectly in every instance. Subject-matter competent lay teachers may approach the task differently and, when subject to observation by experts, may receive lower ratings for the methods they select, but the achievement of their pupils is no worse than the level obtained by graduates of accredited teacher education programs (Jennings, Dembo, & Swensen, 1971). Furthermore, the parity of trained and untrained teachers obtains in tutorial as well as classroom settings. Further, the no-significant-difference result obtains when students who have selected education but not yet taken professional courses are matched with education majors who have finished both their course work and student teaching, but not yet graduated (Bausell & Moody, 1972).

In the past year, a fresh round of public debate about the problems of teacher education has caused the Popham Chimera to be disinterred (Butler, 1983; Greenberg, 1983). The debate now is defined in somewhat different terms: is some training better than no training at all? The continuing practice of employing provisionally certified, short-cut certified, and out-of-field teachers, a strategy that accelerates sharply in times of teacher shortage in a subject area (Masland & Williams, 1983), has afforded researchers some opportunity to gather data that bear on this question. In these studies, teachers with full certification have been shown to have some advantage over teachers with little or no preparation (Bledsoe, Cox, & Burnham, 1967; Copley, 1975). Unfortunately these investigations employ no measure of either student achievement or teacher behavior. Estimates of effectiveness rely mostly on ratings by school principals, who by definition are not blind to the background of their employees. These results seem unconvincing and the case clearly remains open.

It is the nagging questions that give life to this chimera. Would the students of trained teachers pull ahead if the experiments ran longer, as critics have persistently maintained? No one knows. Closer to home, would the Popham findings replicate in physical education? Would a good badminton player, who was a mechanic or a cook by training and vocation, teach beginning badminton to college sophomores just as well as the graduate of a professional preparation activity course taught by Dodds and Locke? No one knows. If the no-significant difference result replicates, what would it mean for preservice preparation? How could we use that information to improve programs? No one knows and, apparently, no one cares.

Happily, for our peace of mind, this chimera is safely just a shadow that passed and was gone. Yet, yesterday there was a footprint in the snow outside the gym. We wonder. . .

A second spook was conjured up recently by a graduate student in the PETE doctoral program at the University of Massachusetts. Kim Graber had been reading through the small body of qualitative research that deals with life inside professional training programs. Included were Becker's *Boys in White* (Becker, Geer, Hughes, & Strauss, 1961), a study of students and professors in medical school, Lortie's classic study of law schools *Laymen to Lawmen* (Lortie, 1959), and Olesen & Whittaker's (1968) account of nurses in training. Graber hit upon the idea of a parallel examination of the subculture formed by physical education majors during preservice teacher preparation. Using a qualitative perspective, familiar events in our program began to have different meaning.

Both students and professors are aware that a certain amount of game playing is involved in obtaining a college degree (Becker, Geer, & Hughes, 1968). Most students are impelled by the categorical imperatives of making the grade in college, of acting so as to obtain a degree in the shortest possible time—with the least possible effort consistent with the best possible prospects for employment (good grades, recommendations, and vocational know-how), and of escaping with the least possible erosion of personal integrity. A bit of faking-it is acceptable, but no student enjoys selling his or her soul for an A. Given these rules, some degree of image management, psyching out, and game playing is expected and even tacitly approved by professors. All good fun, quite harmless, and a part of everyday life (Goffman, 1959; Potter, 1951).

When the detail of life inside teacher training programs is examined closely, however, something less benign may emerge. If in the conduct of their work teachers fail to use skills previously acquired in preservice preparation, that can be explained away by blaming the influence of school socialization. But how are we to account for the same phenomenon when it occurs during the training program? In October, undergraduates learn concepts, skills, and values related to class management, including effective use of time. "Keep students engaged in active learning tasks. No standing in line waiting for a turn!" Majors can answer exam questions, design lesson plans, and analyze management behaviors in both simulations and field observations. Most important, they can teach time-efficient lessons in the on-campus clinical program. They have learned a vital teaching skill, one with strong presumptions about student learning.

Comes February, the students are working on planning and executing physical fitness units. When we go to the gym to watch, what do we see? Children lined up waiting turns all over the gym. What happened to time management? We are not sure, but certainly it is not a case of forgetting. Some management skills may simply be inappropriate for the unique circumstance of our clinical setting. Others may have been incompletely conceptualized by the faculty. For example, having students *not* stand in line produces its own set of managerial problems, some of which are far more threatening to a novice teacher than just wasting a bit of practice time.

More disturbing, however, are clues which lead in a different direction. These suggest that our students learned some management skills just to please us. The underlying value presumption which supports saving time that may then be spent on learning tasks simply is not accepted by some undergraduates. Once freed from the immediate press to gain our favorable evaluation, those students do precisely what they think both practical *and* morally appropriate, which is to have students stand in line and wait.

One explanation of this may lie in how students decide what is practical. Doyle and Ponder (1977) found that teachers develop a "practicality ethic" which governs decision-making in the classroom. With this ethic they screen all suggestions for instruction or curriculum. The process works much like a series of filters with successively finer mesh. Teachers ask "How much effort is involved? Will it encourage discipline problems? Will it be consistent with the kind of person I want to be?" Methods that pass all the tests will be attempted and may be retained. It is vital to understand, however, that teachers can and will learn operations that their sense of practicality dictates will never be put into use.

Our preliminary judgment is that undergraduates have their own practicality ethic. Given what Pooley (1972) and Lawson (1983a, 1983b) have revealed about presocialization in physical education, we can be confident that undergraduates bring no *tabula rasa* to preservice study. Some, at least, come with elaborate, fixed, and highly pragmatic ideas about the work of teaching and coaching. These conceptions of teaching differ sharply from those that teacher educators draw from their background in behavioral sciences. Lortie (1975) has observed that:

> One wonders how effectively such professors communicate with many students who, it appears, see teaching as the 'living out' of prior conceptions of good teaching. Students who conceive of teaching (consciously or not) as expressing qualities associated with revered models will be less attuned to pragmatic and rationalistic conceptions of teaching. The two groups—students and professors—may talk past one another. (pp. 66-67)

At present, no one knows how much of professional preparation is screened out by undergraduates because it conflicts with what they already know about teaching. Perhaps some, perhaps little. We are left with an unanswered question of painful significance. How much of what we have regarded as successful program impact and professional growth in undergraduates has been nothing more than image management designed to keep us happy? The fact that the literature contains not a single study of the undergraduate subculture in physcial education leaves us especially uneasy here. This chimera is decidedly alive and living in our closets.

Our final excursion leads us deeper yet into the twilight zone of preservice chimeras. It has become commonly accepted in the teacher education community that students become increasingly more progressive or liberal in their attitudes toward education during their stay at the university. They then shift to opposing and more traditional views as they pass through student teaching, induction, and the in-service years.

Under the impact of school experience, teachers are thought to become less willing to trust students, more pessimistic about student capacity to take responsibility, more moralistic about violations of class rules, more dogmatic and less flexible in relations with students, more inclined to be punitive in discipline, more inclined to use authoritarian justifications for their actions and, overall, to assume a more custodial attitude which makes student compliance the first item on the agenda of educational intentions (Locke, 1979). That, at least, is the interpretation given to a small mountain of doctoral dissertations on this subject (Locke & Dodds, 1981a).

Both the common interpretation and the data have some limitations. Most studies have employed psychometric measures rather than direct observation of teacher behavior. Further, the invidious caricature of teachers that is implied simply does not fit the people one meets in schools. Finally, our experience indicates that there is no one-way street of influence in the public schools. When the system leans on them, beginning teachers sometimes push back to create a true dialectic of influence and change (Zeichner, 1979).

Nevertheless, few observers would deny that young teachers often do begin with rather liberal attitudes which become at least more tough-minded (some would say realistic), and in some cases truly authoritarian and custodial. There are two common ways of accounting for this shift. In the first scenario, the preservice program is presumed to inculcate values about humanistic teaching, equity, respect for students as people, and the importance of individual differences. Cooperating teachers, pupils, colleagues, and the bureaucratic ecology of the school teach contrary lessons, and because these sources are backed with powerful sanctions, good and valuable impulses acquired in preparation are overwhelmed by the world of work.

In the second scenario, the biography of presocialization plays the central role. Preservice students are seen as *already* possessing traditional values about teaching acquired through their long apprenticeship of observation. Relatively weak treatment in the preparation program produces only cosmetic, superficial changes. Re-entry into schools activates the latent proclivity for custodial behavior; graduates look like the revered models of their youth (and like their colleagues) to the perpetual disappointment of their university mentors. Good and valuable impulses never took root because other values already were in place and the husbandry of teacher education was too weak to plant anew.

Neither scenario has caused much concern among teacher educators. At the worst we are made to appear merely ineffective, while at the best we could claim that we gave it a good try but simply were outnumbered by the toughies down the block. The whole matter would have remained safely at the level of academic debate had not Zeichner and Tabachnick (1981) detected the spoor of a chimera. What if teacher education programs, they ask, really operate at two levels, *on the surface inefficiently liberal, but in a deeper hidden curriculum, effectively traditional*?

Students and professors might be playing a game in which the objective is for the student to read the program's humanistic, liberal rhetoric correctly, and then display appropriate compliance. Meanwhile, in terms of the model established by professors and program structure, the student moves day by day through a world that is implacably traditional in assumptions about education. Whether they come with a conservative bent or not, student majors learn most quickly from the actions, not the words, of professors and administrators. Where they encounter dogmatism, inequity, rigidity, lack of trust, and authoritarianism, those are the values that will be reinforced. Indeed, the program may exert considerable press on individuals who threaten solidarity on this covert aspect of the professional curriculum (Western & Anderson, 1981). In this latter scenario, schools and teacher education programs are seen as working together to provide a powerful conservative indoctrination which ensures the continuation of physical education as it now exists. Given our self-concept as the bastion of liberal ideas in physical education, such a suggestion represents a chimera of awful dimensions.

If you insist on going chimera hunting, you might take a thoughtful look at your own program, or better, have a skilled outsider do it for you. Are there points at which students are treated in ways contrary to the vision of good teaching espoused by the faculty? Is there any evidence that things are done to keep your own undergraduates "busy, happy, and good?" How commonplace is respect for students, sensitivity for inequity, and concern for maintaining a humane learning environment? You will have to answer for your program, and we for ours. If you have a sighting, however, we would appreciate a note to the National Chimera Center at the University of Massachusetts. Fuzzy photographs always are accepted.

CONCLUSION

Is it all worth saving? Given any accounting of the research evidence on teacher education in general (Howey & Gardner, 1983) or physical education in particular (Locke, 1979; Locke, 1983; Locke & Dodds, 1981b), it is difficult to be either optimistic or enthusiastic about salvaging university-based teacher education. We are stuck in the wrong place, doing ineffectual things to the wrong people at the wrong time in their cycle of personal and professional development. Society would be best served if physical educators could, like true professionals, be given autonomy and held truly accountable. But that cannot happen until preservice preparation is enormously upgraded—which cannot happen until a professional culture demonstrably exists (Howsam, 1980). School and university are locked in a closed circle.

Despite a list of reform literature that dates back at least 40 years to the first national commission (Commission on Teacher Education, 1946), Cogan (1975) argues that waiting for our Flexner is too much like waiting for Godot. Unlike Mertens and Yarger (1982), who concluded that teacher education is stuck *in* déjà vu, an honest appraisal of the prospects for macro-improvement suggests more that we are stuck *with* déjà vu.

Can anything be done? Of course! As any proper grandmother would tell you, it is time to settle down and brighten the corner where you are, producing the micro-improvements that constitute progress without revolution. To that end we close with three simple maxims which have proven helpful in our work: Think small, find company, and ask questions.

The proper scope for action in teacher education is *this student, my class, our program, these cooperating teachers, and that school.* Unrealistic expectations simply distract and discourage. There is work to be done, it can be done well, it is worth doing, and there are plenty of models for how to go about it. While it probably is our fate never to discover unambiguous ties between our work as teacher educators and the generic status of physical education in the schools, the perspective of limited scale permits us to define and receive sustaining rewards.

Both the power needed for progress and the self-renewal necessitated by failure are made easier in good company. As a rule of thumb, any time three or more teacher educators get together in a program and give preservice students exactly the same message, the perceived impact of the program rises out of all proportion to the sum of their individual efforts, or even the importance of the message. To paraphrase Arlo Guthrie's wonderful rule from *Alice's Restaurant*, "If one of you does it they'll think you're weird, if two of you do it they'll just think you're both weird, but if three of you do it they'll think it's a movement!" It may be impossible to completely interrupt the turning cycle of interlocking systemic problems, but as little as one teacher, one professor, and one student together can make it perceptibly slow.

Finally, it is best not to take anything for granted in a preparation program. Poke around, get curious, and ask questions. Because hardly anyone else has ever done it, you can quickly become an expert. More important, however, what you learn can serve you well. As an example, in their study of nursing Olesen and Whittaker (1968) found that student nurses had a complete book on which of their peers would make the best nurses once in professional practice. Their list differed from that of their mentors and was based on both different perceptions and different data sources. Which of their peers would students in your program think are destined for excellence? How do they reach that prediction? How do their estimates differ from your own? What could you learn to do better by having access to information about perceptions formed inside the student training cohort? We have absolute faith that as you learn more about how things really are, you will acquire valuable clues about how to do it better.

Think small, find company, and ask questions. Oh yes, and don't let the chimeras frighten you. They cannot really bite (though of course we never have actually met one face to face).

REFERENCES

BAUSELL, R.B. (1976). Teacher training, relevant teaching practice, and the elicitation of student achievement. Doctoral dissertation, University of Delaware. *Dissertation Abstracts International, 37*(5), 2792-A. (University Microfilms No. 76-24, 226)

BAUSELL, R.B., & Moody, W.B. (1972). A factorial study of tutoring versus classroom instruction. *American Educational Research Journal, 9*(4), 591-597.

BAUSELL, R.B., & Moody, W.B. (1973). Are teacher preparation institutions necessary? *Phi Delta Kappan, 54*(5), 298.

BECKER, H., Geer, B., & Hughes, E. (1968). *Making the grade: The academic side of college life.* New York: Wiley & Sons.

BECKER, H., Geer, B., Hughes, E., & Strauss, A. (1961). *Boys in white.* New Brunswick, NJ: Transaction Books.

BLEDSOE, J., Cox, J.V., & Burnham, R. (1967). *Comparison between selected characteristics and performance of provisionally and professionally certified beginning teachers in Georgia.* University of Georgia (ERIC Document Reproduction Service No. ED 015 553)

BRUBAKER, H.A. (1976). *Who should become a teacher: Current selection policies of teacher education institutions.* Bowling Green State University. (ERIC Document Reproduction Service No. ED 115 608)

BUTLER, M.J. (1983). The case for and against teacher education: An essay and suggested readings. *Journal of Teacher Education,* **34**(4), 52-54.

COGAN, M.L. (1975). Current issues in the education of teachers. In K. Ryan (Ed.) *The Seventy-fourth Yearbook of the National Society for the Study of Education: Teacher Education* (pp. 204-229). Chicago: University of Chicago Press.

COMMISSION on Teacher Education. (1946). *The improvement of teacher education.* Washington, DC: The American Council on Education.

COPLEY, P.O. (1975). *A study of the effect of professional education courses in beginning teachers.* Southwest Missouri State University. (ERIC Document Reproduction Service No. ED 098 147)

DEMBO, M., & Jennings, L. (1973). *Who is the "experienced" teacher?* Paper presented at annual meeting of the American Educational Research Association, New Orleans.

DENEMARK, G., & Nutter, N. (1979). *The case for extended programs of initial teacher preparation.* University of Kentucky (ERIC Document Reproduction Service No. SP 015 395.)

DOYLE, W., & Ponder, G. (1977). The practicality ethic and teacher decision-making. *Interchange,* **8**(3), 1-12.

GLASS, G. (1974). Teacher effectiveness. In H. Walberg (Ed.), *Evaluating educational performance.* Berkeley, CA: McCutchan.

GOFFMAN, E. (1959). *The presentation of self in everyday life.* Garden City, NY: Doubleday.

GOOD, T.L., Biddle, B.J., & Brophy, J.E. (1975). *Teachers make a difference.* New York: Holt, Rinehart & Winston.

GREENBERG, J.D. (1983). The case for teacher education: Open and shut. *Journal of Teacher Education,* **34**(4), 2-5.

HABERMAN, M. (1971). Twenty-three reasons universities can't educate teachers. *Journal of Teacher Education,* **22**(2), 133-140.

HOWEY, K.R. (1982). *Charting directions for preservice teacher education.* Paper prepared for the National Commission on Excellence in Education, Washington, DC: Department of Education. (ERIC Document Reproduction Service No. ED 226 004)

HOWEY, K.R., & Gardner, W.E. (Eds.). (1983). *The education of teachers: A look ahead.* New York: Longman, Inc.

HOWEY, K.R., Yarger, S.J., & Joyce, B.R. (1978). *Improving teacher education.* Washington, DC: Association of Teacher Educators.

HOWSAM, R.B. (1980). The workplace: Does it hamper professionalization of pedagogy? *Phi Delta Kappan,* **62**(2), 93-96.

HOWSAM, R.B. (1981). The trouble with teacher preparation. *Educational Leadership,* **39**(2), 144-147.

HOWSAM, R.B., Corrigan, D.C., & Denemark, G.W. (1976). *Educating a profession.* Washington, DC: American Association of Colleges for Teacher Education.

HOPFENGARDNER, J.D., Lashley, T., & Joseph, E.A. (1983). Recruiting preservice teacher education students. *Journal of Teacher Education*, **34**(4), 10-13.

JENNINGS, L., Dembo, M.H., & Swenson, L. (1971). *Competencies of teachers and interns: Implications for teacher education.* Paper delivered at the California Educational Research Association meeting, Los Angeles. (ERIC Document Reproduction Service No. ED 056 998.)

JOYCE, B.R., Yarger, S.J., Howey, K.R., Harbeck, K.M., & Kluwin, T.N. (1977). *Preservice teacher education.* Palo Alto, CA: Booksend Laboratory. (ERIC Document Reproduction Service No. SP 011 438)

LAWSON, H. (Ed.). (1981). *Undergraduate physical education programs: Issues and approaches.* Reston, VA: AAHPERD.

LAWSON, H.A. (1983a). Toward a model of teacher socialization in physical education: The subjective warrant, recruitment, and teacher education. *Journal of Teaching in Physical Education,* **2**(3), 3-16. (Part 1 of a 2-part series.)

LAWSON, H.A. (1983b). Toward a model of teacher socialization in physical education: Entry into schools, teachers' role orientations, and longevity in teaching. *Journal of Teaching in Physical Education*, **3**(1), 3-15. (Part 2 of a 2-part series.)

LOCKE, L.F. (1979). The challenge of change for physical education: The view for supervision. *The Academy Papers* (No. 13). The proceedings of the 50th annual meeting of the American Academy of Physical Education, pp. 65-74.

LOCKE, L.F. (1983). Research on teacher education for physical education in the U.S.A., Part II: Questions and conclusions. In R. Telama (Ed.), *Research in school physical education* (pp. 285-320). Jyvaskyla, Finland: The Foundation for Promotion of Physical Culture and Health. (An English language publication.)

LOCKE, L.F., & Dodds, P. (1981a). *Research on preservice teacher education in physical education: Some preliminary notes.* Unpublished manuscript, University of Massachusetts.

LOCKE, L.F., & Dodds, P. (1981b). Research on teacher education for physical education. *Artus: Revista de Educacao Fisica E Desportos*, Numero 9/11, 51-67. (Appears in both English and Portugese.)

LOCKE, L.F., Mand, C.L., & Siedentop, D. (1981). The preparation of teachers: A subject-matter-centered model. In H.A. Lawson (Ed.), *Undergraduate physical education programs: Issues and approaches* (pp. 33-54). Reston, VA: AAHPERD.

LORTIE, D.C. (1959). Laymen to lawmen: Law school, careers and professional socialization. Harvard Education Review, **29**(4), 352-369.

LORTIE, D.C. (1975). *Schoolteacher.* Chicago: University of Chicago Press.

LYONS, G. (1980). Why teachers can't teach. *Phi Delta Kappan*, **62**(2), 108-112. (Reprinted from *Texas Monthly*, September, 1979.)

MASLAND, S.W., & Williams, R.T. (1983). Teacher surplus and shortage: Getting ready to accept responsibilities. *Journal of Teacher Education*, **34**(4), 6-9.

MERTENS, S.K., & Yarger, S.J. (1982). Escape from déjà vu: On strengthening teacher education. *Journal of Teacher Education,* **33**(4), 8-12.

MOODY, W.B., & Bausell, R.B. (1971). *The effect of teacher experience on student achievement, transfer and retention.* Paper presented at the Annual American Educational Research Association Meeting, New York.

OLESEN, V., & Whittaker, E. (1968). The art and practice of studentmanship: Backstage. In V. Olesen & E. Whittaker (Eds.), *The Silent Dialogue* (pp. 148-199). San Francisco: Jossey-Bass.

PESEAU, B.A. (1982). Developing an adequate resource base for teacher education. *Journal of Teacher Education, 33*(4), 13-15.

PESEAU, B., & Orr, P. (1980). The outrageous underfunding of teacher education. *Phi Delta Kappan*, **62**(2), 100-102.

POOLEY, J. (1972). Professional socialization: A model of the pretraining phase applicable to physical education students. *Quest*, **18**, 57-66.

POPHAM, W.J. (1971a). Performance tests of teaching proficiency: Rationale, development, and validation. *American Educational Research Journal*, **8**(1), 105-117.

POPHAM, W.J. (1971b). Teaching skill under scrutiny. *Phi Delta Kappan*, **52**(10), 599-602.

POTTER, S. (1951). *One-Upsmanship*. New York: Holt & Co.

SCANNELL, D.P., & Guenther, J.E. (1981). The development of an extended program. *Journal of Teacher Education*, **32**(1), 7-15.

SCHLECHTY, P.C., & Vance, V.S. (1983). Institutional responses to the quality/quantity issue in teacher training. *Phi Delta Kappan*, **65**(2), 94-101.

SMITH, B.O. (1980). Pedagogical education: How about reform? *Phi Delta Kappan*, **62**(2), 87-91.

SMITH, B.O., Silverman, S.H., Borg, J.M., & Fry, B.V. (1980). *A design for a school of pedagogy*. Washington, DC: U.S. Government Printing Office. (Stock Order No. 017-080-02098-0)

SMITH, D.C., & Street, S. (1983). The professional component in selected professions. *Phi Delta Kappan*, **62**(2), 103-107.

SYKES, G. (1983). Contradictions, ironies, and promises unfulfilled: A contemporary account of the status of teaching. *Phi Delta Kappan*, **65**(2), 87-93.

TURNER, R.L. (1973). Are educational researchers necessary? *Phi Delta Kappan*, **54**(5), 299.

VANCE, V.S., & Schlechty, P.C. (1982). The distribution of academic ability in the teaching force: Policy implications. *Phi Delta Kappan*, **64**(1), 22-27.

WATTS, D. (1980). Admission standards for teacher preparatory programs: Time for a change. *Phi Delta Kappan*, **62**(2), 120-122.

WEAVER, W.T., (1977). *Educators in supply and demand: Effects on quality*. Paper presented at the Annual Meeting of the American Educational Research Association, New York City. (ERIC Document Reproduction Service No. Ed 143 145)

WEAVER, W.T. (1979). In search of quality: The need for talent in teaching. *Phi Delta Kappan,* **61**(1), 29-32, 46.

WEAVER, W.T. (1981). The talent pool in teacher education. *Journal of Teacher Education,* **32**(3), 32-36.

WESTERN, J., & Anderson, D. (1968). Education and professional socialization. *The Australian and New Zealand Journal of Sociology,* **4**(2), 91-106.

YARGER, S.J., Howey, K.R., & Joyce, B.R. (1979). *In-service teacher education.* Palo Alto: Booksend Laboratory.

ZEICHNER, K.M. (1979, February). *The dialectics of teacher socialization.* Paper presented at the annual meeting of the Association of Teacher Educators, Orlando, FL.

ZEICHNER, K.M., & Tabachnick, B.R. (1981). Are the effects of university teacher education 'washed out' by school experience? *Journal of Teacher Education,* **32**(3), 7-11.

Section 5

Images, Perceptions, And Decision Making In Physical Education

Physical Education, Athletics, And The Mission Of Higher Education

Linda Jean Carpenter
Brooklyn College

Some of us have said that the value and purposes of physical education and athletics in higher education are misunderstood. It is implied that as a result of this misunderstanding, physical education and sometimes athletic programs are not adequately supported by college administrators.

For many reasons, some real and others born of insecurity and defensiveness, some physical educators have responded to a feeling of vulnerability by placing great importance on explaining the *academic* nature and value of physical education programs to colleagues outside of physical education. Others believe that strengthening the athletic program will bring greater support to physical education. Still others adopt the dandelion philosophy, which can be stated as follows: To avoid all mower hardships, the dandelion shortens its neck. The dandelion philosophy finds expression in the withdrawal of physical educators from innovation, controversy, and any overt showing of an aggressive faith in their own self-worth, and a movement toward only that which will keep the administration unaware of their existence.

One might speculate, however, that the allegations of lack of support or commitment to the continued existence of physical education on campus are incorrect. If the allegations are indeed incorrect, the course of action one might take to alleviate the erroneously perceived support may be counterproductive.

The marriage of deed and image is vital. Whatever course of action is selected to maintain the centrality of physical education to the mission of higher education, it must involve a unity of appraisal by both physical educators and their non-physical education administrators. Gracian expressed well the need for a unity of deed and image. To quote in part:

> Do and exhibit your doing. To have worth and to show it is to be worth double. That which is not made apparent is as though it were not.

Let us quickly reaffirm that we are not talking just about image, but *image founded on excellence.*

Physical education has been malleable in its ability to serve the changing needs of society. In the years before World War I, physical education was in large measure a relief from the classroom. Then the war effort required fit young men, and schools found themselves having physical education requirements. This in turn produced an overwhelming demand for physical education teachers.

In the years following the Great Depression, the field of recreation grew. Educational institutions were expected to expose more people than ever to the skills needed for physical activity and recreation. Physical education then became part of the general education requirements of colleges and universities in the years after World War II.

However, during the 1960s higher education generally decreased the number and specificity of general education requirements including physical education. In the 1970s an increasing number of students were unable to find teaching positions. This may have influenced the emphasis placed on specializations within physical education such as motor learning, psychology and sociology of sport, athletic training, coaching, and so forth. The emphasis on specializations may also have been due to a greater degree of research activity in physical education. In addition, the fields of health education and recreation, which historically were related to physical education, often pulled away. Many athletic programs are now housed in departments separate from physical education.

Where do we belong in the 1980s? Are we contributing to the mission of higher education? Perhaps the process of self-appraisal might help answer these questions. Self-appraisal allows one to review the relationship between his or her stated goals and accomplishments. Yet no matter how honest and complete this self-appraisal is, the process is unilateral. One was heard to beseech, "would the gift ye gee' us, to see ourselves as other see us."

This paper is intended to provide a bilateral perspective, a second source, from which to appraise the centrality of physical education and athletics to the mission of higher education. A small questionnaire study was undertaken to obtain subjective responses from non-physical education administrators whose duties include the overseeing of physical education and/or athletic departments. The questionnaire sought information about the relationship of these areas to the mission of the university. All the respondents were either chief executive officers, vice-presidents, or deans.

These responses provide a basis for discussing the degree of unity between perceptions of reality and image. Furthermore, by including this second dimension in the appraisal process, we should better see ourselves as others see us and also have a clearer view of the external expectations placed upon us. The main topics covered in the questionnaire included:

1. The mission of the university—we must know the mission before we develop plans to contribute to it;
2. The contribution to the mission made by physical education;
3. The contribution to the mission made by athletics;
4. Means for physical education to more fully integrate with the mission of the university;
5. Means for athletics to more fully integrate with the mission of the university.

As we discuss what the chief executive officers and deans identified as the five major components of the mission of their institutions, let us also contemplate how we contribute (or fail to contribute, or might better contribute) to the accomplishment of those components by means suitable for this decade and beyond.

Educating—preparing students for life—topped the list with 100% of the institutions considering this a major component. Listed last was research, defined as expanding human knowledge, with only half of the schools regarding it as a major part of their mission. The other three components were listed as:

2. Values—defined as helping students to clarify values (86%);
3. Training—preparing students for jobs (63%);
4. Socialization—creating an environment for students to find their identities (59%).

More than 90% of the schools agreed that *all* five components were part of their missions. How do physical education and athletics contribute to these five agreed-upon components? Several common threads can be found in the subjective fabric of the responses. For instance, it would be fair to say that the respondents saw physical education as directly contributing to the mission of higher education particularly in the areas of socialization, values, and education. Some respondents saw physical education as contributing to the education component through traditional academic avenues. Others indicated their additional understanding of the unique means that physical education can employ to accomplish this goal. These unique means were recognized as being able to educate for a total preparation for life by coupling knowledge with practice. For example, one response was, "Physical education strives to educate students to live physically healthy lives through *knowledge* of the biological sciences and through the *activities* of physical education." Another said, "Physical education offers a chance to *learn* about and *practice* healthful *life patterns*." Regardless of how the respondents characterized the role of physical education, none questioned its direct contribution to the stated mission of higher education.

In contrast, athletics was seen as only tangentially contributing to the mission of higher education. A few respondents saw a slight contribution to the development of values while others suggested athletics may make some contribution to the nonstated mission of providing a forum for competitive energies. But most respondents saw athletics as contributing only indirectly through the public relations efforts of the institution.

Many persons within higher education have perceived an inconsistency in committing institutional assets to a public relations program such as athletics which does not, in itself, substantially reflect or contribute to the mission of the university. This is an interesting issue for future discussion. It is important to restate, however, that physical education was considered by administrators to be a direct contributor to the stated mission; only a few stated such a belief about athletics.

Now that we have established, at least through this small questionnaire, that college administrators acknowledge the contributing role of physical education, let us review their suggestions to even more fully integrate our efforts with the mission of higher education.

Nearly all the respondents suggested that athletics should resolve its ongoing identity crisis between educational and commercial goals in favor of education. This is easy to suggest but difficult to accomplish. A decade ago I conducted a much larger study and in this overlapping issue found the same responses to the same degree. However, the degree of commercialism has not remained static in the last 10 years. The suggestions for change to educational goals come from persons (college presidents) who typically remain silent on the issue in public and are given to those whose domain of power grows in direct relation to the growth in commercialism and their ability to remain free of university restraint (athletic directors).

Even in institutions with Division-III athletic programs we find a disconnection between athletics personnel, physical educators, and the rest of the college community. The comments of the respondents indicate a belief that the disconnection of athletics is intentional while that in physical education is benign. Whatever the case, both physical educators and athletics personnel need to work together and demonstrate their commitment to the mission of the university.

It is my belief that as physical educators we can accomplish this only if we first acknowledge and internalize our own self-worth and value as contributors to the mission of higher education. Then we must reject the dandelion philosophy and take an active, albeit sometimes vulnerable, role in finding ways to accomplish the mission of higher education in the 1980s and beyond. We must dare to lead, not duck to survive.

Decision Making In Physical Education In Higher Education: Theory And Application

Herberta M. Lundegren
The Pennsylvania State University

This presentation encompasses a look at the theoretical background of decision making, the characteristics of the decision maker, approaches to decision making, the decision-making process, and applications to decisions made in physical education in higher education.

DEFINITIONS

Let me begin with some definitions in order to focus on the concepts that form the basis for this paper. These concepts represent a large body of theory encompassing many ideas and arguments, not all of which are compatible. However, it is important to synthesize and, if not to agree, at least to understand the perspective taken.

- *Decision-making* can be most simply thought of as "choosing among various alternatives" (Edginton & Williams, 1978, p. 236).
- *Decisions* are reasoned judgments.
- *Conflict* is a discord of actions, feelings, or effects. For the most part it is considered a useful social element. Conflict is *not* inherently bad.
- *Conflict resolution* refers to conflict management. Conflict itself is essential, but unmanaged conflict gets out of hand and becomes bad for the parties involved. Conflict management puts conflict in perspective and helps to make sense of it.
- *Power*, by classical definition, "is the probability that one actor within a social relationship will be in a position to carry out his own will despite resistance, regardless of the basis on which this probability rests" (Weber, 1947, p. 152). An expansion of this definition in terms of structure is that "power is the potential ability of an actor or actors to select, to change and to attain the goals of a sound system" (Clark, 1968, p. 46). This definition implies that the actors operate in one or more status positions within the system. It brings in the concept of controlling resources within the system in order to influence change. Power, through

influence, is brought to bear on decisions, which are identified as choices between alternative goals. Another way of putting it is that influence is the ability to control power.

Thus we see a relationship established between power, influence, and decisions. In this configuration we see a decison-making structure develop that is defined as the patterned distribution of influence in a social system (Clark, 1968). The other relationship between these concepts that is important to establish is that decisions, when made, can either resolve or cause conflicts. Thus the two concepts may be thought of as interactive, and the process of dealing with conflict becomes linked to decision making.

DECISION THEORY

The steps in the decision-making process lead to problem solving. Since these processes involve cognitive processing, decision theory has grown out of both psychology and economics. There are a number of theories extant in the organization literature relating to these origins such as behavioral decision theory, psychological decision theory, social judgment theory, information integration theory, and attribution theory. The economics-based theories address the probability and utility of decisions leading to a prescription of how decisions should be made; that is, they indicate, on the basis of mathematical analysis and logical reasoning, the steps to follow in making a rational decision. The psychologically based theories are more concerned with how people know what the decision should be; they involve human interaction and human judgment processes and focus on knowing about the source of decisions rather than on the results. In a sense, they are descriptive and deal with how people actually make decisions, what prevents them from making rational ones, and under what circumstances they will make comparatively rational decisions (Etzioni, 1964; Little, in progress). As educators, we tend to lean toward the psychological models and see decision making as linked to problem solving and thus to goal achievement. Physical educators are extremely interested in the properties of the environment that influence the behavior of others, and in judgments about these events, so that they can make decisions involving learning environments and learning outcomes.

THE DECISION MAKER

Who are they—the actors generally involved in decisions—and what are the characteristics of these actors or decision makers? Clark (1968) identifies four types:

1. producers of the commodity being distributed—faculty;
2. consumers who receive the commodity—students;
3. entrepreneurs who initiate, mediate, bargain, and compromise in decisions between various sets of producers and consumers—central administration, sometimes the university senate;
4. enactors who supervise the implementation of a decision—administrators in the college.

All of these people make decisions within their spheres of influence, and these decisions affect the general welfare of the whole organization. The relative power of the decision relates of course to the resources controlled by the decision maker and the perceived influence that may give him or her. If a person is perceived to have control of resources, and indeed does, the person is said to have manifest influence and high power; conversely, if the person is not perceived to have and indeed does not have access to resources, then he or she is without influence. The person who is not perceived as having access to resources but who actually controls some resources has potential influence. In contrast, the person who is perceived to have access to resources but who actually has none has reputed influence. An important point here is that those without influence are the ones who are most active in trying to change the structure of decision making. The less crucial the decision, the more likely those with reputed influence will act.

If we apply this theory to the structures we are most familiar with, we will identify the dean, and in many cases the department heads, as having manifest influence; some students feel they are without influence but actually have potential influence; certain administrative staff have reputed influence; and the faculty have both potential and manifest influence, although they do not think so. The more the actors perceive they are without influence, the more apathetic they become and the fewer crucial decisions they will make. The more this happens and the more the dean alone is perceived to have power, the more autocratic the system becomes because the other actors are actually abdicating their power. The more centralized the decision-making structure, the more predictable the outputs and the more the outputs reflect those who are dominant—in our example, the dean.

The bottom line here is that if one wants to keep effective decision making at all levels, those with potential influence should exercise it and not default to those with reputed influence. Further, they should attempt to change the percentage of control of resources in their favor. For example, department heads might try to control a larger percent of the budgets so as to shift the bulk of fiscal resources to them and away from the dean, letting it be known to the constituency that the shift occurred. If the actors in our educational system would only consider the possibility of these shifts in the university at large and in the college specifically, decision making would take on a fresh look, be more effective, and be seen as a viable responsibility of everyone at all levels of influence.

Kinds of Decision Makers

What are decision makers like? Let us take a brief look first at some kinds of decision makers we have all encountered but wish we had not. Is the decision maker with manifest potential in your life one of these? Worse, have you ever felt yourself acting like one of these? Incidentally, perhaps decision makers behave in one of the following ways because a decision, when made, will reflect where the real power lies, and the decision maker does not want that to happen if he or she does not have control. Nevertheless, in day-to-day decision making we may encounter the following.

The Turtle. This is the very slow decision maker. All factors seem to be in line, the decision should be imminent, but the turtle is afraid of being hasty. The situation might change, (what if. . .) and weeks go by—all spontaneity is gone and one has almost forgotten why he or she needed a decision.

The Rabbit. This one hops from one decision to another. If one does not like the decision, wait a minute; it will change. Everything is settled on Friday afternoon, but on Monday morning everything is different. If the rabbit says to go ahead and renovate the office, one should wait a week before processing the work order because there may be three more changes in that time.

The Bear. This one overpowers and states a position in a firm, authoritative, "because I say so" way. The bear asks if there are any questions and is surprised that there are none. He or she brooks no other opinions and possesses the ultimate in manifest influence. Such authority suppresses creativity; spontaneity and decisions are not openly questioned. In this situation, conflict is often masked and trouble is not far away.

The Weasel. Results of bad decisions are never the weasel's fault. He or she smiles sweetly at all good outcomes and blames all other outcomes on someone else. "I did not have all the facts." "She typed it wrong." "I just received it yesterday." "The faculty is apathetic." "The department head did not give it to me."

There are other examples, but the point is these types of decision makers represent decision-making characteristics that are all too easy to assume and that will lead to conflict, dilution of power, dissolution of influence, and weak decisions. In fact, assuming such traits changes the decision maker quickly from one with manifest influence to one without influence. The worst possible scenario that could result from putting decision makers of these types in charge is that the department (college, team) goes down with them.

What are the characteristics of a good decision maker? They are essentially those which we identify with a good administrator. An effective decision maker is:

- able to adapt to rapid change;
- well informed about the department, the college, the university;
- willing to modify his or her behavior;
- willing to modify the organization to reflect modern realities;
- aware of psychological and social forces acting on the organization;
- able to surface positive emotions and deal with negative ones;
- aware of strengths and weaknesses of self and employees;
- able to create an atmosphere of openness and trust within which decisions are made; and
- willing and able to take risks and also encourage others to do so (Bannon, 1981).

The Decision-Making Process

The decision-making process itself can be summarized in four steps (Edginton & Williams, 1978; Newman, Summer, & Warren, 1967):

Making a Diagnosis. This step involves determining that some sort of action is necessary, how complicated the decision will be, and how much risk to take in terms of the organization and all of those affected by the decision.

Finding Alternative Solutions. Brainstorming is a technique sometimes used by creative decision makers, both as an individual procedure and as a group procedure with faculty and staff. It also allows consultation with experts or getting input from those who will be affected by the decision.

Analyzing and Comparing Alternatives. This evaluation can involve reviewing past experiences, experimenting with different alternatives, and submitting the possibilities to research—possibly by developing a model of the decision and testing it out. Such a model might be developed on the line of a PERT chart or an Edginton and Williams (1978) decision tree in which the possible decisions are diagrammed in a time sequence in terms of alternative approaches and potential results of each choice, and utilizing a feedback loop to revise the decision. One can also use the flow chart found in systems analysis. It is useful to list the advantages and disadvantages of each alternative decision or to list the driving forces and impediments to implementation. The best decision is one that accomplishes the most for the department most efficiently while meeting the criteria for the decision.

Selecting a Plan to Follow. If the other steps are followed effectively, then the members of the college or department will be committed to the plan. This is usually accomplished by having them participate in the decision-making process. In this fourth step, the decision is implemented and all who must be informed of the decision are notified.

If these steps are followed, the decision, when made, will be effective and will demonstrate the following characteristics:

- a clear definition of the issue about which the decision is made;
- group input in the decision-making process;
- a consideration of the alternatives and a plan for implementation of the alternative selected;
- utilization of resources available in making the decision;
- a commitment to the decision by those affected by it;
- a time frame for implementation and designation of who is responsible for carrying it out; and
- a description of a means to evaluate whether or not it has been implemented appropriately (Turner, 1977).

Even when these steps are attended to, sometimes the decision fails and that leads us to ask why. What are some factors that act as blocks to effective decisions? Turner (1977) suggests:

- past history of the group, the organization, the faculty, and so forth, involving unresolved issues and feelings;
- a struggle for power and influence within the group and between those with line responsibilities;
- fear of the implications and consequences of the decision;
- inappropriate methods used in decision making (i.e., being authoritarian when facilitation was indicated);
- assumptions and expectations not being checked out;
- failing to deal with conflict, and resistance to change and questions from the group that the decision would affect.

I would add that a lack of knowledge about how things work in the institution is a key block to both good decision making and to acceptance of the decision.

DECISION MAKING IN PHYSICAL EDUCATION

What kinds of executive decisions are made by the administrator in physical education in higher education? These include:

- allotment of fiscal resources;
- whom to hire, whom to keep, and whom to promote;
- allotment of space;
- whether to keep the basic skills requirement;
- assignment of teaching and research time;
- curriculum changes;
- what responsibilities to delegate, and to whom.

How does the theory developed here relate to making these decisions? Let us make one application of it to a common decision all administrators must face—and perhaps the most difficult one to face—the question of who to keep on the faculty. In a time of reduced resources that puts pressures on universities to cut and merge departments and on colleges to cut personnel and programs, what factors can guide the administrator in making these hard decisions?

First of all, we need to identify the actors in this scenario. The faculty members being evaluated (producer), the students (consumers), peers (entrepreneurs), immediate supervisors of the person (enactors), and external professionals (entrepreneurs) all contribute input into the decision. These actors represent various levels of influence. In this case the faculty member is being judged on the resources he or she has in the critical areas of teaching, research, and service. The students and peers at least have potential influence (and perhaps more), the administrator has manifest influence, and the external referees have potential influence far beyond what many faculty members realize.

Let us refer to the four-step decision-making process outlined earlier: in step 1 the action required is predetermined by university policy; tenure review is mandated. In step 2 both group (the peer and college committees) and individual (student, peer, and professional evaluations lend input to the solution. The faculty member is asked for his/her own input by preparing a dossier that presents, in the best light possible, all of his or her professional accomplishments.

In step 3 for the peer committee, the procedure of weighing alternatives and making comparisons is highly important. A comparison of the contents of the dossier with job expectations for the position must be made as objectively as possible. If minimum standards are met there, then factors must be weighed concerning this person's contribution to the department's goals and mission. It is here that the blocks to effective decision making can surface. Of those already listed, the most likely candidates include past history of the group, fear of the implications of the decision, assumptions not checked out, and inadequate information as well as incorrect perceptions about how things work. However, after considering all the input and determining that the criteria for decision are met, the decision is made by the peer group. At this point the group will be committed to the decision and will pass it on to the administrator. They have completed all steps required of them.

The administrator then begins the decision-making process at step 3, using the input gained from the peer committee plus his or her knowledges about the department and its fiscal resources, its stability within the college, potential for change, and perceived need for the department's products in the university. Fundamental to the decision is a comparison of the individual's contribution to the achievement of the goals and mission of the university. For example, if its primary goal is to be a superior research university, what does that mean for two individuals up for tenure review, one a research-graduate faculty member and the other a teacher-coach? The former has a strong record of publication and good teaching evaluations whereas the latter has strong teaching evaluations, a solid background in skill workshops, and no publications. Should they both be tenured?

The administrator must also compare the case with the college's standard for tenuring faculty in other departments, and the dean must compare across colleges and weigh pressures from central administration to avoid "tenuring in." Are the qualifications of both individuals who are considered here compatible with those from outside the unit? Part of the decision-making process is to assess the risk of the final decision. In this case there is a risk in not tenuring the person. This risk might be that the position line is lost and the department is not allowed to replace the person. If replacement is possible, can a replacement be found who is stronger than the person now holding the position, and would he or she bring fresh new ideas to the department? The alternate risk is that tenuring will further lock in the department. Will decision to tenure reduce flexibility too much? In dealing with these risks, the department head and the dean are somewhat free of the emotional ties that cause blocks to effective decisions at the peer level. They also have access to more information and a better understanding of how things work.

Considering all of these facts, the administrator makes a decision to award or deny tenure. The last step in the process is accomplished, the decision is implemented, the peer committee is notified, and the decision is passed up the line from the department head. If it is the dean who acts as administrator, the decision is passed to the university promotion and tenure committee and thus to the president if positive and back down to the department head if negative. In any case, the notification about the decision must be made if the process is to be completed appropriately.

SUMMARY

We have seen, then, how theory leads to practice—how decision making is linked to power, conflict, and influence. The link between control of resources, influence, and decisions and their effective implementation has also been shown. Further, we have seen that the effective decision maker considers all of these relationships and is able to elicit trust while acting in light of strengths and weaknesses of faculty members. Willingness to take risks makes the decision maker adaptable to rapid change, and change is a condition that is all too familiar in higher education today.

We have also considered the decision-making process itself, how it is blocked and how it is facilitated, and what constitutes effective decision. Finally, we have applied it all to the promotion and tenure decision-making process. Decision making is a skill that is essential to any administrator, who draws upon all of the expertise and information available, considers alternative solutions, weighs the consequences of each and, finally, makes the decision.

We in physical education are experts in skill development and rooted in games play where decisions are made in rapid succession; so we are undaunted in our pursuit of mastering this skill in an administrative arena. Our training speaks to reasoned judgments, and our experience to choosing wisely among alternatives—having processed the input and attending to feedback. What better model could there be for successful decision making?

REFERENCES

BANNON, J.J. (1976). *Leisure resources: Its comprehensive planning*. Englewood Cliffs, NJ: Prentice-Hall.

BANNON, J.J. (1981). *Problem solving in recreation and parks* (2nd ed.). Englewood Cliffs, NJ: Prentice-Hall.

BOULDING, E. (Ed.). (1981). *Conflict management in organizations*. Ann Arbor, MI: Foundation for Research on Human Behavior.

CLARK, T.N. (1968). *Community structure and decision-making: Comparative analyses*. San Francisco: Chandler.

EDGINTON, C.R., & Williams, J.G. (1978). *Productive management of leisure service organization*. New York: Wiley & Sons.

ETZIONI, A. (1964). *Modern organizations*. Englewood Cliffs, NJ: Prentice-Hall.

LITTLE, S.L. (in preparation). *Conflict resolution and social power theories applied to decision-making in a major community leisure event*. Doctoral dissertation, The Pennsylvania State University.

NEWMAN, W.H., Summer, C.E., & Warren, E.K. (1967) *The process of management* (2nd ed.). Englewood Cliffs, NJ: Prentice-Hall.

TURNER, N.W. (1977). *Effective leadership in small groups*. Valley Forge, PA: Judson Press.

WEBER, M. (1947). *The theory of social and economic organization*. New York: Oxford University Press.

Perceptions Of Physical Education
In Higher Education

Benjamin H. Massey
University of Illinois

Samuel R.D. Massey
United Presbyterian Church

Physical education in higher education, like the proverbial elephant, suffers from differences in perceptions. Three blind men were asked to examine an elephant. The first blind man stood at the head of the elephant, grasped the trunk, thought it was a snake, and attempted to beat it to death. The second man grasped the ear, thought it to be a piece of leather and, needing shoes, tried to cut it off. The third, feeling a leg, concluded that it was the trunk of a tree and attempted to chop it down.

Perceptions are important. They are the reality by which we live. They are the basis for our attitudes, decisions, and actions. This is as true for physical education in higher education as for any other phenomenon. Three persons can center their discussion on physical education and its place in higher education, even using the same terminology, but because of differences in perception they will not be talking about the same thing. Hence a meeting of the minds in a genuine sense is virtually impossible. Oliver Wendell Holmes, speaking to this dilemma in the *Autocrat of the Breakfast Table*, pointed out that what I think I am saying, what the listener thinks I said, and what I actually said are all different.

Our purpose here is to set forth in an organized and coherent form those perceptions of physical education in higher education which are most frequently encountered and which appear to reflect the thinking of a substantial segment of the population. Hopefully, such an effort will heighten one's sensitivity to the importance of recognizing differences in perceptions when trying to communicate with others, and will stimulate research to gain a better understanding of existing discrepancies in perceptions of the field and its place in higher education, origins of the perceptions, and implications of decision making regarding the centrality of physical education in higher education.

Perceptions often are hazy and ill defined, difficult to verbalize and more difficult to quantify, because they are qualitative in nature. This possibly explains the dearth of studies in this area. Only one study was found in the physical education research literature with the word "perception" in its title; it dealt with the perceptions high school girls had of the purposes of physical education at their school (Clifton, 1957).

In the absence of directly related studies, we turned to less directly related sources for circumstantial data, namely selected studies about the attitudes of college students toward the general physical education program (Broer, 1965; Campbell, 1968; Keogh, 1962, 1963) and studies in which the views of academic deans and administrative officers were solicited concerning the purposes and objectives underlying the general program (Pelton, 1966; Shea, 1961; Wagner, 1963). Also examined were texts and other materials which presented the views of philosophers, educators, and physical educators on physical education and physical activity. The final source was anecdotal material accumulated over more than 50 years of association with higher education: newspaper clippings, public addresses, and personal experiences reflecting spontaneous, incidental views that individuals held of physical education in higher education.

Obviously, no two people observe a phenomenon in exactly the same ways, and there are as many different perceptions of a phenomenon as there are individuals to perceive it. Despite variations, however, there often seems to be considerable commonality among selected groups of individuals. The degree of contact and the amount and quality of observation are important of course, but also important are background experiences. For example, identical twins who were raised in the same home and had the same schooling are likely to perceive physical education in similar fashion. On the other hand, persons who differ in age, sex, physical ability, schooling, and ethnic background are likely to view physical education quite differently. It is interesting that in those parts of the country largely settled by the English (e.g., Virginia and the Carolinas), physical education traditionally has been viewed as synonymous with sport. In contrast, in those sections of the country settled by the Swedes and Germans (e.g., the north central states), greater emphasis has been placed on gymnastics and the health aspects of exercise. For various reasons such ethnic influences do not play the influential role today that they once did, but certain other influences are important. The following logically can be assumed to be significant factors:

- Individual traits: physique, physical capabilities, temperament, and health.
- Familial influences: parental attitudes, ethnic background, religious persuasion, and sibling traits, attitudes, and behaviors.
- Community influences: peer pressures, recreational resources such as outdoor areas, parks, and gymnasia.
- School: physical education experiences, image projected by physical educators, and peer, faculty, and administrator attitudes.
- Public media: television, radio, newspapers, and journals.

The single most important factor affecting an individual's perception of physical education in higher education is the kind of contact he or she has had with programs of physical education in higher education. If one has not gone to college, the contact will have been indirect—through the public media and the anecdotes of relatives or friends who have attended college. One who has attended college will be influenced by the kind of institution, its size and mission, and the nature of the contacts with physical education. In some institutions, intercollegiate athletics is the sum total of the physical education program, but in larger institutions an individual may be involved in one or more aspects of a program: intercollegiate athletics, intramurals, a basic instructional program often referred to as the required or general instructional program, physical education as a degree major, and graduate major study.

The perceptions that have been identified have been categorized and listed according to the phases of physical education with which one might have had some contact, namely athletics, basic instruction, the undergraduate degree program, and graduate study. In addition to these listings, however, are those perceptions about physical education considered to be generally held, irrespective of program phase.

In listing the perceptions (see Table 1), no attempt has been made to provide substantiating data because to do so would be lengthy and tedious. The literature reviewed is readily available and the anecdotal material is undoubtedly familiar to many physical educators.

A review of the listings immediately brings to one's attention the fact that not all the perceptions listed are compatible; some even directly conflict with others. Such differences not only can obstruct communication but they can also have serious implications for decision making regarding physical education's place in higher education and the role it plays in a particular institution. The first step toward effective communication regarding physical education in higher education is to identify clearly the

Table 1

Perceptions of Physical Education In Higher Education

General Perceptions
Physical education, irrespective of program phase, generally is perceived as:

focusing on human concerns
involving vigorous body activity
requiring participation
an activity in which success is determined by physical skill, vigor, and stamina
involving groups of individuals
involving instruction

Athletics
Physical education as athletics is perceived as:

conducted for exceptional, athletically talented students
having social value, contributing particularly to the education of participants (i.e., character building, ethical behavior, courage)
wholesome entertainment, enriching the quality of campus life
boosting student and faculty morale
rallying alumni, the public, and legislators to the support of the institution
good advertisement by giving the institution visibility
bringing in revenue
being for nonintellectual, nonacademically inclined students
a program to prepare professional athletes
exploiting the participants
prostitution of a fine educational modality

Intramural Program
Perceptions of the intramural program are that it:

is physical exercise
is recreation
is for the not-so-talented athletes
has social value

Table 1 (Cont.)

Basic Instructional Program (general program)
Perceptions of physical education as a basic instructional program are that it:

provides athletic participation for the unskilled
provides necessary regular exercise for the sedentary
is sport skills instruction
rounds out the education of the student, particularly in social and behavioral aspects
is health and fitness education
is an essential part of a liberal education
requires no intellect

Undergraduate Majors Program
The program for majors is perceived as:

preparation of athletic coaches
teacher preparation
taking courses in sport skills
a program for the academically limited
a program for the strong, physically talented
a haven for blue-chip athletes
an academic discipline directed to human movement

Graduate Study
The graduate program in physical education is perceived as:

advanced study of games and sport
advanced teacher preparation
program for athletic coaches
advanced study and research in a discipline (kinesiology, sport sciences)

---

perceptions of physical education held by the parties involved. With this base, those involved can agree upon what they wish to disagree upon. Time and energy can be saved and antagonisms can be avoided.

In closing, we would like to speculate briefly on the permanency of the perceptions of physical education listed here. The perceptions are those most frequently and persistently encountered, some of which go back to the early 1900s. However, their future may be much less permanent. Higher education today is in a state of unrest. Rapidly advancing technology with ever improved modes of communication may very well bring to an end the univerity and college scene we have today. Residence halls, campuses, and class attendance will become obsolete. Universities will be research factories. And all instruction (i.e., dissemination of factual information), will be by direct communication from knowledge barns into homes, offices, and community centers. Orwell's 1949 perception of physical education in 1984 might well portend the higher education of the future.

Thirty-to-forty group! yapped a piercing female voice. Thirty-to-forty group! Take your places, please. Thirties to forties! Winston sprang to attention in front of the telescreen, upon which the image of a youngish woman, scrawny but muscular, dressed in tunic and gym shoes, had already appeared. Arms bending and stretching! she rapped out. Take your time, by me. *One* two, three, four! One, two, three four! Come on comrades, put a bit of life into it! *One*, two, three, four! *One*, two, three four!. . .

You can do better than that. You're not trying. Lower, please! *That's* better, comrade. Now stand at ease, the whole squad, and watch me.

'There, comrades! *that's* how I want to see you doing it. Watch me again. I'm thirty-nine and I've had four children. Now look.' She bent over again. 'You see my knees aren't bent. You can all do it if you want to,' she added as she straightened herself up. 'Anyone under forty-five is perfectly capable of touching his toes.' (Orwell, 1949, p. 268)

REFERENCES

BROER, M.R. (1955). Evaluation of a basic skills curriculum for women students of low motor ability at the University of Washington. *Research Quarterly*, **26**, 15-27.

CAMPBELL, D.E. (1968). Student attitudes toward physical education. *Research Quarterly*, **39**, 456-462.

CLIFTON, M.A. (1957). *Perceptions of physical education: Perceptions of the purposes of a physical education program in a selected secondary school.* Unpublished doctoral dissertation, Stanford University.

KEOGH, J. (1962). Analysis of general attitude toward physical education. *Research Quarterly*, **33**, 239-244.

KEOGH, J. (1963). Extreme attitudes toward physical education. *Research Quarterly*, **34**, 27-33.

ORWELL, G. (1949). *1984.* New York: Harcourt Brace Jovanovich.

PELTON, B. (1966). *A critical analysis of current concepts underlying general physical education programs in higher education.* Unpublished doctoral dissertation, University of Southern California.

SHEA, E.J. (1961). The purposes of physical education in higher education. *Proceedings*, College Physical Education Association. Washington, DC: AAHPER.

WAGNER, A.L. (1963). *The concept of physical education in selected liberal arts colleges.* Unpublished master's thesis, State University of Iowa.

Section 6

Physical Education: Research, Professional Preparation, And Outreach Education

Sport And The Charter
Of American Higher Education:
A Case Study Of Skidmore College 1960-1980

Donald Chu
Skidmore College

The charter of American higher education and the incorporation of intercollegiate sport into early 20th-century institutions of higher learning have been discussed in earlier papers (Chu, 1979, 1982). It was suggested that because the period at the turn of the 20th century was a financially troubled one, and Americans traditionally had a low regard for higher education, there was a need to seek resources. This need, coupled with the paucity of well established, well understood definitions of higher education's legitimate goals and appropriate programs, presented an opportunity to establish sport as a formal enterprise of higher learning. Rather than serving primarily as a means of educating the students, as the ''character building'' rationalization would suggest, the major reason for formally incorporating intercollegiate sport on the American college campus was to compete effectively against many other colleges and universities for relatively scarce funds and students apparently very interested in intercollegiate athletics.

As previous discussions of the charter and programs in higher education would suggest, a closer look at the notion of centrality is required. Are there clearly understood objectives of higher education and programs either proximal to or distal from those objectives? Certainly the rapid incorporation of intercollegiate sport within the first three decades of the 20 century would suggest that radically different programs might be rationalized into what was primarily a place for cognitive development. There was apparently little in the way of a core understanding of legitimate programs in American society which prevented sport's inclusion on campuses faced with the apparent resource-attracting capabilities of athletics. Rather, as previous papers and as Skidmore College's own recent history might suggest, the matter of centrality requires further examination.

Given the pluralism of American society, with sons and daughters of German, English, Swedish, and other immigrants going to college, there has by necessity developed a range of purposes for American higher education. While rationalists might identify one set of objectives and programs as most central to the institution of higher learning, such attempts are rendered hazardous by the diversity of higher education (Carnegie

Commission, 1973; Harris, 1972). As the history of Skidmore College demonstrates, the programs and purposes of American institutions of higher learning vary not only by institution but also over time, even within the same school, and by the needs of the various groups that were important to the survival and development of the institution.

SKIDMORE COLLEGE'S HISTORY

Skidmore is a young institution. Founded in 1903 by Lucy Skidmore Scribner as the 2-year "Young Women's Industrial Club," it was granted its New York State absolute charter as a degree-granting college in 1917. Yet this brief history has witnessed major changes in the purposes and programs as well as the population served by the institution. Originally developed to fill women's need for self-supporting skills within a curriculum conducive to mental, social, and cultural development (Hoffman, 1981), Skidmore has profoundly altered its structure, its programs, and its recruiting strategies to meet the changing requirements for survival and development.

While the period from 1900 to 1930 saw the rapid growth of campus athletics and the "golden age of sport," there was little intercollegiate sport at Skidmore. The years from 1915 to 1920 saw only formal offerings in physical education which suited the population of young women. Increasingly, Skidmore attracted students from many geographic areas and slowly increased its enrollment—from 176 in 1917 to 276 in 1919 to 390 in 1922. By the early 1960s the trustees, faculty, and administration agreed that the student population should be enlarged. The "baby boom" generation was now ready to attend college, and there was increasing awareness of the need for additional disciplines and the recognition that a certain size population was needed to support additional faculty. Thus the decision was made to enlarge the student body to approximately 2,000 by the early 1970s (Mosley, 1965).

Concurrent with discussions concerning enlargement of the student body, the trustees of the college were planning to construct a new campus entirely apart from the original campus in downtown Saratoga Springs (Reed, 1961). The bequest of lands from the late trustee J. Erik Jonsson provided the opportunity to solve maintenance problems, caused by decay of the campus' old house-like structures, and space problems, caused by construction of NY Interstate 87 which separated the college from expansion and recreational areas. In October 1961 the trustees voted to construct a new campus just north of Saratoga Springs on what was formerly the Jonsson Estate.

Although the decision to build had long been made, by January 1969 the new campus was still largely in the planning stages (Liguori, 1969). Clearly, construction plans were affected by the question of coeducation. Though the inclusion of males had been considered as early as 1912 by then President Charles Henry Keyes (Saratogian, 1912), the inclusion of significant numbers of men within the student population did not occur until surveys demonstrated support for it among students, faculty, and administration. Skidmore's primary educational planning group, the Committee on Educational Policy and Planning (1968-69), charged with studying the coeducation proposal, concluded:

> While there is no necessary connection between coeducation and formal education in general, there is a sort of formal education which ought necessarily to involve both men and women. This is an education which intends to be structurally and substantively liberal. Liberalism,

in its very best sense, celebrates diversity. . .A liberal arts college. . . must actively seek out and appropriate ways of multiplying its students' perspectives and educational options. It cannot be but obvious that the presence of the full range educational responses of men to women, and vice-versa, comprises a very significant element of the diversity so integral to a liberal education.

This body, primarily comprising faculty members, concluded that Skidmore's liberal arts tradition would be enriched by a larger and more heterogeneous community. In addition, the inclusion of males in the student population might lead to a more stable community with beneficial effects upon the social, cultural, and athletic objectives of the college in addition to its more strictly academic and professional goals. Co-curricular education and the liberal arts were rationalized as beneficiaries of the move to coeducation. In its study document presented to the faculty for consideration, the Committee on Educational Policy and Planning formally expressed the spirit of coeducation then sweeping the nation's single-sex schools. Between 1966 and 1968, 18 all male and 35 all female colleges took steps toward coeducation. Bennington, Connecticut College, Elmira, Vassar, and Sarah Lawrence all admitted men. More important, the committee expressed great reservation about Skidmore's ability to attract 2,000 well qualified students and to offer a high quality education "unless we recruit and enroll men as well as women from the population of secondary school seniors" (Committee on Educational Policy and Planning, 1970).

In summary, because of the old campus' deteriorating facilities, limitations on potential expansion, and the Jonnson bequest, the decision was made in 1961 to build a new campus for a population enlarged to the 2,000 necessary to support the faculty and disciplines to be added to Skidmore's curriculum. Ten years later the probability of requiring male applicants affected the shape of the new campus and facilitated an increased emphasis on the liberal arts aspects of the traditional professional/liberal arts Skidmore curriculum. Later, this new pool of potential students was to feed the growth of sport programs and facilities expected by the students of the 1980s.

THE PROBLEM OF RESOURCES: EFFECTS ON THE CHARTER OF HIGHER EDUCATION

Given the financial and enrollment resource uncertainties of American colleges and universities, institutions in this century have had to alter their very conception of higher education. Whereas traditional views of higher learning were strictly cognitive in scope, the American charter of higher education's legitimate programs and purposes have come to include physical and spiritual objectives. Need for the resources necessary for growth, and sometimes even for survival, has led to an enlargement of the claims for legitimate function among schools in the United States. Such a view of the American campus stands in stark contrast to the regularly funded and consistently populated Oxbridge models for higher education in the United States (Chu, 1982).

Whereas the period from 1890 to 1930 saw the most rapid rise of sport's incorporation within the formal responsibilities of American higher education, the same motivation—the acquisition of resources necessary for development and expansion—facilitated Skidmore College's rapid development of sport opportunities in the 5 years from 1978 to 1983.

Even during the heady years of higher education's relative prosperity in the 1960s, and lurking in the shadows of developing plans for the new campus expansion of Skidmore College, there remained a potential for severe financial difficulty. Despite the college's high reputation, the basic indicator of economic stability—the level of endowments—still gave cause for concern. Endowment figures of $2.1 million in 1962, $2.8 million in 1967, $3.5 million in 1972, and $3.9 million in 1977 placed an annual burden for operating funds on student tuitions. Enrollment figures, always of great importance, became critical and immediately significant given the changes in American higher education during the 1970s (Financial Report 1981-82).

The admittance of women to Ivy League universities and prestigious liberal arts colleges such as Williams and Amherst in the 1970s eroded the potential student applicant pool for all women's colleges. This diminution in the quantity of potential students contributed to a lowering of top-notch applicants at Skidmore. The most capable female students were no longer excluded from Princeton or Yale. The resulting ripple effect decreased the academic qualification required of all applicants to colleges other than those applying to the most elite schools.

The late 1960s and early 1970s were particularly worrisome years for the administration at Skidmore. The college's net balance showed a deficit of $78,000 in 1967. The fragmented campus, its old and new portions separated by the city of Saratoga Springs, diminished the attractiveness of Skidmore to potential students.[1] In 1973 freshman enrollment dropped to 500, down 37 from 1968. Especially troublesome were declines in male enrollment, from 73 in 1973 to 67 in 1975, and reduced yield rates (total enrolled students divided by total accepted students) for this same period. All this occurred during a period of planned expansion of the college population, particularly males, so as to provide gender balance (Admissions Office, interview, November 1983). Further concern for the college was indicated by Provost Edwin Mosley (1971), who worriedly noted the financial conditions of higher education in general and Skidmore in particular. Projected deficits of $200,000 to $600,000 at Skidmore forced him to consider possible cutbacks in faculty. Short dips in enrollments by 71 in 1972 (1,965 projected vs. 1,894 actual) and by 186 in 1973 (2,017 projected vs. 1,831 actual) also caused serious concern among the faculty (Levine, 1974).

There seemed, then, to be a widely held recognition of Skidmore's precarious condition and the need to make the college more attractive to the students who would provide necessary tuition dollars. In the years to come, the college was to respond vigorously to this challenge. It became obvious that Skidmore's potential student pool was different from its historical applicants in more than gender. These new students expected programs to differ from what had historically been available at Skidmore. A college so reliant upon tuition had little choice but to respond rapidly.

THE DEVELOPMENT OF INTERCOLLEGIATE SPORT PROGRAMS

As was the case in many women's colleges, inter-campus sport at Skidmore more closely resembled the "limited competition" model of women's sport than the highly organ-

---

[1]The first major building constructed on the Jonsson lands was the library in 1966.

ized men's intercollegiate model. During the early 1960s, infrequent competitions in archery, bowling, field hockey, riding, skiing, swimming, synchronized swimming, and tennis occurred without the regular daily practice schedules and multi-game schedules that were the norm for men's sports (Department of Physical Education 1961-62, 1962-63). The early college teams were typically directed by the students themselves and required less commitment of the student's and coach's time. In field hockey, the collegiate cooperative spirit that pervaded the women's sport of the earlier era led to the formation of regional teams—a practice far from the intra-regional campus rivalries and fiercely competitive norms of men's intercollegiate athletics. Total athletic budgets of $500 or less were typically absorbed within the expenses of the Department of Physical Education until the academic year 1974-75, and it was not until the following year that intercollegiate athletic expenses were listed separately for purposes of institutional accounting.

Intercollegiate sport at Skidmore grew from athletic budgets (minus personnel costs) of $500 or less prior to 1974-75 to $19,405 in 1977-78 and to $165,481 during the academic year 1983-84 (Department of Physical Education and Dance, 1974-75, 1977-78, 1983-84). Whereas the college fielded 11 teams in 1976-77 with 229 available student positions, 3 years later 9 teams were added and an additional 132 student positions became available.

Despite the tremendous pace of intercollegiate expansion, upper-level administration remained relatively naive about the requirements of Division III sports. Responding to queries concerning additional projected capital costs of coeducation on the new campus, and though recognizing that a "weakness in physical education facilities and programs would handicap our admissions recruitment efforts," President Joseph Palamountain projected additional costs of only $750,000 for the construction of a building or part of a building, one or two more playing fields, and tennis courts (Palamountain, 1970).

Although college administration and faculty in the late 1960s and early 1970s clearly recognized the need for strenuous efforts to attract students, they did not recognize the immediacy of the need to expand sport programs or the scope of required growth. The naiveté of the college administration to the requirements and popularity of varsity athletics lead to a situation in which the growth in intercollegiate sports was less directed by college administrators than by the forces of student desires and the wishes of particular coaches. According to Palamountain, there was no conscious decision to build up intercollegiate sport, there was no directive "from up on high" to develop sport— "In fact it took me quite by surprise. . .sport's growth has been a real grass roots one." Palamountain credited the desires of students with the development of sport (Palamountain, personal interview, October 1983).

These sentiments were echoed by the new chair of the Department of Physical Education and Dance, Dr. P Timothy Brown, who observed that "things were happening due to circumstances as opposed to planning." Students were developing teams without a coherent plan for an overall athletic program appropriate for the institution (Brown, interview, October 1983). With general support, but also with somewhat vague notions about the shape of Skidmore's intercollegiate sport program for the 1980s, the administration typically deferred athletic decisions to the Department of Physical Education and Dance and to the students whose insistence had been the original motivator for the development of sport in the 1970s. With little athletic tradition and without the precedents for faculty/administrative control typically accompanying established sport programs, the Department of Physical Education and Dance found itself in an uncomfortable adversarial position with new student sport advocates. Without an assumption and acceptance of physical education's legitimate responsibility for the overall development of the sport structure, advocates of athletics among the student body and admissions office sometimes accused the department of dragging its feet about developing sport on the campus (Becker, interview, October 1983).

Given the lack of direction from the administration, the lack of consensus over authority (which often arises in the absence of established tradition and precedent), and the energy-robbing frictions resulting from "the stab and parry" relationship between students and the department, intercollegiate sport in the 1970s grew rapidly in response to student demands but without a coherent intercollegiate formula—the number of sports, size of teams, type of teams, and cost of sport—consistent with Skidmore's philosophy. The lack of centralized control led to difficult and controversial practices, for example the employment of a part-time coach in men's basketball (1979-1980) who enrolled two players whose great basketball talents were not matched by their commitment to a college education. Winning was not everything but it was certainly more important to these players than academics.[2]

Despite the administration's general feeling in 1970 that the sport program would need attention in order to project the best image of Skidmore, the question of authority was not sufficiently impressed upon the administration even 10 years later. Even in 1977, the state of Skidmore's intercollegiate athletic program was described by consultants as "chaotic." Furthermore, the consultants who were brought in to evaluate the entire physical education and athletic program described the campus' indoor facilities as "deplorable" (Consultants Report, 1977). Noting that athletes sometimes paid for their own entry fees and meals, the consultants said, "If the program is not first class, it should not exist. The appearance of an athletic team often indicates the caliber of an institution to the outsider."

The conditions of the sport facilities and programs at Skidmore as reported by the consultants was not news to the Department of Physical Education and Dance, whose Annual Report of 1979-1980 reviews reports from the previous 5 years. Beverly J. Becker, chair, cited central administration's lack of attention to problems in facilities, athletic philosophy, lines of authority, and accident insurance. The consultants' report merely documented further the neglect of sport programs and facilities, which in the department's view had been pointed out in annual reports as early as 1974-1975—with no action taken by the central administration (Becker, interview, October 1983). Roughly 20 years after the decision to enlarge the student population to 2,000 and to construct a new campus, and almost 10 years after the decision to formally admit males, Skidmore found itself without the sport facilities and programs that these new students expected. While there had been for at least 10 years a general agreement to improve athletic opportunities, the college by 1980 was still burdened by an inadequate shell of a field house, was without a commitment to construct an acceptable replacement, and had no established tradition of athletic control or understanding of the appropriate scope of program.

---

[2]Three of the five starters dropped out of school, and the two players enrolled under the college's external degree program (and who were closest to the coach) withdrew from school upon that coach's resignation.

Against this backdrop two events were to catalyze change in the complexion of sports at Skidmore. In the spring of 1977, the persuasive and charismatic Louise Wise was appointed director of admissions. As chair of Skidmore's coeducational study group, the task force of coeducation, Wise became well aware of the student-recruiting problems caused by inadequate sport facilities and programs. Such shortcomings placed the college at a disadvantage relative to competing schools. The broad constituency of the task force included trustees, central administration, faculty, alumni, and students, and the very force of Wise's persuasiveness added impact to the Task Force Report, issued in February 1977 before her appointment as director of admissions. According to Wise, the lack of adequate sport opportunities at the college "would diminish Skidmore in the eyes of potential students." The significance of sport opportunities in her view was not that they would actually be used by all of the potential students interested in Skidmore's programs and facilities. Yet their very presence or absence was an indication of institutional quality (Wise, interview, November 1983).

For an institution so dependent upon tuitions for its survival, for a school with less than $4 million in endowment at the time of her appointment, Wise's warnings and suggestions about necessary and attractive programs and facilities carried great weight, perhaps more weight than all the pleas for help filed by the Department of Physical Education in its annual reports as early as 1974.

The second event which served to catalyze the growth of sport at Skidmore was the resignation of Dr. Becker as chair of the Department of Physical Education and Dance. Dr. Becker's resignation initiated a search process that enlightened the administration about the inadequacy of existing facilities and procedures. As candidate after candidate over the 2-year search period remarked in disbelief about the inadequacy of the field house, the lack of clear lines of authority, and the lack of coherence in the college's philosophy of athletics, the central administration became increasingly convinced of the need for urgent change. Dean of the Faculty Eric Weller wrote in the Annual Report (1979-80):

> Trying to attract and hire a new chair for the department who will also serve as Athletic Director, given the present facilities, has been a great eye-opener. Many of our candidates wondered why students would come to the college at all. . . .His job in moving the department in new directions to new levels of achievement, as well as our own job of attracting and retaining students in the college at large, cannot be successful for long without that new facility.

Finally convinced by the director of admissions and the candidates for chair of the Department of Physical Education and Dance that the problem was urgent, the administration decided in 1980 to construct a $6 million sport center. The 2-year search for a department chair ended with the hiring of Dr. P. Timothy Brown, who was given increased power over sport matters and the parallel title of director of athletics. In effect, he was given the mandate to make Skidmore's sport and recreation programs "representative and competitive" with the schools against which Skidmore competed for students (Brown, interview, October 1983). From its regional affiliation with the Northern Athletic Conference, Skidmore became a member of the NAIA in 1981, the ECAC in 1982, and was to apply for NCAA Division III status in 1984.

SKIDMORE COLLEGE AS A CASE STUDY

The period from 1960 to 1980 saw the expansion of intercollegiate sports at Skidmore, some 60 years later than at many other American institutions of higher learning. As Burton Clark (1970) has demonstrated with Swarthmore, a crisis of enrollments exacerbated the financial problem of minimal endowments at the turn of the century. In order to attract students, social activities and sports were strengthened and made a more formal part of the institution.

Similarly hampered by minimal endowment and heavy reliance upon enrollments and tuition dollars, yet with ambitious plans to expand, Skidmore faced the problem of instituting vigorous fund-raising efforts to acquire resources. Endowment, capital improvement drives, and bond sales did much to increase Skidmore's long-term financial stability and resources available for construction. As already noted, however, another response to the need for resources has been the use of sport programs and facilities as an instrument to reshape the college's image so that it might appeal to the students of the 1980s.

In the course of this study we were given a glimpse of the decision-making process. Though recognized as a potential problem area for at least 10 years at Skidmore, athletics and sport-related matters did not really concern the college's administration until the early 1980s. Sports development at Skidmore has been far from a carefully planned, centrally orchestrated growth. Instead, it has been largely a student-initiated expansion. Facilities and programs have been built in response to student needs and vociferously voiced desires. Central administration has largely only reacted to the expressed needs of the constituency—the lifeblood of the institution.[3]

Due to the manner in which sport was developed at Skidmore, the relative lack of coherence in athletic philosophy, policies, and programs that existed in the late 1970s should come as no surprise. Sound programs typically require a period of maturation in which tradition develops the precedents necessary for stability. The Skidmore sport case study serves as a good illustration of how an institution can lose control over its sport programs. Given the emotional zeal of student sport promoters and some coaches, and the lack of firm directives and expressed concern from central administration about intercollegiate sport, a power vacuum may develop and forceful individuals may assume control. In Skidmore's case, an ambitious basketball coach recruited questionable players to win games and in the process alienated members of the college community. Due to the high visibility of intercollegiate sport, these programs must be governed from the highest levels of administration. If control is to be left to middle-level administration, power must be clearly delegated. Without strong control over college sport at some level of administration, sport's visibility may give particular coaches and sport teams disappropriate power over the symbolic representation of the institution's image.

As noted by Provost David Marcell, "Students want all of the features of a collegiate situation," and as noted by President Palamountain, students seem to "want to know

---

[3]In this manner the liberal arts features of the college were also enhanced. Responding to student program desires and the will of the faculty, Skidmore came to further emphasize the liberal arts aspects of the college's historical mission. In the view of the provost of the college, Skidmore's academic change of focus in the 1960s and 1970s has been due more to a process of accretion than to any centrally planned initiative from above.

sport is taking place though a fraction may actually see it.'' The administration of the college at many levels has learned that sport programs and facilities for recreation have become a necessary part of the charter of higher education in America. Popular expectations concerning the programs and objectives of our institutions of higher learning have come to incorporate the sport programs still foreign to the Oxbridge forerunners of the American colleges. Athletics have become an essential element in the definition of higher education to the American public. Stereotypical images of institutions have far-reaching effects on the recruitment and behaviors of actors in the institution (Cronback, 1974). Though they may be inaccurate, stereotypical images still have far-reaching effects on the institution itself.

Recognition of the general public's expectations was especially important to Skidmore as it sought new students from a more diverse group. Preconceived notions of the college as an effete institution for career-oriented women would not serve the college well in the 1970s and 1980s. Rather than attracting the vocationally oriented female as it had prior to 1971, realities of enrollment needs turned the college toward a new pool of potential applicants—a female *and* male population who expected the Ivy League tradition of colleges that could boast of good sport programs and facilities. No longer would an esoteric image of the college as a specialized training ground for vocationally oriented, cultured women attract the numbers of students required for college survival and development. That image had to be altered, and sport played a major role in altering Skidmore's image.

If there is indeed anything instructive from this review of Skidmore College and sport, it is that at least for this school there is not yet one notion of centrality. Instead there are many notions of what is most important to the institution. The definition of centrality changes with time and with the person being asked. The diversity that marks the American population similarly demands diversity of programs and purposes in institutions of higher education. While solid financial security might buffer some schools from having to respond to the needs and desires of the population, that is not the general rule. Instead the rules of change and diversity lead to many conceptions of centrality. Although the college's ''professional'' focus had been a major factor in Skidmore's image, and its culturally concerned female students had provided its life-blood, both components of the college have changed to satisfy the inexorable demand for resources in a changing world.

REFERENCES

CARNEGIE Commission on Higher Education (1973). *The purposes and the performance of higher education in the United States*. New York: McGraw Hill.

CHU, D. (1979). Origins of the connections of physical education and athletics at the American university: An organizational interpretation. *Journal of Sport and Social Issues*, **3**(1), 22-32.

CHU, D. (1982). The American conception of higher education and the formal incorporation of intercollegiate sport. *Quest*, **34**, 53-71.

CLARK, B. (1970). *The distinctive college: Anhock, Reed, Swarthmore*. Chicago: Aldine.

COMMITTEE on Educational Policy and Planning (1968-69). Statement on coeducation at Skidmore. Skidmore College.

COMMITTEE on Educational Policy and Planning. (1970, May). *Coeducation at Skidmore, a feasibility study presented to the faculty.* Skidmore College.

CONSULTANTS Report (1977, May). *Evaluation of the department of physical education and dance.* Skidmore College.

CRONBACH, L.J. (1974). Stereotypes and college sororities. *Journal of Higher Education,* **15**, 214-216.

DEPARTMENT of Physical Education and Dance (1961-62, 1962-63, 1977-78, 1983-84). *Annual report.* Skidmore College.

HARRIS, E. (1972). *A statistical portrait of higher education.* New York: McGraw Hill.

HOFFMAN, A.H. (1981). *History of an idea.* Washington, DC: University Press of America.

KEYES, (1912, April). Dr. Keyes here, enthusiastic over Skidmore school. *Saratogian,* p. 1.

LEVINE, E. (1974, April). *Third faculty report: The administration's 1974 long-range plan.* Committee on Educational Policy and Planning, Skidmore College.

LIGUORI, V. (1969, January). Memo to CEPP membership. Skidmore College.

MOSLEY, M. (1965, May). Annual report to the board of trustees by the dean of the faculty. Skidmore College.

MOSLEY, M. (1971, May). Annual report from the provost and dean of faculty. Skidmore College.

PALAMOUNTAIN, J. (1970, February). Memo to Erwin Levine, chairman committee on the educational policy and planning. Skidmore College.

REED, H. (1960-61). An overview of the first year of the committee on educational policies and planning. Skidmore College.

SKIDMORE College (1981-82). *Financial Report,* Author.

WELLER, E. (1979-80). Annual report, office of the dean of faculty. Skidmore College.

Insurance Against The Nation's Risk: Extended Professional Preparation For Physical Education

L. Marlene Mawson
University of Kansas

"Our nation is at risk." The media hyped a story in April 1983 that educators already knew. The headlines introduced a new national issue in a four-word title, "A Nation At Risk," the Federal Department of Education's report on the status of education in the United States. Terrance Bell, secretary of education, called on the National Commission on Excellence in Education to examine the condition of American public schools and to project measures for educational reform. While it is unfortunate that it took a federal report with political overtones to catch the attention of the media, educators may be able to capitalize on the publicity the report has generated.

"A Nation At Risk" is not the most scientific study with carefully controlled samples, but it does share a concensus with six other contemporary studies on the status of American education, including the Carnegie Foundation's "The Condition of Teaching" (1983a), the College Board's "Education Equality Project" (May, 1983), the Twentieth Century Fund Task Force on Federal Elementary and Secondary Education Policy (May, 1983), and the National Science Board Commission on Precollege Education (1983). Both *The Paideia Proposal* (1982), created by a group of leaders in American education, and a nationally sampled inside look at America's schools by Goodlad (1984) not only analyze the present status of education but also offer suggestions for its future.

These reports have verified the deplorable conditions in American education that we as educators are well aware of. Despite the present inertia in the educational scene, we have an opportunity to move education as a cultural institution to greater levels of excellence. The time for strategic maneuvers likely will be short, for it is really a tinge of political advantage that has brought the educational plight to the limelight. The excitement may abate sharply once the upcoming political offices have been won. Therefore, as physical education professionals we must plan and adopt a strategy that will effectively enhance the well-being of young American citizens through the educational structures we will offer in the 21st century. It is important that we observe the issues highlighted by the various status-of-education reports in 1983 and translate the implications for physical education in our nation's schools.

First, we should review all the reports to gain an understanding of the issues of con-census. Then a brief review of new curricular trends in physical education during the 1970s will form the philosophical basis for physical education content in the future; the structure of the program format for the professional preparation of physical educators will be viewed from the perspective of extended programs as a new phenomenon in educational reform.

THE NATIONAL REPORTS ON THE STATUS OF AMERICAN EDUCATION

A Nation At Risk

The Federal Commission on Excellence in Education consisted of an 18-member group, 6 of them representing higher education and 4 others representing elementary and second-ary education. The Commission gathered data for its report during 18 months of study conducted in 1981 and 1982. The culminating report, entitled "A Nation At Risk," was published in April 1983 and highlighted issues affecting education today that must be corrected unless we are to have a nation of illiterate citizens who cannot cope in society. The issues included the question of increased high school graduation re-quirements, specifically in English, mathematics, science, social studies, and computer science; competency testing and higher standards for academic performance in public schools and colleges; more time devoted to the five basics already mentioned—whether by lengthening the school day (or the school year) or by decreasing the time spent in other pursuits; improvement in the preparation of teachers and in the teaching profes-sion itself; and the provision of fiscal support and leadership by elected officials and educators for upgrading education.

The Carnegie Report

The Carnegie Foundation for the Advancement of Teaching released a report in August entitled "The Condition of Teaching: A State-by-State Analysis" (1983a) which com-pared the conditions in public schools in 1982-83 with those of 10 years earlier. General-ly, the data revealed that school enrollments had dropped and funding per student had increased 182%, yet teacher salaries had slipped 12% and the number of teachers had increased by 1.4%. The analysis of the future of the teaching profession was grim. It was predicted from the Carnegie study that the nation will be short of 8,000 new teachers in 1983 and will be short of 31,000 more teachers by 1986. This crisis is oc-curring in education because salaries are lower than in any other profession requiring col-lege degrees, and therefore the number of people who wish to enter the teaching pro-fession has dropped from 19% of college freshmen in 1970 to 5% in 1982. Their attributes were not found to be very good either: The Scholastic Aptitude Test scores for the 1983 high school seniors interested in teaching were 32 to 48 points below the average, a drop of 5 to 16 points since 1972. Apparently the future teachers of America are not among the academically bright students entering colleges today.

The Carnegie Foundation, led by its president, Ernest Boyer, published a sequel to "The Condition of Teaching" in October 1983. In this report entitled "High School: An Agenda For Action," the Foundation-recommended content for a 12-discipline core curriculum, including health education (but not physical education), outlined new expectations for high school teachers (including monetary incentives for excellence in teaching and release from the duty of monitoring students) and suggested changes in higher education preparation programs such as education scholarships for top high school graduates and initiation of 5-year teacher preparation programs (Carnegie Report, 1983b).

The College Board Report

The College Board, a national association of 2,500 institutions that sponsor the Scholastic Aptitude Test, published a document in May 1983 called "Academic Preparation for College: What Students Need to Know and Be Able to Do." The College Board identified six basic subjects to be required in high school from its "Educational Equality Project," a 10-year drive to raise academic standards. English, visual and performing arts, mathematics, science, social studies, and foreign language were recommended. The only physical activity included was dance as a performing art. High school preparation for studying dance in college required comprehension of dances of various cultures and historical periods, analysis of dance technique, style and choreography, evaluation of dance performances, and ability to express oneself through dancing or choreography (The College Board, 1983).

Twentieth Century Fund Task Force

The report of a private research foundation, the Twentieth Century Fund, proposed in May 1983 that the federal government should take the lead in a new national commitment to excellence in education. Robert Wood, former secretary of HEW during the Johnson administration, chaired the task force for this organization's research. This report suggested that while state and local communities should remain accountable for the learning in schools, the federal government should assume the task of preventing mediocrity in the nation's educational system. The task force estimated that the federal government would need to allocate an additional $6 billion per year to offset the "risk" of quality education becoming obsolete. Presently, $6.4 billion has been the subsidy for the nation's schools (Twentieth Century Fund, 1983).

The National Science Board Commission

"Educating Americans For the 21st Century" was published by the National Science Board Commission on Precollege Education in 1983. The recommendations of this commission were biased toward mathematics, science, and technology as high school preparatory requirements. This group's analysis of the status of education reflected the increase in technological advances through 1985, but it ignored the social and humanistic requirements in educating citizens for a good life.

The Paideia Proposal

Mortimer J. Adler (1982) published *The Paideia Proposal* in 1982, the ideas for which were composed by a small group of national leaders in education, among them E.L. Boyer of the Carnegie Foundation. *The Paideia Proposal* pointed out that Americans currently expect 12 years of schooling to be a civil right for everyone in this country. The proposal outlined a one-track system of education during the 12-year schooling and three basic objectives for school: personal growth and self-improvement, preparation for self-responsibility as a citizen, and preparation for earning a living in this society. Interestingly, although 12 years of physical education were recommended for personal health and release of energy, the authors recognized that students learn best when coached. Therefore, they recommended that classroom teachers observe athletic coaches as a model for instructional methods. They even suggested that classroom teachers coach their brighter students after school, much like athletic coaches do.

Goodlad's Study of Schooling

A Place Called School, authored by John Goodlad (1984), detailed the findings and implications of an extensive study of schooling in the United States during the second half of the 1970s. Twenty data collectors visited 38 schools and more than 1,000 classrooms to gather data from teachers, parents, and students in grades K-12. The data revealed a steady rise in class time devoted to physical education and increased numbers of physical education teachers. During the 5-year period the study also noted that more emphasis was given to students with superior athletic ability. Students in the study said that their "friends" were the best thing about going to school and that "sport activities" was the second best thing about school.

These seven reports on the status of American education have recorded similar information and have uniformly singled out the major defects in the educational system. Our schools *are* at a crisis point, and we as professionals who prepare teachers need to evaluate physical education programs and to determine whether they offer appropriate learning for people of the 21st century.

These seven status reports on education in America have offered remedies for obsolete teaching and planning of curricular subjects stemming from inadequate preparatory curricular standards in colleges. But it is alarming that only three of the reports mention physical activity programs. The College Board Report suggested that dance be included as an art experience; *The Paideia Proposal* recommended 12 years of physical education for personal health and release of energy; and Goodlad's status report indicated that physical education and athletics has become more popular with students in the last decade. It is apparent that physical education professionals must agree on a disciplinary direction and proclaim that position to an American public which has accepted health spas, racquet clubs, and other athletic commercial endeavors, yet remains either unaware or unsupportive of this same physically oriented goal for their children when offered in an educational setting.

TEACHING PHYSICAL EDUCATION: 1980s STATUS AND 21st-CENTURY GOALS

Physical education leaders have argued the disciplinary nature of their profession since the "Battle of the Systems" in 1889. During the decade of the '70s the issue centered on the compatibility of research theories and the practical application of these knowledges in teaching. The 1980s college preparatory curricula in physical education are being influenced by those ideas, and this trend may give direction for 21st-century goals in physical education.

As early as 1972, Morford argued that physical educators could not claim to be true professionals because they did not use research theories as the basis for practicing teaching methods and procedures. Later, physical education professionals, publishing their perspectives in *Quest*, analyzed why physical educators as well as others questioned the professional status of the discipline. Lawson (1979) pointed out that until physical educators learned to monopolize and monitor their body of theoretical knowledge, they could not reach a professional level. He suggested combining the pedagogical and scientific perspectives both for teaching professionals and for research scientists. Broekhoff (1979) believed that the dichotomy was caused by the fact that physical educators, unlike teachers of other subjects, do not teach the academic content in the public school that they study in their teacher preparation discipline. Physical education teachers teach physical activity, or the art of movement and performance, and not the scientific theory of exercise. He contended that teaching itself is an art and not a science.

In 1981 NASPE attempted to extend scholarly research to the public school physical education class through a project labeled "Basic Stuff" (Bain, 1981). The publications were discussed by physical educators in the September 1982 issue of *JOPERD*. Kneer (1982) pointed out that the "Basic Stuff" series has been the most popular, best selling publication in AAHPERD history. The publications were reportedly being used in college professional courses, as resources by secondary and elementary school physical education teachers, and as supplementary texts in school libraries. Lockhart (1982) felt that NASPE had put forth a strong effort in the "Basic Stuff" series for the marriage of theory and practice in physical education as a new approach to preparing teachers in the 1980s.

THE DILEMMA OF EXPANDED TIME FOR SPECIALIZED KNOWLEDGES IN EDUCATION AND PHYSICAL EDUCATION

The several national reports of 1983 in their call for educational reform echo the efforts of physical educators to adjust and adapt to a society that is changing from an industrial state to one of advanced technology and specialized information. Developing the skills of the future professionals, either in education or in fields that complement it, requires immediate planning if those professionals are to prepare literate and functional citizens and leaders.

The national reports are unanimous in demanding higher quality in preprofessional training of teachers. The Carnegie Foundation's recommendation of 5-year teacher preparation programs has already been endorsed by the American Association of Colleges for Teacher Education (AACTE, 1982) and has been initiated by teacher education programs at three major universities. The University of New Hampshire began its Five-Year Program in 1973 (Birrell, 1978), the University of Kansas initiated its Extended Program in 1981 (Scannell, 1980), and the University of Florida was to start its new program, PROTEACH, in the fall of 1984 (Smith, 1980).

THE AACTE ALTERNATIVE MODELS OF
EXTENDED TEACHER PREPARATION PROGRAMS

The American Association for College Teacher Education has proposed seven alternatives for designing teacher preparation curriculum extended beyond 4 years. The various plans included:

- Four-Plus-One (B.S.)
- Four-Plus-One (internship)
- Five-Year (B.A. and master's degree)
- Five-Plus-One (master's degree plus internship)
- Four-Plus-Two (B.A., M.A., and Ed.S.)
- Four-Plus-Three (B.A., and internships with Ed.D.)
- Three-Plus-Three (B.A. and teaching doctorate)

The New Hampshire Extended Program

The University of New Hampshire graduated its first class of Five-Year-Program (Birrell, 1978) education students in 1975, using the four-plus-one (internship) model. Physical education majors at New Hampshire seeking K-12 certification are among six specialization areas which may opt for either the extended preparation program, which includes an entire 5th year as a teaching intern in the schools, or the traditional 4-year program with one semester of student teaching. The program exposes students to actual teaching experiences in public schools as early as their sophomore year, in a course called "Exploring Teaching." During the first 4 years, students take courses in their respective subject matter specialties and, in addition, select a series of minicourses from four general content areas of professional education taught as learning modules. The program features field-based experiences and a strong liberal arts and subject-matter content. Admission to the internship year requires New Hampshire students to have earned a 2.5 GPA in their major and a 2.2 overall.

The Kansas Extended Program

The University of Kansas began its Extended Teacher Preparation Program in 1981 with a model similar to the four-plus-one (internship) model, as outlined by AACTE. Students in the Kansas model participate in field experiences each year in the public schools from their first semester in college through student teaching *and* an internship during the 5th year. The 5-year program has a balance of courses required in liberal arts, in the major subject area, and in the professional education component. The unique difference in preparatory study in the Kansas program is the progressive stages of field-based teacher preparation, identified as introductory, acquisition, mastery, and generalization stages.

Physical education majors, like all teacher preparation students at Kansas, must attain an overall GPA of 2.5 to continue in the teacher preparation program after the sophomore year and must have earned a 2.75 GPA (the minimum GPA for entrance into graduate school) before continuing into the 5th year, full-time teaching experiences.

After 4 years the student receives a bachelor's degree; but it is during the 5th year that teaching certification and at least 15 semester hours of elective graduate course credit are earned.

The Florida Extended Program

PROTEACH is the extended teacher preparation program offered by the University of Florida beginning in the fall of 1984 (Smith, 1980). The Florida program has trimmed the professional education proportion of teacher preparation considerably in favor of the subject area content. Like those at New Hampshire and Kansas, the Florida extended program will culminate in an internship in the schools.

SUMMARY

The several reports reflecting the seriousness of the troubled status of education across the nation have given physical education in higher education an unprecedented opportunity to identify and solidify its unique mission. Amidst the controversy surrounding the philosophical basis of physical education within the past decade is the recognition that physical education should be considered as both an art and a science. This duality of art and science within the discipline could enhance the aim of graduating more qualified and creative teachers and supplying better theorists of our scientific knowledge base. It appears that a 5th year of additional time in undergraduate professional preparation, if planned effectively, may give future teachers a better exposure to physical education research findings applying these findings to their field-based practice even before graduation. The rigors of the newly sanctioned 5-year teacher preparation programs which prepare intelligent new physical educators to apply scientific knowledges could be the type of insurance the nation needs to help ease the current risk evident in its educational system.

> Mirror, mirror, on the wall
> Who's the fairest of them all?
> Is it English, science, or math?
> Or is computer science our future path?
>
> Will it be technology for two thousand and four?
> Or will human movement really mean more?
> Will self-sufficient citizens only read books?
> Or will school curricula have a performance-based look?
>
> Physical education of our citizens can be one insurance
> To prevent an "obsolete education" occurrence.
> The greater risk to our nation's schools
> Is *not* playing on courts, fields, and pools.

REFERENCES

AACTE Task Force on Extended Programs. (1982). *Educating a profession: Extended programs for teacher education*. Unpublished monograph.

ADLER, M.J. (1982). *The Paideia proposal*. New York: MacMillian.

BAIN, L. (1981, February). Introduction to basic stuff. *Journal of Physical Education and Recreation*, pp. 33-34.

BIRRELL, S. (1978, February). Learning to teach: A continuous process. *New Hampshire Magazine*, pp. 1-3.

BROEKHOFF, J. (1979). Physical education as a profession. *Quest*, **31**, 244-254.

CARNEGIE Foundation. (1983a). *The condition of teaching: A state-by-state analysis*. Princeton: Princeton University Press.

CARNEGIE Foundation. (1983b). *High school: An agenda for action*. Princeton: Princeton University Press.

COLLEGE Board. (1983, May). Academic preparation for college: What students need to know and be able to do. *Chronicle of Higher Education*.

GOODLAD, J.I. (1984). *A place called school*. New York: McGraw-Hill.

KNEER, M. (1982, September). Basic stuff: A collaborative project for a 'new game'. *Journal of Physical Education, Recreation and Dance*, pp. 27-38.

LAWSON, H.A. (1979). Paths toward professionalization. *Quest*, **31**, 231-243.

LOCKHART, B. (1982, September). The stuff series: Why and how. *Journal of Physical Education, Recreation and Dance*, pp. 18-19.

MORFORD W.R. (1972). Toward a profession, not a craft. *Quest*, **18**, 88-98.

NATIONAL Commission on Excellence in Education. (1983). *A nation at risk: The imperative for educational reform*. Washington, DC: U.S. Government Printing Office.

NATIONAL Science Board Commission on Precollege Education in Mathematics, Science and Technology. (1983). *Educating Americans for the 21st century: By 1995*.

TWENTIETH Century Fund Task Force on Federal Elementary and Secondary Education Policy. (1983). *Making the grade*. New York: Twentieth Century Fund.

SCANNEL, D.P. (1980). *Progress report on teacher education program review*. Unpublished manuscript, University of Kansas.

SMITH, D.C. (1980). *Developing operation PROTEACH*. Paper presented at conference on Operation PROTEACH, University of Florida.

Revitalization Through Collaboration: Instructional Analysis In Physical Education

Judith C. Young
University of Maryland

Much of the time at professional meetings is devoted either to discussion about the future or to expressions of worry about the state of the profession. The collective awareness and sharing of problems, worries, fears, and professional concerns serve as a basis for revitalization and progress. Currently we are not alone in the educational arena as we address problems. Recent national interest is represented by the "Nation At Risk" report of the National Commission on Excellence in Education, (1983). This and other similar reports (Adler, 1982; Twentieth Century Fund, 1983) have crystallized the general feeling that our schools are not preparing individuals to cope effectively with the modern information society. We as educators must collaborate with policy makers and those implementing change to address the current problems in both reflective and active ways.

Physical education has not been addressed fully or specifically in the previously mentioned reports, but physical educators must consider the implications of any proposals which may be developed in response to such reports. Suggestions have included more academic requirements, longer school days, and more independent work for students. All of these would have an impact on the physical education programs of the future. In addition, increasing academic requirements, reduced job security, lack of enough new teachers, and declining enrollments in elective and required physical education programs in public schools make obsolescence seem highly possible. Physical educators must take this situation as an opportunity to consider how our programs may be enriched to contribute significantly to the development of effective individuals.

Issues of curriculum and public policy are vital and of concern to teachers, but they are not often in the control of teachers. Rather, it is the grass roots activities of teachers that are having direct daily influence on teaching strategies and student learning. The project described here addresses issues at the classroom level that higher education faculty and in-service teachers can work on together in order to make the physical education experience a worthwhile one for teachers and students.

The range and quality of physical education programs in the public schools is extensive. More significantly, there are vast differences in the climate of the physical education programs. Climate, the sum of interactions among teachers, students, administrators, facilities, and curriculum, may be a positive or negative influence on the total program. The differences in these factors that contribute to differences in climate are central to the issue of obsolescence or vitality. Effective teaching and maximum learning are products of a positive climate. This assumption establishes a basis for studying what affects the teachers' feelings about what they do and how these feelings affect their actual teaching behaviors. Teachers' feelings unquestionably are components of climate which operate in conjunction with various other factors to provide a more or less positive learning environment.

One physical education program may be staffed by teachers who are at school every day but who do little to enhance the quality of their own or their students' lives. Their students participate minimally and half-heartedly. Large heterogeneous groups are squeezed into limited spaces and exposed to a repetitive, nonchallenging curriculum. In such a program one sees locked doors, offices cluttered with last year's memos from the principal, a lack of bulletin board displays, and many students just sitting around rather than participating. The teachers feel powerless and unable to control the situation, they lack energy and generally feel frustrated or perhaps even apathetic. Certainly obsolescence would be a blessing in cases like this.

By contrast, a nearby school may share many of the same structural or systematic problems such as limited facilities, large classes, poor scheduling, and inadequate equipment. Yet in this program the climate is vital and lively. Teachers are enthusiastic and energetic; students participate more fully with body, soul, and mind. The facility, although not always new or elaborate, is attractive; bulletin boards are informative and timely; clutter is current and shows involvement with students. Teachers are eager to describe various facets of the program to outsiders; they demonstrate interest in new ideas, personal pride in their work, and general feelings of being in control of the program. These programs are continually revitalized and address problems eagerly and with confidence that they can be overcome.

Those involved in teacher education and staff development must help teachers approach their work in such a way as to encourage the latter as much as possible. Previously this was done quite effectively by preparing comparatively large numbers of new teachers and flooding the market with their enthusiasm and vitality. Experienced teachers felt involved in helping these new teachers make the transition from preservice to the role of an effective teacher. Now we are preparing fewer teachers, who may or may not get teaching positions. We can no longer assist our public school colleagues or influence public school programs only through teacher education programs. Our campus-based teacher education programs and various field experiences are still viable, of course, and certainly we want preservice education to effectively prepare individuals to be teachers capable of coping with current problems and willing to take responsibility for maintaining quality programs. However, the current status of physical education requires a more direct focus on in-service teachers; needed are methods for studying instruction and for reflecting on the activities of teaching and the role of teachers. We must study the teachers in the field in order to find the factors important for establishing and maintaining a positive climate and for supporting the teachers themselves more directly in their day-to-day efforts.

Recently we have seen significant progress in the research on teaching, teacher behavior, and effective schools (Boyer, 1983; Medley, 1977; Peterson & Walberg, 1979). This research provides evidence that variations in teacher behaviors produce variations in student achievements. We also know that teacher expectations affect student achievement (Martinek, Crowe, & Rejeski, 1982). This information is encouraging in that maximizing those behaviors associated with higher student learning and minimizing others is conceptually simple. We also know that teacher behaviors can be changed or developed in a short time (McKenzie, 1981; Siedentop, 1981).

Practically, however, the possibility of easy changes is contradicted by research indicating that in-service teachers are more powerful socializing agents than are our teacher preparation programs for individuals entering the profession. (Locke, 1977; Templin, 1979). Changes in behavior gained in formal preservice or in-service programs seem not to be incorporated into the daily practice of teachers. Student teaching has been viewed as a time for learning much about the role of a teacher but little about teaching and learning (Templin, 1979).

PURPOSE

The project described here was undertaken to address these concerns with the hope of establishing a basis for programmatic research and staff development. The purpose of the project was to develop a collaborative approach to instructional analysis utilizing in-service teachers, student teachers, and university faculty-researchers. More specifically, the goal was:

1. To establish trustful, enduring collaborative relationships between field-based and campus-based educators;
2. To demonstrate theory into practice and application of research findings to preservice and in-service teachers;
3. To increase the objectivity of teachers about teaching generally, their own teaching behaviors, and the responses of their students;
4. To examine the social dynamics of the cooperating teacher/student teacher relationship during the process of instructional analysis.

METHOD

The procedures for this project were carefully designed to meet the objectives as fully as possible and to establish a strong basis for a continuing collaboration. Initially, team building was the highest priority. The goal was to develop an interdependence among those involved, which would serve as a basis for a continuing support group and exchange of ideas.

Previous experiences have indicated that some student teacher/cooperating teacher/supervisor relationships at first may be either dependent or independent. Neither is appropriate, however, because none of the parties involved can fully benefit from the potential knowledge and experience represented in individuals. Dependent relationships produce either students who have no confidence in or awareness of their ability to lead student learning, or students who resent the restrictions placed on them; and in-service cannot benefit from any ideas of the preservice teachers. Independent relationships deprive both the student teacher and the cooperating teacher of the benefits of a true collegiality and the sharing of expertise; further, they are inappropriate socialization experiences for working with others in education settings. Those of us in higher education should be interdependent to the extent that the knowledge we try to generate through our research is grounded and ultimately evaluated in terms of its ability to inform the practice. In addition, the designs for research must be informed by the experiences of teachers in field settings because teachers in this context potentially are subjects and co-researchers at the same time.

The intitial approach to team building involved meeting with a group of teachers from a teacher education center who agreed to participate. Some were cooperating teachers and some were not. Discussion at the first meeting focused on areas of concern to these teachers, concepts of effective teaching, and possible topics for action/research in the gymnasium. Afterward, commitments for continued participation were solicited from the teachers, some of whom also indicated which areas of instructional practice were of greatest interest to them.

Additional meetings were held and academic learning time (ALT-PE) was identified as the focus for this first project. Currently, Hunter's Teacher Decision-making Model (Dodds & Rife, 1983) is being used as the focus of another collaborative project. Teacher commitment to the research effort was further encouraged by intensive involvement in the development of the research protocol and instrumentation. Teachers suggested extensive modifications in previously established instruments, modifications that would help develop a simpler system that could be used more easily. The university researcher's role at this stage was to maintain the conceptual integrity of the ALT-PE construct by presenting the full model and delineating the implications of proposed modifications.

Training teachers and student teachers to use the final instrument required two additional meetings, which included final clarification of instruments, a paper and pencil test for coding reliability, classroom observation, and comparison of observations across the 12 teachers who participated. After the training, teachers worked in pairs to observe and collect data in five classes for each teacher. Following the data collection, the teachers shared results, related these results to previous research, discussed implications for changes in teaching, and evaluated the total process in terms of continuation, modification, or termination.

RESULTS AND DISCUSSION

This project provided data on two levels: that collected by the teachers in actual classes, and that collected by the university researcher. The latter concerned the process of collaboration among teachers and researchers and dynamics of teacher participation in analysis of instruction.

The data collected by the teachers indicated that activity time devoted to planned lesson content ranged from approximately 15% to 60% of the total allocated class time. Students considered to have a low skill level had significantly lower activity times than those described as highly skilled. Students in classes comprised mainly of game situations exhibited lower content-related activity than students in classes with other kinds of learning experiences. Younger students (grades 1-3) exhibited higher learning time than older students. These findings do not differ substantially from those of previously reported studies utilizing the ALT-PE (Dodds & Rife, 1983). Although direct comparison is not possible because of the modifications of the instruments, the similarity suggests that efforts to maintain conceptual integrity were successful. Furthermore, these findings have significant implications for analyzing instructional practices.

The most significant aspects of this project concerned the process of conducting research as a staff development activity. Extensive notes and recordings of meetings throughout the project provided data describing the involvement of teachers in the process of instructional analysis, and their growing awareness of processes that affect their teaching and the students' learning. The teachers examined their own assumptions and sometimes their defensiveness about instructional practices. An initial inability to separate evaluative factors from the analysis of instruction was overcome by the time the actual observations began. After being trained in use of the instrument, teachers seemed to be more willing to examine their classes for information they could gain to make their own value judgments. The final meetings revealed the actions taken and the changes initiated following early observations to alter results in subsequent observations.

While this poses some questions for interpreting the observational data, the implications for the teacher development process are positive. The mechanisms for continuity in these approaches need to be examined; perhaps the key to ensuring permanent incorporation of instructional analysis into teaching is a system of follow-up. To date, some of the teachers involved in this project have continued to use the format frequently while others have been less consistent in their involvement. Teachers can do this type of analysis on their own. We must continue to encourage and establish ongoing mechanisms for collaboration to support instructional analysis. In conclusion, this project had several positive outcomes:

1. Collaboration among teachers and researchers provided positive professional experience.
2. Research activity was integrated into classroom teaching in a meaningful and nonintrusive way.
3. Teachers felt that they looked at the students and class content in new ways and were actively controlling the learning environment.
4. Teachers modified their behaviors without outside direction or mandate.

Yet in spite of the opportunities for improving classroom climate and self-efficacy of teachers, this approach was not without problems. For example:

1. These kinds of programs are very time-consuming and labor-intensive.
2. The approaches used must be idiosyncratic, and therefore the results may not be generalizable or easily interpreted.
3. Methods and designs are complex, and interpretation is difficult.
4. Relationships of trust are difficult to build and maintain but essential to the success of collaborative activity.

These problems, inherent in all field research, must be dealt with if we are to make solid progress toward improving the teaching/learning experience. This project is a small but encouraging beginning for cooperating with our colleagues in elementary and secondary schools to continually revitalize our physical education programs. Activities such as this by which teachers reflect about teaching and increase their feelings of efficacy can help them to become change agents who can enhance physical education programs at all levels. This potential for stimulating change provides the basis for the positive climate, which in turn provides continuing vitality and increased student learning.

REFERENCES

ADLER, M.J. (1982). *The Paideia proposal*. New York: MacMillan.

BOYER, E. (1983). *High schools*. New York: Harper & Rowe.

DODDS, P., & Rife, F. (1983). Time to learn in physical education: History, completed research and potential future for academic learning time in physical education. *Journal of Teaching in Physical Education*, **1**, 1-22.

LOCKE, L. (1977). Research on teaching physical education: New hope for a dismal science. *Quest*, **28**, 2-16.

MARTINEK, T., Crowe, P., & Rejeski, W. (1982). *Pygmalion in the gym: Causes and effects of expectations in teaching and coaching*. West Point, NY: Leisure Press.

MCKENZIE, T. (1981). Modification, transfer and maintenance of the verbal behavior of an experienced physical education teacher. *Journal of Teaching in Physical Education, Introductory Issue*, pp. 48-56.

MEDLEY, D. (1977). *Teacher competence and teacher effectiveness*. Washington, DC: American Association for Colleges of Teacher Education.

NATIONAL Commission on Excellence in Education. (1983). *A nation at risk: The imperative for educational reform*. Washington, DC: U.S. Government Printing Office.

PETERSON, P., & Walberg, H. (Eds.). (1979). *Research on teaching: Concepts, findings, and implications*. Berkeley, CA: McCutcheon.

SIEDENTOP, D. (1981). The Ohio State University research program: Summary reports. *Journal of Teaching in Physical Education, Introductory Issue*, pp. 30-38.

TEMPLIN, T. (1979). Occupational socialization and the physical education student teacher. *Research Quarterly*, **50**(4), 482-493.

TWENTIETH Century Fund Task Force on Federal Elementary and Secondary Education Policy. (1983). *Making the grade*. New York: Twentieth Century Fund.

Rejuvenating General Education Via Personalized Health Fitness

K. Nelson Butler
Salisbury State College

Many colleges and universities around the country are busy reviewing and/or revising their general education curriculum (Gaff, 1980). There are numerous reasons for this, among them: discernment of what constitutes a liberal education in contemporary society, the question of how to fulfill the requirements of general education once it has been determined what that may be, and the need to develop survival techniques in an era of shrinking enrollments.

Physical education service courses, as a required part of the general education curriculum in colleges and universities, have fallen off over the years. Oxendine and Roberts reported in 1978 that only 57% of the institutional respondents in their survey indicated a requirement of physical education for all students prior to graduation. That study also revealed an increasing decline over time in previously reported figures: 83% in 1961, 82% in 1968, and 74% in 1972. No explanations were offered for this decline in enrollment. However, it was stated that in the late 1960s and early 1970s, the trend was toward greater curricular flexibility and student options, and that recently there was a movement to reinstitute required courses across the general education curriculum. How widespread this movement was (or is) is relatively unknown at this point. This surge of interest may have happened coincidentally with general education curriculum perusal. More important, however, is that no contemporary published research has revealed any dynamics vis à vis required physical education in higher education.

Given the issues described above, Salisbury State College took the initiative to review its required physical education curriculum in 1977-78. Historically, the pattern of requirement at Salisbury paralleled many such programs of similar size and mission around the country for a number of years. A minimum number of credits/courses was required in physical education, and they often involved such offerings as activity (fitness), sport skills, or personal health classes.

The requirement at Salisbury State College for a long time was either 3 credit hours chosen from a variety of 1-hour sport skill courses or a combination of a 2-hour personal health course along with a 1-credit sport skill course. Many students opted for the latter. Students and faculty speculated about that choice, some suggesting the health course was a "crip" course and therefore students naturally gravitated to it. Others mentioned that the lack of interest in sport skills was so widespread that students were willing to substitute almost anything. One shocking bit of information was that some students were so turned off because of physical education experiences in secondary or elementary school that they simply did not want additional exposure to it.

Owing to personnel resources, the building of a new physical education facility, and a general concern for emphasizing the positive benefits of physical activity, the Department of Physical Education at Salisbury State College proposed to the College Curriculum Committee a change in the requirement in 1977-78. It simply called for the student to take three 1-hour activity courses. Personal health was no longer accepted as part of the physical education requirement. Many new courses were included in the context of activity classes. The new building afforded the opportunity to add many classes that previously had been precluded. For example, handball/racquetball, expanded dance offerings, and an array of aquatic courses were offered for the first time. One specific course, entitled Individualized Physical Education, focused on the individual's specific physical fitness needs or interests. Course content included fitness assessment, individual program prescription, and exposure to a body of knowledge about the effects of exercise as it related to personal health development. Because it stressed individuality, the course became very popular with students. The Departmental Curriculum Committee recognized not only its popularity but also its viability in maintaining the integrity of physical education as a required course in the general education curriculum of a higher education institution. That is, it seemed to fit at least some of the most important objectives in physical education.

However, by 1980 the entire college was beginning to question the purpose, scope, and sequence of its general education curriculum. The Department of Physical Education once more was asked to review its contribution to this important part of the entire college curriculum. After considerable deliberation of such issues as personnel resources, departmental mission, and physical resources, the department proposed a new requirement in physical education for every student in the college. The new requirement centered on the aformentioned course, Individualized Physical Education, but changed the name to Personalized Health Fitness. The course was somewhat restructured to include a lecture portion during which students were exposed to the concepts of physical fitness and then were required to apply those via a laboratory experience. The lab experience entailed a choice of six separate activities: aerobic dance, cycling, circuit training, jogging, aquacises, and swimming. By introducing the lecture into the course, students were provided a more in-depth understanding of fitness. The lectures concentrated on cardiovascular health, basic diet and weight control, strength and flexibility development, and relaxation theory and technique. The laboratory experience provided opportunities to participate twice a week in an activity of the students' choosing. For optimum development, students were encouraged to engage in additional workout periods during the week.

Prior to beginning the lab activity the students were subjected to a battery of physical assessment procedures. A bicycle ergometer test for cardiovascular condition was employed, as was a strength test (hand dynamometer), flexibility (sit and reach), and an underwater weighing session to determine percent body fat.[1] Once these indices were obtained, the student received an individual profile sheet and counseling from

---

[1]These tests and individual assessments subscribe to the same principles promoted in the JOPERD series (1981). Exercise prescription for the practitioner, *Journal of Physical Education, Recreation and Dance*, **52**(7), 35-46.

the lab instructor about the results and how to effect positive changes. Students repeated the physical assessment procedures at the end of the semester to see if measurable differences had occurred.

The general theory underlying this approach was that physical education involved both cognitive and physical aspects of the learning process. Through the presentation of concepts via the lecture, supplemented by the lab experience, students had a better opportunity to become truly physically educated. Not only were they subjected to the actual physical experiences which bring about positive changes in their being, but they also learned why it is important for that process to take place.

An experimental, pilot semester was initiated in the Spring of 1982 and approximately 250 students enrolled. Enrollment in this pilot semester was not mandatory, but students were allowed to fulfill two-thirds of their general education physical education credit by taking this course. Some logistical problems were encountered, such as the number of students to be assessed at any one period, proper training of all staff and students in the testing procedures, and space problems due to conflicting activities being conducted in the same area.

The initial semester also featured lectures by individuals who had the most expertise in a particular area. For example, one faculty member gave a lecture on strength training, another spoke on weight control, another on flexibility, and so forth. This led to a lack of continuity in presentations, different teaching styles, and varying expectations of students, and thus this part of the course was soundly criticized.

The difficulties encountered in the pilot semester pointed to a need for changes before the first mandatory session was to go into effect that fall. The changes that were made dealt with logistical problems and training procedures, and assigning only one faculty member per section as lecturer.

The course is still in its infancy. More than 400 students are enrolled in some 24 sections. Preliminary evaluation by students suggests that the course is achieving those goals agreed upon by both students and faculty. A formal and systematic ongoing evaluation is in progress. It is the hope of the department that, by offering this new course, it will be more able to fulfill its mission of physically educating students in higher education.

REFERENCES

GAFF, J.G. (1980, Fall). Avoiding the potholes: Strategies for reforming general education. *Educational Record*, 50-58.

OXENDINE, J.B., & Roberts, J.E. (1978). The general instruction program in physical education at four year colleges and universities: 1977. *Journal of Physical Education and Recreation*, **49**(1), 21-23.

Physical Fitness For Public Safety Personnel: An Opportunity For The Profession

Paul Dubois
Bridgewater State College

One mission of higher education is to provide community service. Given the growing pressure on colleges and universities to increase their delivery of practical programs and services, this mission is likely to become increasingly prominent in the decades ahead.

The contemporary phenomenon often referred to as the employee fitness boom gives the physical education profession an ideal opportunity to make a substantial contribution to higher education's community service mission. Many physical education programs are already providing businesses, hospitals, and other private sector organizations with the support needed to develop and implement systematic, high quality fitness programs. In addition, physical education departments are increasingly training health fitness specialists to work in such settings.

As real as the employee fitness boom appears to be, it has yet to make a substantive impact on an important component of the work force: the public sector employee. This condition does not mean that health fitness is any less beneficial in the public sector or that there is no awareness among those employees about the desirability of staying fit. On the contrary, there are often more compelling reasons for public servants to be fit than for workers in private enterprise. For example, few would deny that an optimal level of health fitness must be a top priority for public safety personnel.

The purpose of this presentation is to outline how one college physical education department broadened its program scope by meeting the fitness needs of one of our most vital public safety professionals: the municipal firefighter. Specifically, it provides a rationale for and describes the development and services of a state funded "Resource Center for Firefighter Fitness." It also briefly reviews what I perceive to be the benefits of this agency to the college and department responsible for its operation.

RATONALE

Establishing a state-supported health fitness agency for firefighters can be justified on three counts. First, it can cut program costs. A service that is state subsidized becomes affordable for even the most fiscally hard-pressed municipality. A centralized agency is also fiscally sound in a broader sense: by consistently utilizing a well established operating model and core group of resource professionals, money need not be repeatedly poured into planning, development, and staff training.

Second, institutionalizing a service such as health fitness by creating an agency increases the probability it will be used by potential clients. An established agency is more visible than an exercise science program, particularly if the agency's title identifies with clients the agency wishes to target. Furthermore, an agency suggests to a client the quality of availability; when a client requests some service, the agency will be there to respond quickly.

The third justification revolves around the potential payoffs of a physically fit firefighting force. One possible payoff is health related. Studies consistently show that about 50% of all firefighters die from heart attacks, a figure well above the national average (Balanoff, 1976; Heart Facts, 1980; Ornberg, 1982). Because of current evidence concerning the positive relationship between regular aerobic exercise and the decreased risk of heart disease (Clarke, 1979; Paffenbarger, 1977), any agency that might enhance the fitness level of firefighters may also reduce their risk of disability and death by heart attack.

A second payoff focuses on worker productivity. Firefighting requires a high level of aerobic fitness and musculoskeletal strength, endurance, and flexibility (Davis, Dotson, & Santa Maria, 1982; Sharkey, Wilson, Whiddon, & Miller, 1978). However, simply fighting fires and responding to other emergencies does not provide the firefighter with the conditioning needed to perform his or her job efficiently and safely (Dotson, Santa Maria, & Davis, 1977; Dubois & Otto, 1982). For example, the firefighters in one study displayed an estimated average $\dot{V}O_2$ max of 36 ml/kg/min, a figure well below the minimum recommended professional standard of 45 ml/kg/min (Sharkey, 1977). Thus, along with improving the firefighters' cardiovascular health, such a fitness agency could also help to enhance the firefighters' capacity to perform physical work.

A third payoff concerns the cost effectiveness of firefighter fitness programs. For example, costs can be contained in the area of disability pensions. Massachusetts, the sponsor of the Resource Center for Firefighter Fitness, is one of 25 states with a "heart and lung" law. These laws award liberal disability retirement benefits to any public safety employee who has heart or lung disease. By improving the fitness levels of firefighters, the costs in disability benefits awarded under the heart and lung law would eventually be reduced. Fitness programs can also realize savings by helping to reduce the number of days lost to sickness or injury (Wirfs, 1978), reducing insurance fees (Johnson, 1979), and decreasing employee turnover rates (Peepre, 1980).

PROGRAM DEVELOPMENT

The establishment of a permanent agency for firefighter fitness was to rest on the findings of a 1980 pilot project, which consisted of a 9-month fitness program conducted in a city that employed 250 firefighters. As with subsequent agency funding, the pilot project was supported by the Massachusetts Department of Health, Division of Preventive Medicine. The pilot study showed that a successful firefighter fitness program could be conducted on site, without expensive equipment and expensive facilities (see Tables 1 and 2). Thus the decision was made to formally establish the Resource Center for

Table 1

**Selected Pre- and Posttest Fitness Scores of Firefighters
who Exercised Three or More Times per Week (N = 9)**

Variable	Pretest	Posttest	Percent change
Vertical jump (in.)	15.9	18.4	16%
Situps (2 min)	43.6	58.1	33%
Pushups	33.0	41.0	24%
Sit and reach (in.)	14.4	15.6	8%
Body fat (%)	21.7	18.7	− 16%
Lean body weight (lbs)	136.9	136.2	NC
$\dot{V}O_2$ max (ml/kg/min)	36.2	46.8	29%
Total cholesterol (mg/100 ml)	183.9	203.4	11%
HDL (mg/100 ml)	49.4	54.1	10%

Table 2

Participants' Perceptions of Program Benefits (N = 31)

Item	Agree	Undecided— probably agree
Enhanced sense of well-being	22	6
Feel better physically	25	5
Firefighting w/less fatigue	26	5
More relaxed	19	10
Will exercise after program ends	24	4

Firefighter Fitness (RCFF). Before the RCFF could become fully operational, however, it first went through a 6-month phase of development and promotion. The development component of this phase consisted primarily of producing or purchasing educational and communication materials such as:

- An informational brochure, mailed to all fire departments in the state, describing RCFF services and pointing out the payoffs of a physically fit firefighter service;
- A 113-page manual on physical fitness based on the model program that evolved from the pilot project's evaluation findings;
- A slide presentation describing the model program and summarizing the pilot project's evaluation findings;

- A monthly RCFF newsletter, distributed to all fire departments in the state and including information about RCFF activities, articles about fire departments that have established fitness programs, vignettes on selected fitness or health topics, and opinion pieces.

The promotion component of this 6-month gearing-up phase was conceived along two dimensions. First, because the RCFF needed visibility, there was a need to promote itself. Second, it had to promote the importance and benefits of a physically fit firefighting force. The RCFF brochures and the monthly newsletters served some of these important promotional functions. In addition, information seminars were conducted in various communities throughout the state, focusing on how a community could develop and implement its own firefighter fitness program. Finally, efforts were made to promote the RCFF mission via the media.

PROGRAM SERVICES

Following the 6-month development and promotion phase, the program shifted to providing services. The RCFF's primary service is to help municipal fire departments plan and implement fitness programs. A general program model, derived from the experiences gained in the pilot project, guides the delivery of this service. The model, briefly outlined here, has proven to be both financially flexible and functional within the wide range of organizational and environmental settings that characterize fire departments in Massachusetts.[1]

Elements of the Model

Planning Sessions. The purpose of these sessions is to help fire department personnel and town officials develop fitness programs. Typical agenda items at the sessions include budgeting, procuring exercise equipment, medical screening and exercise program options, and program timeline. It is also at one of these meetings that a firefighter is made fitness program coordinator. Among other tasks, this individual serves as the liaison between the RCFF and the department.

Information Seminar. Once a department is firmly committed to implementing a program, the next step is to conduct an information seminar for the department members, outlining the nature of the fitness program and answering questions.

Medical Screening. The screening process may be as comprehensive as a physician-monitored ECG stress test and blood chemistry analysis, or as basic as written clearance to exercise by the participant's family physician.

Physical Fitness Assessment. Once the firefighters have been cleared for exercise, they complete a battery of tests which includes measures of musculoskeletal strength, endurance, flexibility, body composition, and aerobic power. Follow-up assessments are typically conducted every 3 months.

---

[1]The importance of functionality within the settings lies in the fact that all components of the model are conducted at the work site.

Exercise Prescription/Program. The firefighters are given individualized exercise prescriptions following each of the four fitness assessments. The initial prescription is complemented with a workshop on exercise concepts and techniques each firefighter needs to successfully implement his/her own fitness program. The firefighters are now ready to begin their workouts. Although they can exercise wherever they choose, for several reasons they are strongly encouraged to exercise while on duty. First, the 3- or 4-day work week schedule typical of most firefighters is ideal for ensuring regularity of exercise. Second, co-workers can motivate the firefighter to exercise on those days when he or she might not have the incentive. Third, most fire stations have an exercise area outfitted with equipment that can provide a complete workout.

Education. Two educational strategies are used in the program. One is a series of workshops on such topics as aerobic fitness, nutrition, weight control, temperature regulation, and stress reduction. The second strategy is the use of bulletin board displays in each fire station. The bulletin boards provide information about health and fitness as well as program-related information such as the date of the next scheduled fitness assessment and comparisons of pre- and interim test results.

Counseling. A final important feature of the program is the systematic (i.e., every 2 to 3 weeks) one-to-one counseling the firefighters receive. The counselors, who are trained exercise science students, are each permanently assigned to about 10 firefighters. Their primary responsibilities are to modify exercise prescriptions when appropriate, to serve as health/fitness resource persons, and to encourage and motivate.

Ancillary Services

The RCFF also conducts a number of services which support the primary one of fitness program planning and implementation. These ancillary services include the following:

Adopt a Fire Department. The aim of the ''Adopt a Fire Department'' program is to help reduce the initial costs of a fitness program by encouraging businesses, medical centers, and service organizations to provide the financial or in-kind support needed to enable such a program to succeed. RCFF staff are available to help fire departments identify and link up with potential adopting organizations.

Clearinghouse of Information. The RCFF collects a variety of materials on health fitness, information on firefighter fitness programs, source books, relevant research reports, booklets and pamphlets on health fitness topics, and audiovisual aids. Some such materials may be distributed at large or included in the newsletter; others may be forwarded to a department to meet a specific request.

Training Program. This 30-hour program provides department training officers or other designated personnel with information on the theoretical and applied aspects of physical fitness program operation. Individuals who successfully complete this program gain the competencies needed to make informed judgments about the methods and materials of a fitness program in their department and to take over some program activities normally provided by the RCFF.

BENEFITS

The RCFF has benefited the sponsoring college and department in a number of ways. For the department, it has meant an opportunity to create a new program. Given the reduction in student numbers in some undergraduate programs—teacher training in particular—this opportunity is particularly noteworthy. For instance, it has played a role, albeit a small one, in holding off faculty attrition; the two faculty members who serve as agency director and exercise physiologist share the equivalent of a three-quarter release time from regular classroom assignments. The agency also appears to be serving as a catalyst in developing a department-sponsored health fitness institute that will serve all groups and organizations in the college's sphere of influence.

The RCFF has given both students and faculty members in physical education and health the chance to expand their horizons. It has provided exercise physiology students with excellent field-based experiences. To date, 14 students have received academic credit for their roles as program counselors and numerous others have been involved in fitness testing data collection. For faculty members, the RCFF provides a new professional dimension. Such new dimensions can help to prevent burnout, particularly in an institution in which one's entire workload is teaching.

The RCFF has enhanced the department's potential of entering into new collaborative relationships with other institutions. For example, the RCFF is currently working with a nearby hospital to share in the operation of a fire department fitness program. Among other things, expanding our relationships with other institutions is expected to provide new internship outlets for our students.

The RCFF benefits the college by providing it with an excellent public relations tool. Through the RCFF, the public recognizes that the college's claim of community service is not an empty slogan. Resource center activities help to portray the college as an innovative institution working to meet real social needs. This positive portrayal is not lost on state legislators, who control the college's purse strings, or on students about to choose a college in which to enroll.

The RCFF is currently operating firefighter fitness programs in six communities; four others are in various stages of development. In addition, more than 35 communities have benefited from RCFF seminars and training programs. We believe that the RCFF represents a creative, cost effective strategy for meeting an important social need. At the same time, it is making a valuable contribution to a college, to an academic department, and to the faculty and students who comprise that department.

REFERENCES

AMERICAN Heart Association (1980). *Heart facts, 1980.* Dallas: Author.

BALANOFF, T. (1976). *Firefighter mortality report.* Washington, DC: International Association of Firefighters.

CLARKE, H.H. (1979, April). Update: Physical activity and coronary heart disease. *Physical Fitness Research Digest,* **7**.

DAVIS, P., Dotson, C., & Santa Maria, D.L. (1982). Relationship between simulated firefighting tasks and physical performance measures. *Medicine and Science in Sports and Exercise*, **14**(1), 65-71.

DOTSON, C., Santa Maria, D.L., & Davis, P. (1977). *Development of a job related physical performance test for firefighters*. Washington, DC: U.S. Fire Administration.

DUBOIS, P., & Otto, R. (1982). *Health and fitness for firefighters*. East Bridgewater, MA: Baggia Press.

JOHNSON, R. (1979). *The payoff for business, government and industry*. Presentation at the Conference on Lifetime Fitness, Massachusetts Governor's Committee on Physical Fitness and Sports, Andover, MA.

ORNBERG, R.C., (1982, September). Bodywork: Shaping up. *Firehouse*, **7**, 86-89.

PAFFENBARGER, R.S. Jr. (1977). *Report*. American Public Health Association, Miami Beach, FL.

PEEPRE, M. (1980, December). The Canadian employee fitness and lifestyle project. *Athletic Purchasing and Facilities*, **4**, 10-22.

SHARKEY, B.J. (1977). *Fitness and work capacity*. Washington, DC: Forest Service of the U.S. Dept. of Agriculture.

SHARKEY, B.J., Wilson, D., Whiddon, T., & Miller, K. (1978, September). Fit to work? *Journal of Physical Education and Recreation*, **49**, 18-21.

WIRFS, R. (1978, June). Firefighters. *Job Safety and Health*, **6**, 19-33.

Section 7

NAPEHE
And The Future

The Future Of NAPEHE

Neil J. Dougherty
Rutgers University

I believe that our Association must do three things in order to become a strong force in the profession, and hopefully in academia. The first, and in my opinion the most critical task that we must undertake, is that of clearly identifying the role and focus of the National Association for Physical Education in Higher Education. An organization without a clear and unified concept of its reason for being cannot help but flounder. There has been good cause and, in fact, an absolute need for our early concern for organizational matters. However, the time has come to move beyond housekeeping chores to a clear identification of our professional role. How can we attract the participation of our colleagues when we cannot pinpoint our purpose? How can we market a product that we cannot describe? Our recent conferences have been deliberately designed to highlight many of the issues and, to some degree, the options before us. We must now begin to make choices that can lead to cohesive actions on issues of concern to the organization and the individuals it represents.

If I were to identify a focus at this point—based upon my own perception of the individual and collective histories of the NAPECW, the NCPEAM, and the various district associations—and if allowed the caveat that it reflects only my personal perceptions and not necessarily those of the board, I would suggest as a focus the administrative aspects of post-secondary physical education. I would hasten to add here that the term *administration* is probably more a misnomer than it is an appropriate label. I am actually speaking of administration as it involves every individual professional at all levels, not simply the nuts and bolts of the process with which those of us who hold administrative titles must cope.

How can we maintain the vigor of our profession in the face of budget cuts, program restrictions, and faculty retrenchment? How can we most effectively blend the theoretical and the practical to guarantee not only professional survival but improvement and development as well? How can we take the product information developed by the theorists and researchers in the subdisciplines, incorporate it into viable disciplinary models, effectively transmit it to our students, and market it to the rest of the academic community? These are questions that do or should concern us, both individually and collectively. They provide a focus that is meaningful, common to all and, not insignificantly, can support rather than subvert the goals and concerns of the so-called splinter groups or subdisciplines.

The second major task facing us, I believe, in some ways reflects the general pattern of the physical education profession. We are and have been what I would call a *reactive* profession. We wait until things happen, and then we react to them. We too often view change as a threat to avoid rather than something that we can constructively turn to our own best advantage. We must develop a much more *proactive* posture if we are to survive.

We must look beyond the "how we do it" to "how we can improve it," how we are likely to have to do it in the future, and what we can do to affect and alter the envisioned course of events. Certainly we cannot expect to avoid or ignore problems. Such things as budget cuts and shrinking faculty lines befall all of us sooner or later. What we can do, however, is to maximize the likelihood that decisions about quality and quantity will reflect sound professional criteria and that we, as individuals and as representatives of our respective academic institutions, are prepared to meet and exceed those criteria. The expertise is here, within NAPEHE. I believe that by actively focusing our efforts we can and will have a positive effect on the future of our profession.

The third task is intimately tied to the first two. We must increase both our membership and the involvement of our younger colleagues. I believe that this will be accomplished only when we can point to clear professional goals and can explain how and why this association is the best vehicle for their accomplishment. We have some tremendous assets. A young professional can come to a NAPEHE conference and interact with some of the finest leaders in our profession. Our publications and programs are second to none in quality. The problem we face is one of channeling our efforts toward viable professional goals and then effectively communicating our value and importance to our colleagues and to academia at large.

Our tasks are not simple. They will require a great deal of thought and effort from all of us. However, the results will be reflected in the development of a vital, effective, professional organization worthy of the respect and honor earned by our parent associations and able to help shape the future of physical education in higher education.

The Future Of NAPEHE

Hally B.W. Poindexter
Rice University

The National Association for Physical Education in Higher Education was founded June 2, 1978, through a merger of the National College Physical Education Association for Men and the National Association for Physical Education of College Women. These two organizations—unified by interests, issues, and goals but separated by gender—responded to the social concern for equal rights, opportunities, and privileges for both sexes. An organization emerged which recognized the need to protect the balance and rights of both sexes in decision making while the organization grew to full status as a viable voice for physical education in higher education. NAPEHE is the only professional organization devoted exclusively to the concerns of physical education in higher education.

Our 6-year history reflects polar positions regarding the merger and the formation of NAPEHE. A loss of membership resulted for both groups and, consequently, a small fledgling organization inherited the problems but failed to generate the resources for solutions. Later when we reflect on these early years, I am certain we will not view them as the golden years of the association. We will probably be content to accept the notion that the energies of the dedicated members were well spent in establishing a structure that served and freed the membership to create, research, write, publish, exchange ideas, and enjoy an arena for exploring concepts of physical education in higher education. History will undoubtedly establish that it was a difficult time for most professional organizations and certainly for those concerned with education. Social changes, the winds of international unrest, and economic limitations escalated educational change that was often unfavorable for physical education. The paradox that remains unresolved is that American society developed a love affair with human movement and sport, yet failed to recognize instruction in human movement as an integral part of formal education.

We experienced yesterday so that we would be prepared for today. NAPEHE has approximately 1,000 members. The organization holds conferences and publishes its *Proceedings, Quest,* and *Action Line.* The organization works to encourage scholarly inquiry, provide a forum for discussion of major issues confronting physical education, disseminate research and scholarly contributions in the field of physical education, and give direction to the profession in institutions of higher education. It appears that the reasons for the organization's existence are valid and, given this, every effort should be made to assure the future of NAPEHE.

It seems appropriate to identify one mechanism for expanding the impact of the association. Many ideas and gimmicks might be proposed as measures for bolstering both membership and visibility. Each deserves to be examined and considered. The immediate issue is to enroll more members, encourage wider participation in meetings, and expand the influence of the association in higher education. The members of NAPEHE represent all disciplines of physical education. There are motor control specialists, pedagogy professors, sport sociologists, exercise scientists, and administrators, to name but a few. Each is loyal to his or her discipline and to the profession of physical education, specifically in higher education. Could we meet in concert or concurrently with one or more of the discipline groups? Such meetings would strengthen the professional relationship between NAPEHE and the discipline group, allow members of each association to move freely to the meetings of the other, and minimize the cost of such meetings by having them at the same location.

The scenario might be as follows. NAPEHE meets at Asilomar from June 12-16, 1985. The sport history group arranges to meet several days earlier at the same site. Sport sociology meets immediately following NAPEHE (or perhaps overlaps a day), so that two discipline groups with members who have interests in NAPEHE are brought to a location where they can attend at least two important meetings, exchange ideas, and meet with colleagues in different but related areas. And all of this occurs at a minimal additional cost to the individual or his or her institution.

The intent and the role of NAPEHE is to develop a logistical plan through which we can associate with other groups who have interests in the discipline of physical education. It is conceivable, and perhaps a personal dream, that such discipline interest would grow so that four or five groups might meet—simultaneously with NAPEHE overseeing programming and involving discipline members by interpreting their concerns and interests in higher education. A successful venture will benefit our membership through continued expansion of a knowledge base. NAPEHE can assist any discipline group by the expanded involvement in its association, thus further bridging the gap from the discipline to interpretation and application in higher education. Perhaps once again we can speak openly with our colleagues about mutual concerns and specialized interests.

NAPEHE is coming of age. We are concerned about all disciplines and all professional aspects of physical education. Should it not be the responsibility of NAPEHE to make the overture and establish communication between the scholars and professionals who share many common goals? As Burris Husman said almost 8 years ago, "At best, cooperation can be attained by periodically meeting at the same location." Logistical plans for this effort will be sought from the membership at this meeting and through *Action Line*. It is time for the organization concerned about *all* to seek cooperation from the *many*.

NAPEHE BOARD OF DIRECTORS
1984

President
Neil J. Dougherty, Rutgers University

Past President
Hally B.W. Poindexter, Rice University

Secretary
Mary Lou Remley, Indiana University

Treasurer
Judy Jensen, SUNY, College at Brockport

Vice President for Conferences
Ronald Feingold, Adelphi University

Vice President for Projects and Research
Robert Stadulis, Kent State University

Members-at-Large
Donald Chu, Skidmore College
J. William Douglas, West Virginia University
Benjamin Massey, University of Illinois
Richard A. Swanson, University of North Carolina-Greensboro

Affiliated Associations

Central Association for Physical Education in Higher Education
Mary Young, University of Minnesota

Eastern Association for Physical Education of College Women
Muriel Sloan, University of Maryland

Midwest Association for Physical Education of College Women
Norma Jean Johnson, Indiana University

Southern Association for Physical Education of College Women
Mary Ford, Winthrop College

Western Society for Physical Education of College Women
Virginia Scheel, California State University-Fullerton

Western Men's Physical Education Society
Jim Ewers, University of Utah

Special Appointments

NAPEHE Registered Agent
Roger Wiley, Washington State University

Editor, 1984 NAPEHE Proceedings
Nancy L. Struna, University of Maryland

Editor, Quest
John D. Massengale, Eastern Washington University

Editor, ActionLine Newsletter
Donna Thompson, University of Northern Iowa

NAPEHE Necrologist
Joanne Davenport, Auburn University

NAPEHE Presidents

1984-1986 Neil J. Dougherty

1982-1984 Hally B.W. Poindexter

1981-1982 George Sage

1979-1980 Marguerite Clifton

1978-1979 Jim Ewers and Marianna Trekell

NAPEHE MEMBERSHIP LIST

A

Betty Abercrombie, Oklahoma State University, Stillwater, OK 74074
Ruth Abernathy, Greentree Box 28, Greenbank, WA 98253
Jerry A. Acanfora, St. Andrews College, Laurinburg, NC 28352
Doris Acord, 1083 Griffin Street, Grover City, CA 93433
R. Vivian Acosta, Brooklyn College-SUNY, Brooklyn, NY 11210
Jack Adams, Eastern Kentucky University, Richmond, KY 40475
Martha A. Adams, Pennsylvania State University, University Park, PA 16802
Margaret H. Aitken, Western Washington University, Bellingham, WA 98225
Dorothy J. Allen, Southeast Missouri State University, Cape Girardeau, MO 63701
Robert E. Allen, University of Florida, Gainesville, FL 32611
Louis Alley, 1204 Ashley Drive, Iowa City, IA 52240
Pamela C. Allison, 5500 High Point Road, Greensboro, NC 27407
William L. Alsop, West Virginia University, Morgantown, WV 26506
Lenore K. Alway, 55 Clayton Avenue, Cortland, NY 13045
Virginia Ames, 3200 Bensalem Boulevard, Bensalem, PA 19020
Katherine Amsden, University of New Hampshire, Durham, NH 03824
Eugene W. Anderson, University of Texas, Arlington, TX 76019
Marian H. Anderson, 449 Northridge Road, Santa Barbara, CA 93104
Marjorie J. Anderson, Gonzaga University, Spokane, WA 99258
Pride V. Anderson, 1613 Steven Drive, Hobbs, NM 88240
William G. Anderson, Teachers College, Columbia, NY 10027
Jean M. Appenzellar, Vassar College, Poughkeepsie, NY 12603
Alan C. Applebee, San Jose State University, San Jose, CA 95192
Joy Archer, College of William and Mary, Williamsburg, VA 23185
Dudley Ashton, 2070 Eastern Parkway, Louisville, KY 40402
Joan Askew, Appalachian State University, Boone, NC 28608
Gene M. Asprey, University of Iowa, Iowa City, IA 52242
Ruth Atwell, 5613 Schaddele Drive, Fort Meyers, FL 33901
Janet Atwood, Pennsylvania State University, University Park, PA 16802
Susan Aufderheide, Purdue University, West Lafayette, IN 47907
Sally Ayer, California State University, Fresno, CA 93740

B

Alice Backus, 129 Court Street, Plattsburgh, NY 12901
Thomas Baechle, Creighton University, Omaha, NE, 68178
Anne H. Bages, Pomona College, Claremont, CA 91711
Viola M. Bahls, University of Nebraska, Lincoln, NE 68588
Linda L. Bain, University of Houston, Houston, TX 77004
Wesley D. Bair, Southwest Missouri State University, Springfield, MO 65807
Stuart Baker, Rogue Community College, 3345 Redwood Highway, Grants Pass, OR 97526
Ralph B. Ballou, 1710 Dover Street, Murfreesboro, TN 37130
Helen Barr, Glidden Drive, Sturgeon Bay, WI 54235
J. Shober Barr, 704 N. President Avenue, Lancaster PA 17603
Jean A. Barrett, California State University, Fullerton, CA 92634
Kate R. Barrett, University of North Carolina, Greensboro, NC 27412
Ann S. Batchelder, 6 Wingate Road, Wellesley College, Wellesley, MA 02181
Thomas Battinelli, Fitchburg State College, Fitchburg, MA 01420
Willis J. Baughman, 25 Audabon Place, Tuscaloosa, AL 35401
Mary Ann Bayless, Washington State University, Pullman, WA 99164
Judith C. Beale, Virginia Polytechnic Institute and State University, 214 War Memorial Gym, Blacksburg, VA 24061
Elizabeth Beall, Wellesley Manor, Wellesley, MA 02181
Gladys Bean, 1400 Pine Avenue West #1005, Montreal, PQ Canada, H3A 1E3
Beverly J. Becker, Skidmore College, Saratoga Springs, NY 12866
Charles A. Becker, 3 The Knoll, Armonk, NY 10504
Marian C. Beckwith, University of New Hampshire, Durham, NH 03824
Mary A. Behling, University of Northern Colorado, Greeley, CO 80639
James J. Belisle, Indiana University, Bloomington, IN 47401
Lacey D. Bell, Hampton Institute, Hampton, VA 23668
Mary M. Bell, Northern Illinois University, Dekalb, IL 60115
Betty Sue Benison, 6412 Sam Kiam Avenue, Fort Worth, TX 76133
Bruce L. Bennett, 501 Loveman Avenue, Worthington, OH 43085
Jane G. Bennett, University of Missouri, Columbia, MO 65211
Bonnie C. Berger, 20 Waterside Plaza, Apartment 26K, New York, NY 10010
Wilfred Berger, Arnold College, University of Bridgeport, Bridgeport, CT 06602
Ann Bergman, Quincy College, Quincy, IL 62301
Pearl Berlin, University of North Carolina, Greensboro, NC 27412
Dean Betts, University of Northern Colorado, Greeley, CO 80639
Edith Betts, 1236 Bird Song Ln, Moscow, ID 83843
Bonnie J. Bevans, California State University, Fresno, CA 93740
John E. Billing, University of North Carolina, Chapel Hill, NC 27514
Roger M. Bishop, Wartburg College, Waverly, IA 50677
Kathleen Black, Central State University, Edmond, OK 73034
William O. Blair, 2400 Calmo Court, Santa Fe, NM 87501
Mary E. Blann, Towson State University, Towson, MD 21204

Frances A. Bleick, Route 1, Box 30 S, Hackensack, MN 56452
T. Erwin Blesh, 459 Hartford Turnpike, Hamden, CT 06517
William W. Bolonchuk, University of North Dakota, Grand Forks, ND 58202
Patricia J. Bonner, Milligan College, Milligan, TN 37682
Jean Bontz, 1115 N. Wasatch, Colorado Springs, CO 80903
Patsy C. Boroviak, University of Tennessee, Knoxville, TN 37916
Ronald R. Bos, Virginia Polytechnic Institute and State University, War Memorial Gym,
    Blacksburg, VA 24061
James S. Bosco, University of California, Santa Cruz, CA 95064
Connie Bothwell-Myers, University of New Brunswick, Fredericton, NB, Canada E3B
    5A3
Robert L. Boucher, University of Windsor, Windsor, ON, Canada N9B 3P4
Jean M. Bouton, Towson State University, Towson, MD 21204
Robert T. Bowen Jr., 109 Alpine Way, Athens, GA 30606
Gary W. Bowie, University of Lethbridge, Lethbridge, AB, Canada T1K 3M4
Charles J. Bowles, Willamette University, Salem, OR 97301
Bill C. Bowman, Boise State University, Boise, ID 83725
Mary Bowman, San Jose State University, San Jose, CA 95192
William B. Bradley, Western Illinois University, Macomb, IL 61455
Kathleen Brasfield, P.O. Box 11047, San Angelo, TX 76909
P. Stanley Brassie, University of Georgia, Athens, GA 30605
Elizabeth Bressan, University of Oregon, Eugene, OR 97403
Carol A. Briggs, Plymouth State College, Plymouth, NH 03264
D. Shelby Brightwell, Southeast Louisiana State University, Hammond, LA 70402
Gretchen Brockmeyer, Springfield College, Box 1647, Springfield, MA 01109
Jan Broekhoff, University of Oregon, Eugene, OR 97403
Marion R. Broer, Regents Point, 19191 Harvard Avenue, Irvine, CA 92715
Catherine L. Brown, Ohio University, Athens, OH 45701
Janie P. Brown, Elon College, Elon College, NC 27244
Hubert E. Brown, 823 P Via Alhambra, Laguna Hills, CA 92651
Jamie Brown, Elon College, Elon College, NC 27244
Julia M. Brown, 145 Lathrop Hall, University of Wisconsin, Madison, WI 53706
Clifford L. Brownell, 25 Woodford Court, Avon, CT 06001
Betsy L. Bruce, Hartwick College, Oneonta, NY 13820
Patricia J. Bruce, James Madison University, Harrisonburg, VA 22807
Wayne B. Brumbach, University of California, Santa Cruz, CA 95064
James E. Bryant, 15332 E. Milan Drive, Aurora, CO 80013
Paul Brynteson, Oral Roberts University, Tulsa, OK 74171
Duane Buchanan, Litchfield Park, AZ 85340
Charles Bucher, 4505 Maryland Parkway, University of Nevada, Las Vegas, NV 89154
Elaine Budde, Roanoke College, Salem, VA 24153
Linda K. Bunker, 405 Emmet-Ruffner Hall, University of Virginia, Charlottesville,
    VA 22901
Dorothy Burdeshaw, Mississippi University for Women, Columbus, MS 39701
Donald L. Burgess, University of Saskatchewan, Saskatoon, Sas, Canada, S7N 0W0
Tommy Burnett, Southwest Missouri State University, Springfield, MO 65804
Kay Burrus, HPER Building 296B, Indiana University, Bloomington, IN 47401
Craig A. Buschner, 1006 N. 29th Avenue, Hattiesburg, MS 39401

Nelson Butler, Salisbury State College, Salisbury, MD 21801
Willie Mae Butler, Alabama A&M, Normal, AL 35762

C

John E. Caine, Director of Athletics, University of California, Irvine, CA 92717
Frances E. Cake, Monte Vista Ingalls Street, Clifton Forge, VA 24422
Stratton F. Caldwell, California State University, Northridge, CA 91330
Jan R. Callahan, University of Nebraska, Lincoln, NE 68588
Barbara J. Calmer, 596 E College, Oberlin, OH 44074
Robert A. Carey, 1013 Behmann, Apt. H, Corpus Christi, TX 78418
Gerald P. Carlson, University of Southwest Louisiana, Lafayette, LA 70504
Judith B. Carlson, Appalachian State University, Boone, NC 28607
Iris M. Carnell, Ithaca College, Ithaca, NY 14850
Carlin B. Carpenter, Bluffton College, Bluffton, OH 45817
Judy Kee Carpenter, Oregon State University, Corvallis, OR 97330
Linda Carpenter, Brooklyn College, Brooklyn, NY 11210
Gavin H. Carter, University of New Hampshire, Durham, NH 03824
J.E.L. Carter, San Diego State University, San Diego, CA 92182
Julia Carver, Brigham Young University-Hawaii Campus, Laie, HI 96762
Donald R. Casady, Fieldhouse, University of Iowa, Iowa City, IA 52242
Irma J. Caton, 1300 Angelina Bend, Denton, TX 76201
Mary F. Cave, San Diego State University, San Diego, CA 92182
Sandy Ceveridge, HPR-N245, University of Utah, Salt Lake City, UT 84112
Clarence C. Chaffee, Williams College, Williamstown, MA 01297
Claire Chamberlain, University of Lowell, South Campus, Lowell, MA 01854
Nancy L. Chapman, Illinois State University, Normal, IL 61761
Alyce Taylor Cheska, 906 S. Goodwin Avenue, University of Illinois, Urbana, IL 61801
Agnes L. Chrietzberg, Eastern Kentucky University, Richmond, KY 40475
Carl S. Christensen, 106 Dockst Hall, Northeastern University, Boston, MA 02115
Don Chu, Skidmore College, Saratoga Springs, NY 12866
Gabie Church, 313 Lafitte Drive, Baton Rouge, LA 70819
Betsy Clark, Ithaca College, Ithaca, NY 14850
Bruce A. Clark, University of Missouri, St. Louis, MO 63121
M. Corinne Clark, University of Wisconsin, Whitewater, WI 53190
Marilyn L. Clark, Ferris State College, Big Rapids, MI 49307
David H. Clarke, Indiana University, Bloomington, IN 47405
H. Harrison Clarke, University of Oregon, Eugene, OR 97403
Maurice A. Clay, University of Kentucky, Lexington, KY 40500
Irene Clayton, 7500 W. Dean Road, Apt. 132, Milwaukee, WI 53223
Annie Clement, 420-9 Chandler Drive, Cleveland State University, Aurora, OH 44202
Edith Clemetson, College of Saint Scholastica, Duluth, MN 55811
Marguerite A. Clifton, 1250 Bellflower Boulevard, California State University, Long
  Beach, CA 90840
Richard A. Clower, Western Maryland College, Westminster, MD 21157
Elsie J. Cobb, North Texas State University, Denton, TX 76203
Alden C. Coder, Montclair State College, Upper Montclair, NJ 07043
Max Cogan, Northeast Missouri State University, Kirksville, MO 63501

Homer L. Coker, Central State University, Edmond, OK 73034
Dorothy M. Coleman, 9 Fox Run Drive, Little Rock, AR 72209
Catherine M. Collins, Ramapo College, Mahwan, NJ 07430
Janet H. Collins, Chowan College, Murfreesboro, NC 27855
Miriam Collins, University of Montevallo, Montevallo, AL 35115
Carolyn Colvin, Western Illinois University, Macomb, IL 61455
Richard D. Conant, California State College-Stanislaus, Turlock, CA 95380
Connie M. Conatser, Central Connecticut State College, New Britain, CT 06050
John J. Conroy, 310 Nassau Street, Princeton, NJ 08540
Barbara J. Conry, San Jose State University, San Jose, CA 95192
John M. Cooper, 2431 Barbar Drive, Bloomington, IN 47401   7401
Samuel M. Cooper, Bowling Green State University, Bowling Green, OH 43403
Doris E. Coppock, McPherson College, McPherson, KS 67460
Charles B. Corbin, Arizona State University, Tempe, AZ 85287
Shirley Corbitt, Box 353, Southern Methodist University, Dallas, TX 75275
Theresa M. Corcoran, Boston State College, Boston, MA 02115
Harold J. Cordts, Frostburg State College, Frostburg, MD 21532
Barbara Cothren, Illinois Wesleyan University, Bloomington, IL 61701
Curtis A. Coutts, SUNY-Binghamton, Binghamton, NY 13901
Geraldine Crabbs, 1027 N. Main, Brookings, SD 57006
Virginia Crafts, 1606 E. Oakland Avenue, Bloomington, IL 61701
Carolyn Cramer, Bridgewater State College, Bridgewater, MA 02324
Darrell Crase, Memphis State University, Memphis, TN 38152
Marilyn Crawford, James Madison University, Harrisonburg, VA 22807
Phyllis T. Croisant, 3301 West Daniel St., Champaign, IL 61801
Thomas L. Cronan III, University of Tennessee, Knoxville, TN 37916
Patricia Crowe, Adair Gym, College of William & Mary, Williamsburg, VA 23185
F.P. Cullen, San Diego State University, San Diego, CA 92182
William H. Cullum, California State University, Northridge, CA 91330
Thomas K. Cureton, 906 S. Goodwin, University of Illinois, Urbana, IL 61801
Delores M. Curtis, 1336 Lower Campus, University of Hawaii, Honolulu, HI 96822
Russell Cutler, California State University, Chico, CA 95926
A. Ross Cutter Jr., Whitworth College, Spokane, WA 99208

D

Victor P. Dauer, 5697 Davison Head Drive, Friday Harbor, WA 98250
Joanna Davenport, Memorial Coliseum, Auburn University, Auburn, AL 36830
Mary Sue David, Radford University, Radford, VA 24141
Dorothy R. Davies, 702 Taylor, Carbondale, IL 62901
Elwood C. Davis, 1114 Pacific Avenue, Apt. 301, Everett, WA 98201
Marilyn E. Day, Otterbein College, Westerville, OH 43081
Susan J. Day, Asst. VP Academic Affairs, Winona State University, Winona, MN 55987
Dorothy F. Deach, 1267 E. Riviera Drive, Tempe, AZ 85282
Dorothy Deatherage, California State University, Long Beach, CA 90840
John M. Deck, Eastern Kentucky University, Richmond, KY 40475
Bill L. Degroot, University of New Mexico, Albuquerque, NM 87131

Barbara Delong, Box 67A, Southern Illinois University, Edwardsville, IL 62026
Karen P. DePauw, Washington State University, Pullman, WA 99164
Richard L. Deschriver, East Stroudsburg State College, East Stroudsburg, PA 18301
Joy T. Desensi, University of Tennessee, Knoxville, TN 37996
Helga Deutsch, 906 S. Goodwin Avenue, University of Illinois, Urbana, IL 61801
Joseph Digennaro, Lehman College, Bedford Park Boulevard, Bronx, NY 10468
Jean P. Dillenbeck, 201 West Avenue, Brockport, NY 14420
Margaret J. Dobson, P.O. Box 751, Portland State University, Portland, OR 97207
Ethel Docherty, Western Illinois University, Macomb, IL 61455
Patt Dodds, 155 N. P.E. Building, University of Massachusetts, Amherst, MA 01003
Janice Dodson, Casper College, Casper, WY 82601
Paul Dohrmann, Illinois State University, Normal, IL 61761
Neil J. Dougherty, Rutgers College, New Brunswick, NJ 08903
J. William Douglas, West Virginia University, Morgantown, WV 26506
John G. Douglas, U-110, University of Connecticut, Storrs, CT 06268
Margaret L. Driscoll, 302 Mulberry Drive, Blacksburg, VA 24060
Paul E. Dubois, 42 Kennedy Circle, Bridgewater State College, South Easton, MA
   02375
Gerry A. Dubrule, 555-B Sherbrooke Street, W., McGill University, PQ, Canada
   H3A 1E3
Joan L. Duda, Kinesiology Department, UCLA, Los Angeles, CA 90024
Frances T. Dudenhoffer, Box 3M, New Mexico State University, Las Cruces, NM
   88003
Robert J. Dugan, Aquatics Center, St. Joseph's University, Philadelphia, PA 19129
Margaret Duncan, 812 S. 11th Street, Lafayette, IN 47905
John M. Dunn, Oregon State University, Corvallis, OR 97331
Sue M. Durrant, Washington State University, Pullman, WA 99164

E

Jack A. Ecklund, University of Puget Sound, Tacoma, WA 98416
Jane Ellis, University of Wisconsin, Oshkosh, WI 54901
Lynne Emery, California State Polytechnic, Pomona, CA 91768
Mary Lou Enberg, Northwest 440 Orion Drive, Pullman, WA 99163
Carl E. Erickson, Lamberts Cove Road, Vineyard Haven, MA 02568
Walter F. Ersing, Ohio State University, Columbus, OH 43210
Newman H. Ertell, 14845 Rosemont, Detroit, MI 48200
Anna Espenschade, 428A Avenida Sevilla, Laguna Hills, CA 92653
Anthony J. Evans, Lewis & Clark College, Portland, OR 97219
Gail G. Evans, 21116 Locust Drive, Los Gatos, CA 95030
Harold M. Evans, 25 Prospect Street, Falmouth, MA 02540
Ruth Evans, 33 Smithfield Court, Springfield, MA 01108
Thomas M. Evans, 830 Harris Avenue, Manhattan, KS 66502
Peter W. Everett, Florida State University, Tallahassee, FL 32306
Carl H. Everts, Concordia College, Seward, NE 68434
Jim R. Ewers, University of Utah, Salt Lake City, UT 84112
Marvin H. Eyler, 10408 43rd Avenue, Beltsville, MD 20705
Melvin H. Ezell Jr., The Citadel, Charleston, SC 29409

F

Anne R. Fairbanks, Skidmore College, Saratoga Springs, NY 12866
Helen E. Fant, Louisiana State University, Baton Rouge, LA 70803
Tilia J. Fantasia, Westfield State College, Westfield, MA 01086
Jane Farr, Marywood College, Scranton, PA 18509
Margaret E. Faulkner, Towson State University, Towson, MD 21204
Nancy Fee, Indiana University, Bloomington, IN 47401
Patricia K. Fehl, 284 Coliseum, West Virginia University, Morgantown, WV 26506
David A. Feigley, Rutgers University, New Brunswick, NJ 08903
Ronald S. Feingold, Adelphi University, Garden City, NY 11530
William R. Fenstemacher, 291-B Malvern Court, Lakewood, NJ 08701
Bonnie Jill Ferguson, University of Delaware, Newark, DE 19716
Stephen K. Figler, California State University, Sacramento, CA 95819
Bernice R. Finger, P.O. Box 6, Montvallo, AL 35115
Ruth White Fink, 53 Oakwood Drive, Chapel Hill, NC 27514
Angela M. Fisher, 24 Overlook Road, Ardsley, NY 10502
Sylvia E. Fishman, Hunter College, 695 Park Avenue, New York, NY 10021
Josephine F. Fiske, 501 Kenilworth Drive, Towson, MD 21204
Mary P. Fitzpatrick, Auburn University, Auburn, AL 36830
Rhita Flake, California State University, Fresno, CA 93740
Clarence M. Flory, 1015 W. Sloan, Stephenville, TX 76401
M. Lorraine Flower, Eastern Illinois University, Charleston, IL 61920
Richard B. Flynn, University of Nebraska, Omaha, NE 68132
Barbara E. Forker, Iowa State University, Ames,IA 50010
Harry L. Forsyth, Box 2820, South Dakota State University, Brookings, SD 57007
Jean L. Foss, Asst. Vice Chancellor, University of Wisconsin, Lacrosse, WI 54601
John S. Fowler, Campus Box 354, University of Colorado, Boulder, CO 80309
Connie Fox, University of Georgia, Athens, GA 30606
Kathleen Fox, San Diego State University, San Diego, CA 92182
Warren P. Fraleigh, SUNY-Brockport, Brockport, NY 14420
Margaret K. Franco, Queens College, Flushing, NY 11360
Barbara J. Franklin, California State University, Long Beach, CA 90840
B. Don Franks, University of Tennessee, Knoxville, TN 37916
John W. Fredericks, 400 Fourth Street, Petaluma, CA 94952
Dorothy G. Frie, Northeastern State University, Tahlequah, OK 74464
John A. Friedrich, Duke University, Durham, NC 27705
Reuben B. Frost, Box 132, Fort Garland, CO 81133
Don Fry, University of Saskatchewan, Saskatoon, Canada 57N 0W0
Patricia A. Frye, 11 Hill Center, Ithaca College, Ithaca, NY 14850

G

P.J. Galasso, University of Windsor, Windsor, ON, Canada N9B 3P4
Sandra L. Gallemore, Georgia Southern College, Statesboro, GA 30460
Jeanne C. Galley, Emporia State University, Emporia, KS 66801
Robert Gandee, University of Akron, Akron, OH 44325
Robert A. Garcia, School of Education, Stanford University, Stanford, CA 94305
Robert N. Gardner, Box 124, Lincoln University, Lincoln, PA 19352

Joan M. Garrison, Washington University, St. Louis, MO 63130
Joann D. Garside, Birmingham-Southern College, Birmingham, AL 35218
Arlene E. Garton
Susan J. Gavron, Bowling Green State University, Bowling Green, OH 43403
C.P. Gazette, Eastern Washington University, Cheney, WA 99004
Leo L. Gedvilas, University of Illinois-Chicago Circle, Chicago, IL 60680
Bertha R. Geiger, Dickinson State College, Dickinson, ND 58601
James E. Genasci, Springfield College, Springfield, MA 01109
Barbara E. Gench, Box 24782, Denton, TX 76204
Katherine Geyer, 2121 Meadowlark Road, Manhattan, KS 66502
Diane L. Gill, University of Iowa, Iowa City, IA 52242
Robert Gillis, Adrian College, Adrian, MI 49221
Elizabeth G. Glover, University of Oregon, Eugene, OR 97405
Eunice I. Goldgrabe, Concordia College, Seward, NE 68434
Richard D. Gordin Jr. UMC 70, Utah State University, Logan, UT 84322
Richard D. Gordin, Ohio Wesleyan University, Delaware, OH 43015
R. Scott Gorman, Berry College, Mount Berry, GA 30149
Russ Gorman, Illinois State University, Normal, IL 61761
Geoffrey R. Gowan, 333 River Road, Coaching Association of Canada, Ottawa, ON,
    Canada K1L 8B9
Barbara A. Gowitzke, McMaster University, Hamilton, ON, Canada L9G 1E8
Marie M. Grall, Pole 162 Box 85, Harvey Lake, PA 18618
Jim Gratz, Manchester College, North Manchester, IN 46962
Charles A. Gray, Alma College, Alma, MI 48801
Miriam Gray, Route 1, Nevada, MO 64772
Flo Grebner, George Williams College, Downers Grove, IL 60515
Susan L. Greendorfer, 51 Gerty Drive, Motor Behavior Lab, Champaign, IL 61820
H. Scott Greer, 1419 Winfield Road, Bloomington, IN 47401
Leonard O. Greninger, University of Toledo, Toledo, OH 43606
Mary P. Griffin, Winthrop College, Rock Hill, SC 29733
Norma Sue Griffin, 125 Mabel Lee Hall, University of Nebraska, Lincoln, NE
    68588
Betty R. Griffith, California State University, Long Beach, CA 90840
Joseph J. Gruber, 216 Seaton Building, University of Kentucky, Lexington, KY
    40506
Mercedes Gugsiberg, 1248 Lobo Place N.E., Albuquerque, NM 87106
William F. Gustafson, San Jose State University, San Jose, CA 95192
Luell Weed Guthrie, 850 Esplanada, Stanford, CA 94305
Steven P. Guthrie, 1573 Jefferson #3, Eugene, OR 97402

H

Eileen Hackman, Elmhurst College, 190 Prospect Avenue, Elmhurst, IL 60126
Sue A. Hager, Bowling Green State University, Bowling Green, OH 43740
Ara Hairabedian, Fresno State University, Fresno, CA 93740
Patricia Ann Hale, 1902 Warren Street, Apt. 107, Mankato, MN 56001
Allan W. Hall, University of Akron, OH 44325
Diane W. Hall, University of South Florida, Tampa, FL 33620
Gene Hall, Culver-Stockton College, Canton, MO 63435

Susan J. Hall, Oregon State University, Corvallis, OR 97331
Wayne Halliwell, 205 Hampshire Road, Beaconsfield, PQ, Canada H9W 3N9
Samuel C. Halstead, 110 Misty Court, Cary, NC 27511
Doris R. Hamer, Southeast Missouri State University, Cape Girardeau, MO 63701
Walter S. Hamerslough, Loma Linda University, Riverside, CA 92515
Xandra Hamilton, Butler University, Indianapolis, IN 46208
Dale Hanson, Lambert 117, Purdue University, West Lafayette, IN 47907
Margaret W. Harbison, East Texas State University, Commerce, TX 75428
Dorothy W. Harkins, Eastern Kentucky University, Richmond, KY 40475
William Harper, Purdue University, West Lafayette, IN 47907
Doris E. Harrington, Alfred University, Alfred, NY 14802
Wilma M. Harrington, University of Georgia, Athens, GA 30602
Janet C. Harris, University of North Carolina, Greensboro, NC 27412
Ruth W. Harris, 3060 CCRB 401 Washtenaw, University of Michigan, Ann Arbor,
  MI 48109
Virginia Hart, Box 431, Mars Hill College, Mars Hill, NC 28754
Betty G. Hartman, Kent State University, Kent, OH 44242
John L. Haubenstricker, IM Sports Circle, Michigan State University, East Lansing,
  MI 48824
Betty Haven, Indiana University, Bloomington, IN 47405
Helen Hazelton, Pennswood Village, Apt. F106, Newtown, PA 18940
Richard E. Heeschen, University of South Florida, Tampa, FL 33620
John M. Heffernan, Brown University, Providence, RI 02900
Jane H. Heidorn, Anderson Hall, Northern Illinois University, Dekalb, IL 60115
Mary A. Heintz, Longwood College, Farmville, VA 23901
Helen M. Heitmann, 5731 Woodlands Drive, Western Springs, IL 60558
Don Hellison, P.O. Box 751, Portland State University, Portland, OR 97207
Doris E. Henderson, Illinois State University, Normal, IL 61701
Joy L. Hendrick, HPER-112, Indiana University, Bloomington, IN 47401
Keith P. Henschen, University of Utah, Salt Lake City, UT 84112
Myrtis E. Herndon, Hiram College, Hiram, OH 44234
Hortense Hester, Livingston University, Livingston, AL 35470
Carolyn Hewatt, Belmont Hall 222, University of Texas, Austin, TX 78723
Dorothy E. Hicks, Box 156, Marshall University, Huntington, WV 25701
Patricia E. Higginbotham, College of Education, University of Central Florida, Orlando,
  FL 32816
Donald Hilsendager, Temple University, Philadelphia, PA 19122
Chalmer G. Hixson, Wayne State University, Detroit, MI 48202
Julia Hobby, Box 3311 DSU, Delta State University, Cleveland, MS 38733
Marjorie Hodapp, Mankato State University, Mankato, MN 56001
Jean Hodgkins, 6885 Del Playa Drive, Goleta, CA 93017
Hodgson, 2663 Tallant Road, c/o Samarkand, Santa Barbara, CA 93105
Shirl Hoffman, University of Pittsburgh, Pittsburgh, PA 15668
Dorothy S. Holman, 45 Pleasant, Danbury, CT 06810
Frances Holton, Box 6178 College Station, Durham, NC 27708
Owen J. Holyoak, University of Florida, Gainesville, FL 32611
Eleanor T. Hopper, Kennesaw College, Marietta, GA 30067
Dorthalee B. Horne, Shoal Bay, Lopez, WA 98261

Jean G. Horner, RT1, Box 22OH, Forest Grove, OR 97116
Astrid E. Hotvedt, University of Notre Dame, Notre Dame, IN 46556
Alvin J. Hovland, University of Wisconsin, Madison, WI 53706
Evelyn B. Howard, Northeastern University, Boston, MA 02181
Glenn W. Howard, 11 Eastland Road, Glencove, NY 11542
Louise S. Howarth, 313 Columbia Avenue, Clarke Summit, PA 18411
Ruth A. Howe, Bemidji State University, Bemidji, MN 56601
Jackie Hoyt, California State University, Los Angeles, CA 90032
Vickery E. Hubbard, 66 Berkshire Terrace, Amherst, MA 01002
Joseph H. Huber, 208 Greenbrook Drive, Stoughton, MA 02070
Patricia Huber, William Paterson College, Wayne, NJ 07470
Laura J. Huelster, 606 S. Ridgeway, Champaign, IL 61820
Georgia M. Hulac, Washington State University, Pullman, WA 99164
Joan S. Hult, University of Maryland, College Park, MD 20742
Dennis Humphrey, Southwest Missouri State University, Springfield, MO 65802
Burris F. Husman, 5037 Dover Court, Columbia, MD 21044
David M. Hutter, Bethany College, Bethany, WV 26032
Robert S. Hutton, University of Washington, Seattle, WA 98195

I

Roy Ilowit, Long Island University, C.W. Post Center, Greenvale, NY 11548
Melva E. Irvin, California State University, Fresno, CA 93740
Elkin Isaac, University of the Pacific, Stockton, CA 95211

J

Thomas Jable, William Paterson College, Wayne, NJ 07470
Eloise M. Jaeger, University of Minnesota, 104 Burton, Minneapolis, MN 55455
Clair W. Jennett, 6636 Winterset Way, San Jose, CA 95120
Barbara E. Jensen, 73 Bayberry Road, Hampden, MA 01036
Judy Jensen, SUNY-Brockport, Brockport, NY 14420
Sara S. Jernigan, 623 N. Cherokee, Deland, FL 32720
Harvey M. Jessup, Tulane University, New Orleans, LA 70118
Ann E. Jewett, University of Georgia, Athens, GA 30602
Barbara Johnson, Kentucky Wesleyan College, Owensboro, KY 42301
Chic Johnson, Southwest Missouri State University, Springfield, MO 65802
Joan D. Johnson, California State University, Los Angeles, CA 90032
Joann Johnson, University of Minnesota, Duluth, MN 55812
Leon E. Johnson, University of Missouri, Columbia, MO 65211
Norma Jean Johnson, Indiana University, Bloomington, IN 47405
William Johnson, P.O. Box 143, Cheshire, OR 97419
Judith E. Johnston, Box 22120A, Eastern Tennessee State University, Johnson City,
   TN 37601
Ernest Jokl, University of Kentucky, Lexington, KY 40500
Annie Lee Jones, Eastern Illinois University, Charleston, IL 61920
Dow W. Jones, Tarrant County Junior College, Hurst, TX 76053
J. Richard Jones
John O. Jones, c/o M.J. Simpson, 2108 S. Main, Sioux Falls, SD 57105

Lloyd M. Jones, 30 Leahey Avenue, South Hadley, MA 01075
Margaret A. Jones, Georgia State University, Atlanta, GA 30303
Margaret L. Jones, Illinois State University, Normal, IL 61761
Lavernia Jorgensen, University of North Dakota, Grand Forks, ND 58201
Cathy E. Joseph, Nicholls State University, Thibodaux, LA 70301

K

Jo K. Kafer, Box 158, Virginia Tech Athletic Association, Blacksburg, VA 24060
Ervin E. Kaiser, North Dakota State University, Fargo, ND 58102
Eveline E. Kappes, Baylor University, Waco, TX 76798
Janet H. Keefe, Danvers, MA 01923
Paul V. Keen, 1205 Oklahoma, Norman, OK 73069
Betty A. Keenan, Iowa State University, Ames, IA 50011
Dennis J. Keihn, Macalester College, St. Paul, MN 55105
Louis F. Keller, 1340 Keston Street, St. Paul, MN 55100
Barbara J. Kelly, University of Delaware, Newark, DE 19720
Sue N. Kelly, City College of New York, New York, NY 10031
Joan Kemp, Columbia College, Columbia, SC 29203
Edward F. Kennedy, 725 Foch Boulevard, Williston Park, NY 11596
Grace C. Kenney, Gettysburg College, Gettysburg, PA 17325
James W. Kent, University of Delaware, Newark, DE 19711
Betty Keough, Illinois State University, Normal, IL 61761
Mary E. Keyes, McMaster University, Hamilton, ON, L8S 4K1, Canada
Thomas R. Kidd, University of Nebraska, Omaha, NE 68182
Emelia L. Kilby, George Mason University, Fairfax, VA 22030
Joy W. Kistler, Greenacres, Fayette, MO 65284
Erik Kjeldsen, University of Massachusetts, Amherst, MA 01035
Kathryn L. Klein, Sonoma State University, Rohnert Park, CA 94928
Seymour Kleinman, Ohio State University, Columbus, OH 43210
Stephen E. Klesius, University of South Florida, Tampa, FL 33620
Marian E. Kneer, 5731 Woodland Drive, Western Springs, IL 60558
Annelies Knoppers, Michigan State University, East Lansing, MI 48824
Walter S. Knox, Box 365 A, Route 6, Jacksonville, TX 75766
Jane Kober, 1006 11th Street, Denver, CO 80030
William B. Koch, Ithaca College, Ithaca, NY 14850
Rosina M. Koettin, 131 Henderson, Cape Girardeau, MO 63701
Janet L. Koontz, Douglas College-Rutgers, New Bruswick, NJ 08903
Robert Korsgaard, Ball State University, Muncie, IN 47306
Hyman Krakower, Wellington, H/250, West Palm Beach, FL 33409
Patricia Krebs, Adelphi University, Garden City, NY 11530
Ellen F. Kreighbaum, 3550 Blackwood Road, Bozeman, MT 59715
R. Scott Kretchmar, White Building, Pennsylvania State University, University Park, PA 16802

L

Dolly Lambdin, Bellmont 222, University of Texas, Austin, TX 78712
Mary B. Lampe, University of Minnesota, Minneapolis, MN 55455
Jerry Landwer, Texas Christian University, Fort Worth, TX 76129
Ernest K. Lange, University of New Mexico, Albuquerque, NM 87131
Franklin R. Langsner, 6711 Park Heights Avenue, #414, Baltimore, MD 21215
Richard A. Lauffer, North Carolina State University, Raleigh, NC 27650
Rudolph H. Lavik, 1185 Maple Avenue, Tempe, AZ 85281
Norman S. Lawnick, University of Missouri, Columbia, MO 65211
Karl J. Lawrence, Colgate University, Hamilton, NY 13346
Barbara R. Lawson, 913 Valentine Drive, Sherman, TX 75090
Hal A. Lawson, 109 Phillips, Miami University, Oxford, OH 45056
Patricia A. Lawson, University of Saskatchewan, SK, Canada S7N 0W0
John D. Lawther, University of North Carolina, Greensboro, NC 27400
John S. Laycock Jr., Anne Arundel Community College, Arnold, MD 21012
Loretta Lebato, McNeese State University, Lake Charles, LA 70609
Betty Leblanc, Texas A&M University, College Station, TX 77840
Mary Lou Lecompte, University of Texas-Austin, Austin, TX 78712
Amelia Lee, Louisiana State University, Baton Rouge, LA 70803
Mabel Lee, 2248 Ryons Street, Lincoln, NE 68502
Carolyn Lehr, University of Georgia, Athens, GA 30602
Hazel M. Leland, Yakima Valley Community College, Yakima, WA 98907
Eugene E. Lepley, Indiana University of Pennsylvania, Indiana, PA 15701
Paul M. Lepley, Northeastern University, Boston Bouve College, Boston, MA 02115
Harold A. Lerch, 302 Florida Gym, University of Florida, Gainesville, FL 32611
David L. Leslie, Fieldhouse, University of Iowa, Iowa City, IA 52242
Ruth Levinson, 4521 Claire Avenue, Apt. 16, Lincoln, NE 68516
Audrey E. Lewis, Tennessee State University, Nashville, TN 37203
K. Ann Lewis, Northern Illinois University, Dekalb, IL 60115
Laretha J. Leyman, SUNY-Cortland, Cortland, NY 13045
Mary L. Life, Louisiana State University, Baton Rouge, LA 70803
Walter B. Lingo, Box 41101, Lansing Community College, Lansing, MI 48901
Alar Lipping, Miami University, Oxford, OH 45056
Taras N. Liskevych, University of the Pacific, Stockton, CA 95211
Richard W. Litwhiler, Georgia Southwestern, Americus, GA 31709
Robert D. Liverman, Illinois State University, Normal, IL 61761
Lawrence F. Locke, University of Massachusetts, Amherst, MA 01003
Mabel Locke, Box 6087, Carmel Valley Manor, Carmel, CA 93921
Margaret Locke, Elmira College, Elmira, NY 14901
Aileene S. Lockhart, Texas Woman's University, Denton, TX 76204
Joyce O. Locks, Winona State University, Winona, MN 55987
Aimee M. Loftin, Western Illinois University, Macomb, IL 61455
Ben Lombardo, Rhode Island College, 600 Mt. Pleasant Avenue, Providence, RI 02908
E.M. Loovis, Cleveland State University, Cleveland, OH 44115

William T Loughlin, 1 The Link, Massapequa, NY 11758
James Loveless, 105 N. Arlington, Greencastle, IN 46135
John M. Lowe Jr., Westchester State College, Westchester, PA 19380
Reba Y. Lucey, Seattle University, Seattle, WA 98122
Elizabeth Ludwig, 3561 N. Murray Avenue, Milwaukee, WI 53211
Angela Lumpkin, University of North Carolina, Chapel Hill, NC 27514
Herberta M. Lundegren, 267 Recreation Building, Pennsylvania State University, University Park, PA 16802
Minnie L. Lynn, 300 Home Savings and Loan, c/o Sayre, Canton, OH 44702
John S. Lyon, Stevens Institute of Technology, Hoboken, NJ 07030
Mary E. Lyon, Central Missouri State University, Warrensburg, MO 64093
Rose M. Lyon, California State University, Fresno, CA 93740

M

Donald MacIntosh, Queens University, Kingston, ON, Canada, K7L 3N6
Marlin M. Mackenzie, Box 100, Teachers College, Columbia University, New York, NY 10027
Anne D. Mackey, P.O. Box 127, Bayside, NY 11361
Matthew G. Maetozo, Lock Haven State College, Lock Haven, PA 17745
Bonnie Magill, 2828 East 17th Street, Joplin, MO 64801
Lucille Magnusson, 113 White Building, Pennsylvania State University, University Park, PA 16802
Michael Maksud, Oregon State University, Corvallis, OR 97331
Andrew W. Maluke, University of Akron, Akron, OH 44325
Victor H. Mancini, Ithaca College, Ithaca, NY 14850
Kay A. Manuel, Agnes Scott College, Decatur, GA 30030
Laura S. Mapp, Bridgewater College, Bridgewater, VA 22812
Donna R. Marburger, 2315 Spring Creek Drive, Laramie, WY 82070
Jean Marsh, 6140 Sinbad Place, Columbia, MD 21045
Fred L. Martens, University of Victoria, Victoria, BC, Canada V8W 2Y2
Rainer Martens, 906 S. Goodwin, University of Illinois, Champaign, IL 61820
Cecilia Martin, Colorado State University, Fort Collins, CO 80523
Dorothy A. Martin, 2002 Prairie Lane, Emporia, KS 66801
Milton Martin, Westmar College, Lemars, IA 51031
Ray H. Martinez, East Carolina University, Greenville, NC 27834
John W. Masley, 502 N. Sixth, Charleston, IL 61920
John D. Massengale, Eastern Washington University, Cheney, WA 99004
Benjamin H. Massey, Freer Gym, University of Illinois, Urbana, IL 61801
M.D. Massey, University of Rhode Island, Kingstown, RI 02881
Helen E. Matthews, University of North Alabama, Florence, AL 35630
David F. Matuszak, 31430 Marbeth Road, Yucaipa, CA 92399
Pat J. Mauch, University of North Dakota, Grand Forks, ND 58202
L.M. Mawson, University of Kansas, Lawrence, KS 66045
Robert A. McCall, Rural Route 1, Box 230, Goreville, IL 62939
Ann McConnell, Southeast Missouri State University, Cape Girardeau, MO 63701
King J. McCristal, 1409 Mayfair Road, Champaign, IL 61820

Betty F. McCue, 1728 W. 34th Place, Eugene, OR 97405
Thomas E. McDonough Sr., 512 Emorty Circle, N.E., Atlanta, GA 30300
Rosemary McGee, University of North Carolina, Greensboro, NC 27412
Martin H. McIntyre, Box 4070, Texas Technical University, Lubbock, TX 79409
Joanne L. McKeag, Slippery Rock State College, Slippery Rock, PA 16057
Mary Ellen McKee, Western Illinois University, Macomb, IL 61455
Kate McKemie, Agnes Scott College, Decatur, GA 30030
Barry C. McKeown, Box 19259, University of Texas-Arlington, Arlington, TX 76019
Nancy A. McNames, Kellogg Community College, Battle Creek, MI 49016
Merrill J. Melnick, SUNY-Brockport, Brockport, NY 14420
Vincent J. Melograno, Cleveland State University, Cleveland, OH 44115
Betty Menzi, Eastern Michigan University, Ypsilanti, MI 48197
Eleanor Metheny, 6625 Spring Park, Los Angeles, CA 90056
Dora H. Metrelis, Southern Connecticut State College, New Haven, CT 06515
Mike W. Metzler, 113 Memorial Gym, Virginia Polytechnic Institute & State University, Blacksburg, VA 24061
Faith J. Meyer, 8 Williams Street, Boothbay Harbor, ME 04568
Ruth A. Meyer, 8542 Sylvan Lane, Kalamazoo, MI 49002
Carlton R. Meyers, SUNY-Buffalo, Buffalo, NY 14214
Donna M. Miller, University of Arizona, Tucson, AZ 85721
Henry G. Miller, 4420 N. 4th Street East, Lancaster, CA 93534
Kenneth D. Miller, Florida State University, Tallahassee, FL 32306
Frank J. Misar, Stevens Institute of Technology, Hoboken, NJ 07030
Beverly F. Mitchell, 367 Wesleyan Drive, Wesleyan College, Macon, GA 31201
Carolyn B. Mitchell, P.O. Box 13016, Stephen F. Austin State University, Nacogdoches, TX 75962
Elmer D. Mitchell, University of Michigan, Ann Arbor, MI 48103
Nancy K. Mitchell, Douglas College-Rutgers, New Brunswick, NJ 08903
Rudy Moe, Brigham Young University, Provo, UT 84602
Mohamed Ali Mohamed, P.O. Box 6677, Sharjah, United Arab Emirates
Kofie Lea Montgomery, 238 Zink Hall, Indiana University of Pennsylvania, Indiana, PA 15705
Nicholaas J. Moolenijzer, University of New Mexico, Albuquerque, NM, 87131
Elizabeth Moore, Vickers Ranch, Lake City, CO 81235
Jane Moore, Room 2055 MC, Auburn University, Auburn, AL 36830
Margaret A. Moore, Moorhead State University, Moorhead, MN 56560
Roy B. Moore, 151 Bermuda Drive, Mankato, MN 56001
Alfred F. Morris, Rehab Center, 1207 South Oak Street, University of Illinois, Champaign, Il 61820
Karen J. Morris, 410 Alatna Drive, University of Alaska, Fairbanks, AK 99701
Stephen D. Mosher, 31 Chestnut Street, Amherst, MA 01002
Alfreda Mosscrop, 21 Cloyde Street, Manchester, NH 03104
Jane A. Mott, 610 Northridge Drive, Denton, TX 76201
Mary L. Mott, California State University, Fresno, CA 93740
Nicholas P. Moutis, 293 Alden Street, Springfield College, Springfield, MA 01109
Marilyn Mowatt, Smith Gym, Washington State University, Pullman, WA 99164
Lou J. Moyer, Northern Illinois University, Dekalb, IL 60115

Fred A. Mulhauser, Wayne State University, Detroit, MI 48202
Marie R. Mullan, University of Georgia, Athens, GA 30602
Martha Mullins, Eastern Kentucky University, Richmond, KY 40475
Mary J. Mulvaney, University of Chicago, Chicago, IL 60637
Iveagh Munro, 1535 Summer Hill Avenue, Apt. 201, Montreal, PQ, Canada
Richard A. Munroe, University of Arizona, Tucson, AZ 85721
Mary J. Murray, Northeast Louisiana University, Monroe, LA 71209
Lois J. Mussett, Mankato State University, Mankato, MN 56001
Maryann Myrant, Academic Affairs, Towson State University, Towson, MD 21204

N

William J. Napier, Loma Linda University, Loma Linda, CA 92354
Virginia A. Neal, Lewis & Clark College, Portland, OR 97219
Barbara A. Nelson, 669 Beautyview Court, Columbus, OH 43214
Jonathan E. Nelson, Northern Michigan University, Marquette, MI 49855
Katherine H. Nelson, 2008 Post Road, Madison, WI 53706
Richard C. Nelson, Biomechanics Lab, Pennsylvania State University, University Park,
   PA 16802
Jerry Nestray, Sam Houston State University, Huntsville, TX 77341
John E. Nixon, 732 Alvardado Court, Stanford, CA 94305
Marie Nogues, 995 Hawthorne, Lafayette, CA 94549
Cheryl C. Northam, McNeese State University, Lake Charles, LA 70609

O

Dianne O'Brien, 221 Nickell Heights, Paducah, KY 42001
Doris O'Donnell, MHL 202, University of Nebraska, Lincoln, NE 68588
James E. Odenkirk, Arizona State University, Tempe, AZ 85287
Mary Jo Oliver, California State Polytechnic University, Pomona, CA 91768
Gareth R. Olson, University of Denver, Denver, CO 80208
Janice K. Olson, 111B Lambert Hall, Purdue University, West Lafayette, IN 47907
Ray Oosting, Trinity College, Hartford, CT 06100
Wayne Osness, University of Kansas, Lawrence, KS 66045
Maurice E. Ostrander, University of Minnesota, Minneapolis, MN 55400
Marjorie G. Owen, 3028 Ashley Court, Bensalem, PA 19020
Joseph B. Oxendine, Temple University, Philadelphia, PA 19122

P

Cal Papatos, Box 96, Island Park, NY 11558
Linda L. Parchman, Arkansas State University, Jonesboro, AR 72467
Lee H. Park, Southeast Missouri State University, Cape Girardeau, MO 63701
Jae S. Park, Ball State University, Muncie, IN 47306
Barbara Passmore, Indiana State University, Terre Haute, IN 47809
Patricia Paterson, Hamline University, St. Paul, MN 55104
Joan M. Paul, Southeastern Louisiana University, Hammond, LA 70402
Margaret Paulding, 100 High Rock Avenue, Saratoga Springs, NY 12866

Gregory Payne, San Jose State University, San Jose, CA 95192
Kathleen M. Pearson, Western Illinois University, Macomb, IL 61445
Dean A. Pease, Shepherd College, Shepherdstown, WV 25443
Ana Maria Pellegrini, Rua Harmonia 942, Cidade Universitari 05435, Sao Paulo,
  Brazil C P 5349
Barry C. Pelton, 7 Houston, University of Houston, Houston, TX 77004
Kenneth A. Penman, Washington State University, Pullman, WA 99164
Marian E. Penny, RR 6, Millstream Road, Victoria, BC, Canada
Ellen L. Perry, Pennsylvania State University, University Park, PA 16801
Patricia M. Peterson, 28 Harris Avenue, Albany, NY 12208
Ray Petracek, Faculty of Education, University of Regina, Regina, SK, Canada S4S
  0A2
Hazel G. Pflueger, Montgomery College, Rockville, MD 20850
Joan A. Phillip, Youngstown State University, Youngstown, OH 44555
Madge M. Phillips, University of Tennessee, Knoxville, TN 37916
Odell Phillips, 987 Spanish Grove, Richmond, KY 40475
A.H. Pilch, Western Carolina University, Cullowhee, NC 28723
Ralph Piper, 3123-D Via Serean N., Laguna Hills, CA 92651
Frank Pleasants, University of North Carolina, Chapel Hill, NC 27514
Ruth Podbielski, Indiana University of Pennsylvania, Indiana, PA 15705
Hally B.W. Poindexter, P.O. Box 1892, Houston, TX 77251
Virginia Politino, 135-B Marina Drive, Edison, NJ 08817
Bernard Pollack, 1018 E. 29th Street, Brooklyn, NY 11210
Geri Polvino, Eastern Kentucky University, Richmond, KY 40475
Frederick Ponder, Livingstone College, Salisbury, NC 28144
M. Joan Popp, Northern Illinois University, Dekalb, IL 60115
Jose Portela-Suarez, University of Puerto Rico, Rio Piedras, PR 00923
Thomas Porter, St. Olaf College, Northfield, MN 55057
Archibald T. Post, Head O Tide, Newry, ME 04261
Frank R. Powell, Metropolitan State College, 1006 11th Street, Box 25, Denver, CO
  80204
John T. Powell, School of Human Biology, University of Guelph, Guelph, ON, Canada
  N1E 485
Roberta B. Powell, Slippery Rock State, Slippery Rock, PA 16057
J.T. Powers, U.B. Box 34L, Baylor University, Waco, TX 76798
Gregory L. Price, California State College, San Bernardino, CA 92407
Reginald L. Price, California State College, San Bernardino, CA 92407
Jan Progen, 911-B W. Bessmer, Greensboro, NC 27408
Florence Prybylowski, University of Wisconsin, Oshkosh, WI 54901
Martilu Puthoff, University of Northern Colorado, Greeley, CO 80639
B. Jean Putnam, Summer Session, Central Washington University, Ellensburg, WA
  98926

R

Howard W. Raabe, 1809-739 S.W. St. Claire, Portland, OR 97200
Amy L. Rady, 420 E. 55th Street, New York, NY 10022
Muhamad Ali Rahni, Northwestern State University, Natchitoches, LA 71497

Ernest P. Rangazas, SUNY-Plattsburgh, NY 12901
Jack E. Razor, 1900 Association Drive, AAHPERD, Reston, VA 22091
Lorraine A. Redderson, Lander College, Greenwood, SC 29646
Glen P. Reeder, Middle Tennessee State University, Murfreesboro, TN   37132
Jim Reedy, 206 Student Athlete Complex, Georgia Institute of Technology, Atlanta,
    GA 30332
Thomas E. Rees, P.E. Skills Room 122, University of Iowa, Iowa City,   IA 52242
Mary L. Remley, HPER 179, Indiana University, Bloomington, IN 47401
Matthew C. Resick, 16-E Cape Shores Drive, Cape Canaveral, FL 32920
Michael J. Reynolds, P.O. Box 663, Ballarat C.A.E., Mt. Helen, Victoria, 3350
    Australia
Howard D. Richardson, Indiana State University, Terre Haute, IN 47809
William W. Richerson, Northeast Missouri State University, Kirksville, MO 63501
Kathryn Riddle, 534 W. Cooper, Maryville, MO 64468
George L. Rider, 1010 23rd Street Road, Greeley, CO 80631
Marie I. Riley, Coleman Gymnasium, University of North Carolina, Greensboro, NC
    27412
Lewis B. Ringer, Youngstown State University, Youngstown, OH 44555
Janet A. Rintala, 2425 Old North Road, Denton, TX 76201
Stuart Robbins, 4700 Keele Street, York University, Downsview, ON, Canada M3J 1P3
Nancy K. Roberson, 11830 Westline Ind. Dr., College Division, Mosley Co., St. Louis,
    MO 63141
David Robertson, SUNY-Plattsburgh, Plattsburgh, NY 12901
Joann Robertson, 2215 Brophy Hall, Western Illinois University, Macomb, IL 61455
Glenn E. Robinson, South Dakota State University, Brookings, SD 57006
Patricia S. Robinson, 164 Bailey, Bailey Island, ME 04003
Fred B. Roby, University of Arizona, Tucson, AZ 85721
Harry J. Rockafeller, 10 Landing Lane, New Brunswick, NJ 08900
Larry V. Roe, 390 Ponderosa Drive, Athens, GA 30605
Candace Roell, 1827 Sunny Drive, Apt. E 27, Bradenton, FL 33507
Kathleen A. Rohaly, University of Richmond, Richmond, VA 23173
Diane Ross, 109 Parkview Road, Fullerton, CA 92635
Saul Ross, University of Ottawa, Ottawa, ON, Canada K1N 6N5
Steven M. Rostas, 466 S. Pleasant Street, Amherst, MA 01002
Anne L. Rothstein, P.O. Box 672, Newton, CT 06470
Joanne Rowe, Box 1967, University of Alabama, University, AL 35486
Robert O. Ruhling, College of Health, University of Utah, Salt Lake City, UT 84112
Rose Mary Rummel, James Madison University, Harrisonburg, VA 22807
Margaret Ryder, N. P.E. Building, University of Maryland, College Park, MD 20742

S

Margaret J. Safrit, 1502 Windfield Way, Middleton, WI 53562
George H. Sage, University of Northern Colorado, Greeley, CO 80639
Erika Sander, University of Wisconsin, Milwaukee, WI 53201
James P. Santomier, 635 E. Building, New York University, New York, NY 10003
Miriam Satern, University of North Carolina, Greensboro, NC 27412
Roslyn Scheer-McLeod, Notre Dame College, Cleveland, OH 44112

Ruth Schellberg, 50 Skyline Drive, Mankato, MN 56001
Jack H. Schiltz, Virginia Commonwealth University, Richmond, VA 23284
Herb Schmalemberger, University of California, Davis, CA 95616
Patricia A. Schmitt, Del Mar College, Corpus Christi, TX 78404
R.N. Schmottlach, Ball State University, Muncie, IN 47306
M. Gladys Scott, RR 2, Box 74, Iowa City, IA 52240
Phebe M. Scott, Illinois State University, Normal, IL 61761
Janet A. Seaman, California State University, Los Angeles, CA 90032
Don C. Seaton, University of Kentucky, Lexington, KY 40500
Helen M. Sedelmeyer, Adelphi University, Garden City, NY 11530
Jeffrey O. Segrave, Skidmore College, Saratoga Springs, NY 12826
Herman B. Segrest, Texas Technical University, Lubbock, TX 79409
William S. Senior, Claflin College, Orangeburg, SC 29115
Charley H. Shannon, Box 10965 ASU Station, Angelo State University, San Angelo, TX 76909
Catherine F. Shaw, Box 332, Lake Erie College, Painesville, OH 44077
John H. Shaw, Syracuse University, Syracuse, NY 13200
Edward J. Shea, Southern Illinois University, Carbondale, IL 62901
Henry A. Shenk, 1235 Kentucky Street, Lawrence, KS 66044
George E. Shepard, 2210 Carol Woods, Chapel Hill, NC 27514
Ginny L. Shider, Department of Administration, SUNY-Brockport, Brockport, NY 14420
Mabel J. Shirley, 409 Lincoln Pky. #A, Northfield, MN 55057
Alice M. Shoman, Northern Michigan University, Marquette, MI 49855
David A. Shows, Stephen F. Austin State University, Nacogdoches, TX 75962
Frederick D. Shults, Oberlin College, Oberlin, OH 44074
Barry B. Shultz, University of Utah, Salt Lake City, UT 84112
Ronald A. Siders, University of Florida, Gainesville, FL 32611
Daryl Siedentop, 309 Pomerene, Ohio State University, Columbus, OHG 43210
Peter O. Sigerseth, University of Oregon, Eugene, OR 97401
Caroline Sinclair, 1600 Westbrook Avenue, Richmond, VA 23227
Becky L. Sisley, 310 E. 48th, Eugene, OR 97405
Edward R. Slaughter, 1843 Edgewood Lane, Charlotesville, VA 22901
Yvonne Slingerland, Wichita State University, Wichita, KS 67208
Muriel R. Sloan, 1120 Francis S. Key Hall, University of Maryland, College Park, MD 20742
Barbara B. Smith, Longwood College, Farmville, VA 23901
Johanne M. Smith, 48 John Street, North Quincy, MA 02171
Nettie D. Smith, 101 Fern Road, East Brunswick, NJ 08816
Richard J. Smith, University of Oregon, Eugene, OR 97403
Ronald A. Smith, 101 White Building, Pennsylvania State University, University Park, PA 16802
Sarah L. Smith, Rutgers University, New Brunswick, NJ 08903
Shirley A. Smith, California State University, Chico, CA 95929
Jeanne E. Snodgrass, 13 Marwood Court, Rockville, MD 20850-2906
Raymond A. Snyder, UCLA, 405 Hilgard, Los Angeles, CA 90024
Edlo Solum, 1005 W. Second, Northfield, MN 55057
Robert P. Sorani, Sonoma State University, Rohnert Park, CA 94928

Robert W. Sorge, Northern State College, Aberdeen, SD 57401
Ruth M. Sparhawk, University of Southern California, Los Angeles, CA 90007
Raymond E. Sparks, Sparks Farm, E. Wallingford, VT 05742
Betty Spears, 56 Van Meter Drive, University of Massachusetts, Amherst, MA 01002
William R. Spieth, Georgia Southern College, Statesboro, GA 30458
George B. Spitz, 22 Hawthorne Road, Southampton, NY 11968
John H. Spurgeon, University of South Carolina, Columbia, SC 29208
Robert E. Stadulis, 1560 Vine Street, Kent, OH 44240
Loretta M. Stallings, George Washington University, Washington, DC 20052
Lorraine Stark, Box 129, Southern Illinois University, Edwardsville, IL 62026
Thomas W. Steele, 32 Parker Avenue, Cortland, NY 13045
Barney Steen, Calvin College, Grand Rapids, MI 49506
Thomas B. Steen, Ohio State University, Columbus, OH 43210
Harriet E. Stewart, 67-1/2 N. Franklin, Delaware, OH 43015
Sharon Kay Stoll, PEB 208, University of Idaho, Moscow, ID 83843
Marjorie E. Stone, 1200 Commercial, Emporia State University, Emporia, KS 66801
Linda Stonecipher, Skidmore College, Saratoga Springs, NY 12866
Eula M. Stovall, California State University, Fullerton, CA 92634
Robert Strauss, 715 Stadium D, Trinity University, San Antonio, TX 78284
Robert L. Strehle, 888 Harvard Avenue, Claremont, CA 91711
Clinton H. Strong, Indiana University, Bloomington, IN 47405
Raymond Struck, 44 Clemmon Street, Box 71, Hanover, IN 47243
Nancy L. Struna, University of Maryland, College Park, MD 20742
Ginny L. Studer, SUNY-Brockport, Brockport, NY 14420
G.A. Stull, University of Minnesota, Minneapolis, MN 55455
Mary Sturtevant, PE & Dance, Tufts University, Medford, MA 02155
Ann Strutts, California State University, Northridge, CA 91330
Walter L. Sunderhaus, P.O. Box 10832, Eugene, OR 97440
Jon D. Sunderland, Gonzaga University, Spokane, WA 99258
Robero N. Sunger,
Gladys Swanson, 1615 Waverly Avenue, Duluth, MN 55811
Richard A. Swanson, University of North Carolina, Greensboro, NC 27412
Colleen Sweeney, P.O. Box 3067, Boise, ID 83703

T

Gladys Taggart, 1426 N. Vassar, Wichita, KS 67208
Hazael G. Taylor, Hood College, Frederick, MD 21701
William L. Terry, 3943 Kenwood, Spring Valley, CA 92077
Edwyna P. Testerman, Box 41087, University of Southwestern Louisiana, Lafayette,
    LA 70504
Alfred S. Thomas, Central Michigan University, Mount Pleasant, MI 48858
Carolyn E. Thomas, University of Buffalo, Buffalo, NY 14214
Nelson Thomas, Calkins Hall, Loma Linda University, Riverside, CA 92515
Paul Thomas, University of Windsor, ON, Canada, N9B 3P4
Peggy Thomas, Southwest Missouri State University, Springfield, MO 65809
Carol A. Thompson, Baldwin-Wallace College, Berea, OH 44017
Donna Thompson, 101 E. Gym, University of Northern Iowa, Cedar Falls, IA 50613

Margaret M. Thompson, 906 S. Goodwin, University of Illinois, Urbana, IL 61801
Pat L. Thomson, California State University, Cedar and Shaw Avenue, Fresno, CA 93740
Mary L. Thornburg, Bridgewater State College, Bridgewater, MA 02324
Kenneth G. Tillman, Trenton State College, Trenton, NJ 08625
Carl E. Tishler, Texas A&M University, College Station, TX 77840
Ross E. Townes, Box 19656, North Carolina Central University, Durham, NC 27707
Marianna Trekell, University of Illinois, Champaign, IL 61820
Joan Tudor, Chapman College, Orange, CA 92666
Phyllis Turbow, 11842 Della Lane, Garden Grove, CA 92640
M. Malissa Turner, Box 747, Southeastern Louisiana University, Hammond, LA 70402
Joann L. Tyler, Otterbein College, Westerville, OH 43081

U

Ann Uhlir, Texas Woman's University, Denton, TX 76204
Elizabeth C. Umstead, University of North Carolina, Greensboro, NC 27412
Dan Unruh, San Jose State University, San Jose, CA 95192
Wynn Updyke, Indiana University, Bloomington, IN 47401

V

Martha Van Allen, Westfield State College, Westfield, MA 01086
Martha E. Van Steenderen, University of Wisconsin, Whitewater, WI 53190
Alvin J. Van Wie, College of Wooster, Wooster, OH 44691
Nancy M. Vananne, University of Northern Colorado, Greeley, CO 80639
George Vanbibber, 22 Hillside Circle, Storrs, CT 06268
Lawrence E. Vance, Seattle University, Seattle, WA 98122
William G. Vandenburgh, California State University, Hayward, CA 94542
Edna R. Vanderbeck, McCormack Hall, Illinois State University, Normal, IL 61761
Betty Vandersmissen, Memorial Hall, Bowling Green State University, Bowling Green, OH 43403
Anky A. Vanderstok, 1701 E. Little Creek Road 203, Norfolk, VA 23518
Harold J. Vanderzwaag, University of Massachusetts, Amherst, MA 01003
Shirley Vanvalkenburg, Kent State University, Kent, OH 44242
Linda K. Vaughan, Five Wingate Road, Wellesley, MA 02181
C. Lynn Vendien, 111 Rockyhill Road, Hadley, MA 01035
Lucille Verhulst, 5330 Bahia Blanca, Laguna Hills, CA 92653
Margo Verkruzen, Towson State University, Baltimore, MD 21204
Barbara L. Viera, Carpenter Sp. Building, University of Delaware, Newark, DE 19711
Eric Vlahov, University of Tampa, Tampa, FL 33606
Kathryn E. Vonderau, University of Wisconsin, Whitewater, WI 53190
A. Henry Vonmechow, SUNY-Stony Brook, Stony Brook, NY 11794

W

Hazel M. Wacker, 8 Highland Avenue, Maplewood, NJ 07040
Bernice Waggoner, 328 Chico Drive, Las Vegas, NM 87701
I.F. Waglow, 1219 S. Central Avenue, Flagler Beach, FL 32036

Catharine J. Wakefield, Box 79086, Saginaw, TX 76179
Margaret C. Walker, 475 Pine W. Avenue, McGill University, Montreal, PQ, Canada, H2W 1S4
Tony Wallingford, University of Ohio, Cincinnati, OH 45204
Eleanor A. Walsh, California State University, Northridge, CA 91330
Leta I. Walter, San Jose State University, San Jose, CA 95192
Ned L. Warren, 2847 Sherwood Drive, Brunswick, GA 31520
Donald J. Watkins, Pennsylvania State University, State College, PA 16802
Jan C. Watson, Appalachian State University, Boone, NC 28608
Robert G. Waxlax, St. Cloud State University, St. Cloud, MN 56301
Carlos L. Wear, 7815 Euper Lane, Fort Smith, AR 72903
Robert E. Wear, 4 Hoitt Drive, University of New Hampshire, Durham, NH 03824
Ann Webb, Pembroke State University, Pembroke, NC 28372   NC   28372
Robert J. Weber, SUNY-Cortland, Cortland, NY 13045
Gail E. Webster, Athens University Unit, GRC, 850 College Station Road, Athens, GA 30610
Randolph W. Webster, P.O. Box 17, Okemas, MI 48864
Fred A. Wegner, University of Wisconsin, 2000 Observatory Drive, Madison, WI 53706
R.W. Wehr, Georgia State University, University Plaza, Atlanta, GA 30303
J. Edmund Welch, West Virginia Institute of Technology, Montgomery, WV 25136
Janet Wells, Tully Gym, Florida State University, Tallahassee, FL 32306
Katharine F. Wells, 61 Forest Street, Needham, MA 02192
Janice Wendt, University of Houston, Houston, TX 77004
Barbara H. West, University of Utah, Salt Lake City, UT 84112
Eula L. West, San Francisco State University, San Francisco, CA 94132
Arthur Weston, 200 Central Park S., New York, NY 10019
Marylinda Wheeler, California Polytechnic State University, San Luis Obispo, CA 93407
K. Gail Whitaker, San Francisco State University, San Francisco, CA 94132
Christine White, 40 Highland Terrace, Taunton, MA 02780
Doris L. White, University of California, Berkeley, CA 94720
Jess R. White, P.O. Box 240, Arkansas State University, State University, AR 72467
Ralph L. Wickstrom, P.O. Box 248, Ripon, WI 54971
Carol J. Widule, Purdue University, West Lafayette, IN 47907
Judy Wilder, University of Wyoming, Laramie, WY 82071
Roger C. Wiley, N.W. 340 Janet Street, Pullman, WA 99163
Samuel L. Wilkey, Friends University, Wichita, KS 67213
Robert Wilseck, California State College, California, PA 15419
Marjorie U. Wilson, 7646 Hampshire Avenue N., Brooklyn Park, MN 55428
Sam Winningham, California State University, Northridge, CA 91330
Douglas C. Wiseman, Plymouth State College, Plymouth, NH 03264
Mildred Wohlford, 13826 Lake Shore Point, Sun City, AZ 85351
Robert A. Wojcik, Health Technology, J. Sargeant Reynolds Community College, Richmond, VA 23241
Harold H. Wolf, California State University, Sacramento, CA 95819
J. Grove Wolf, 4201 Somerset Lane, Madison, WI 53711
James E. Wolfe, Dean Junior College, Franklin, MA 02038
Frances Wood, University of Arkansas, Fayetteville, AR 72701
Nan E. Wood, P.O. Box 705, Lock Haven, PA 17745

Shirley J. Wood, Iowa State University, Ames, IA 50011
Stephen L. Woodcock, Endicott College, Beverly, MA 01915
Janet Woodruff, 3198 Portland Street, Eugene, OR 97405
Lilyan B. Wright, 260 Green Valley Road, Langhorne, PA 19047
Rollin G. Wright, 906 S. Goodwin, University of Illinois, Urbana, IL 61801
William H. Wright, Norfolk State University, Norfolk, VA 23504
Emily H. Wughalter, New York University, 239 Green Street, 635 East Building, New York, NY 10003
Gerald B. Wyness, San Francisco State University, San Francisco, CA 94132

Y

Sherill L. York, Iowa State University, Ames, IA 50011
Florence Young, Central Missouri State University, Warrensburg, MO 64093
Mary L. Young, 224 Cooke, University of Minnesota, Minneapolis, MN 55455
Olive G. Young, 101 W. Windsor Avenue, Apt. 1205, Urbana, IL 61801
Sophie T. Young, 213 Phillips Street, Thunder Bay, ON, Canada P7B 5G9
Virginia E. Young, P.O. Box 178, Livingston University, Livingston, AL 35470
Lois J. Youngen, University of Oregon, Eugene, OR 97403
Carl I. Youngworth, 1204 Pine Street, Yankton, SD 57078

Z

Linda B. Zaichkowsky, Northeastern University, 360 Huntington Avenue, Boston, MA 02115
Joan Zardus, Salem State College, Salem, MA 01960
Earle F. Zeigler, Thames Hall, University of Western Ontario, London, ON, Canada, N6A 3K7
Robert G. Zeigler, Towson State University, Towson, MD 21204
Rico N. Zenti, Northern Michigan University, Marquette, MI 49855
M. Nadine Zimmerman, Anderson Hall 229, Northern Illinois University, Dekalb, IL 60115

QUEST

QUEST

The Journal of the National
Association for Physical Education
in Higher Education (NAPEHE)

Editor: John D. Massengale, EdD
Eastern Washington University

Associate Editor
Wilma Harrington, PhD
University of Georgia

Book Review Editor
Nancy L. Struna, PhD
University of Maryland

Designed to stimulate professional development in physical education, *Quest* focuses on the critical issues facing today's physical
education faculty and students. Each issue contains theoretical and
practical articles synthesizing recent research developments in the
sport sciences and other subdisciplines of human movement. Also
included are commentary and constructive analyses of the physical
education profession. As a forum for scholarly and creative thought
about the profession, *Quest* is an excellent resource for academicians, teachers, and administrators.

Editorial Board
William G. Anderson, *Columbia University*; Robert K. Barney,
University of Western Ontario; Anne Marie Bird, *California State
University-Fullerton*; Warren Fraleigh, *State University of New
York-Brockport*; Janet C. Harris, *University of North Carolina-
Greensboro*; Donald Hellison, *Portland State University*; Shirl
Hoffman, *University of Pittsburgh*; Carole Oglesby, *Temple
University*.

Additional Information
Frequency: Semiannual (May and November)
Subscription Rates: Individuals: 1 year—$14; 2 years—$26;
3 years—$38 • Institutions or libraries: 1 year—$20; 2 years—$38;
3 years—$56
Foreign Shipping Rates: Surface Mail: Add $2/year • Air Mail:
Add $8/year

Human Kinetics Publishers, Inc. • Box 5076W • Champaign, IL 61820